BPM
Excellence
in Practice 2008
Using BPM for Competitive Advantage

BPM Excellence in Practice 2008

Using BPM for Competitive Advantage

Innovation and Excellence in
Business Process Management and Workflow

LAYNA FISCHER

Future Strategies Inc.
Lighthouse Point, Florida, USA

BPM Excellence in Practice 2008: Using BPM for Competitive Advantage

Copyright © 2008 by Future Strategies Inc.

ISBN10: 0-9777527-3-9

ISBN13: 978-0-9777527-3-7

Published by Future Strategies Inc., Book Division

2436 North Federal Highway, #374, Lighthouse Point FL 33064 USA
954.782.3376 / 954.782.6365 fax
www.FutStrat.com
books@FutStrat.com

Cover: www.nissosdesign.it

Publisher's Cataloging-in-Publication Data

ISBN: 978-0-9777527-3-7
Library of Congress Control Number: 2008932797

BPM Excellence in Practice 2008: Using BPM for Competitive Advantage
(Print Edition)
/Layna Fischer

p. cm.

Includes bibliographical references and appendices.

1. Technological Innovation. 2. Organizational Change. 3. Business Process Management.
4. Information Technology. 5. Total Quality Management. 6. Management Information systems.
7. Office Practice-Automation. 8. Knowledge Management. 9. Workflow. 10. Process Analysis

Fischer, Layna.

Table of Contents

Section 5: South America

Section 6 Appendix

Introduction
BPM Excellence in Practice:
Using BPM for Competitive Advantage

Layna Fischer, Editor and
Awards Executive Director

The prestigious annual **Global Excellence Awards for BPM and Workflow** are highly coveted by organizations that seek recognition for their achievements. Now evolved into their 18th year, originally starting with, and moving through, imaging, documentation, knowledge management and more, as our industry moved forward, these awards not only provide a spotlight for companies that truly deserve recognition, but also provide tremendous insights for organizations wishing to emulate the winners' successes.

These winners are companies that successfully used BPM in gaining competitive advantage within their industries.

CRITERIA

The criteria for submitting an entry are fairly simple: the project should have been operational for six months prior to nomination, and have been installed within the past two years. The submission guidelines, however, are more detailed. To be recognized as winners, companies must address three critical areas: excellence in *innovation*, excellence in *implementation* and excellence in strategic *impact* to the organization. Details at www.bpmf.org.

Innovation

Innovation encompasses the innovative use of technology for strategic business objectives; the complexity of the underlying business process and IT architecture; the creative and successful deployment of advanced workflow and imaging concepts; and process innovations through business process reengineering and/or continuous improvements.

- Innovative use of BPM technology to solve unique problems
- Creative and successful implementation of advanced BPM concepts
- Level of integration with other technologies and legacy systems
- Degree of complexity in the business process and underlying IT architecture

Implementation

Hallmarks of a successful *implementation* include extensive user and line management involvement in the project while successfully managing change during the implementation process. Factors impacting the level of difficulty in achieving a successful implementation include the system complexity; integration with other advanced technologies; and the scope and scale of the implementation (e.g. size, geography, inter-company processes).

- Successful BPM and/or workflow implementation methodology
- Size, scope and quality of change management process
- Scope and scale of the implementation (e.g. size, geography, inter-and intra-company processes)

Impact

Impact is the bottom line, answering the question, "What benefit does BPM deliver to my business? Why should I care?"

- Extent and quantifiable impact of productivity improvements
- Significance of cost savings
- Level of increased revenues, product enhancements, customer service or quality improvements
- Impact of the system on competitive positioning in the marketplace
- Proven strategic importance to the organization's mission
- Degree to which the system enabled a culture change within the organization and methodology for achieving that change

Using BPM for Competitive Advantage

Examples of potential benefits include: productivity improvements; cost savings; increased revenues; product enhancements; improved customer service; improved quality; strategic impact to the organization's mission; enabling culture change; and—most importantly—changing the company's competitive position in the market. The visionary focus is now toward strategic benefits, in contrast to marginal cost savings and productivity enhancements.

While successes in these categories are prerequisites for winning a Global Excellence Award, it would reward all companies to focus on excelling in *innovation*, *implementation* and *impact* when installing BPM and workflow technologies. Companies must recognize that implementing innovative technology is useless unless the organization has a successful approach that delivers—and even surpasses—the anticipated benefits.

Trends

At the **Global Awards for Excellence in BPM and Workflow** ceremony held at the BPM TechShow in Nashville TN, Analyst Connie Moore of Forrester Group noted the following trends in reviewing the submissions:

- Multiple, complex processes automated
- Workflow integrated with CRM and ERP
- Portal implementations (B2E, B2B, B2C)
- Supply chain automation
- E-gov and customer self-service initiatives
- Emphasis on straight-thru processing
- Sophistication in the Asian market

True visionaries are not content with merely achieving benefits; they are proactively driven to raise the standard for excellence in their industry—in essence, *using BPM for competitive advantage.*

SUBMIT AN ENTRY

Submissions for the annual **Global Excellence Awards for BPM and Workflow** open in the September timeframe. The Awards program is managed by Future Strategies Inc., the Awards Director is Layna Fischer in collaboration with Derek Miers of BPM Focus.org, with sponsorship from WfMC, OMG and BPM.com.

General information and guidelines may be found at www.bpmf.org or contact:
Layna Fischer, Layna@FutStrat.com
Future Strategies Inc., www.FutStrat.com
Phone +1 954 782 3376, Fax +1 954 782 6365

TABLE OF CONTENTS AND CHAPTER ABSTRACTS

Guest Chapters:

Nathaniel Palmer, Executive Director Workflow Management Coalition (WfMC), President, Transformation+Innovation, USA
For 18 years the **Global Excellence Awards for BPM and Workflow** have covered virtually every economic environment, from bubble to bust. The first modern process era emerged from the economic downturn of the early 1990s. Then, after years defined by relentless cost-cutting, the new charter for business shifted toward enhancing capacity to address the return of customer demand. Nathaniel Palmer looks at the changes through the perspective of chapters published in this book.

Dr. Michael zur Muehlen, Stevens Institute of Technology, USA
Dr. zur Muehlen takes another look at organizational structures and their development. He previously studied their variety of disciplines, such as sociology, psychology, and economics. He notes that the goal of organizational research still lies primarily within the field of business administration and is the development of viable and efficient structures for enterprises as self-contained economic units. The term itself *organization* can be viewed through an institutional or an instrumental lens. The institutional view describes an organization as a self-contained entity that has a specific structure. The traditional American organizational literature is dominated by the institutional notion of organization. In contrast, for example, German organizational literature focuses primarily on the instrumental view, i.e. the act of organizing an enterprise. This paper notes how new fronts have been opened for management by recent advances in thinking and attitude.

Dr. Timothy D. Kehoe, Irene N. Chang, David S. Czulada, Howard Kong, Dr. Dino Konstantopoulos, MITRE; with Linus Chow, Charles Medley, Oracle.
Current Air Force (AF) Command, Control, Communication, *Computers, and Intelligence* (C4I) systems are costly to integrate because they were not initially designed to work together, and many integration efforts still provide point-to-point solutions between tightly coupled systems. The Department of Defense (DoD) is moving toward net-centricity and the AF Air and Space Operations Center (AOC) Enterprise Service Bus (ESB) Risk Reduction Study investigated industry best practices for streamlining the integration process using a Service Oriented Architecture (SOA). The Government study team engaged with three industry vendors and their partners, evaluated ESB interoperability characteristics, explored the business process management workflow orchestration technology, and developed a proof-of-concept prototype for information exchange within the AOC.

Section 1: Europe

Silver Award, nominated by BizAgi
In view of the challenge to comply with MiFID – Market in Financial Instruments Directive – requirements by November 2007, infoCaja began the process to select a BPM technology so that its affiliate banks could adapt as soon as possible to the regulations. They wanted an agile and efficient business solution which would

also support evolution of the guidelines in the long term. The processes automated with BizAgi at infoCaja, a company that provides shared services for its five affiliate banks (Cajastur, Caja Canarias, Caja Castilla la Mancha, Caja Murcia, y Caixa de Balears), supports the MiFID client order handling process trough a multi-bank, individually administered environment (e.g., each bank can define and modify the tests and their validity).

Thus infoCaja, supported by Pricewaterhouse Coopers and the agility of BizAgi, was able to implement the automation of this process in less than 4 months, and went live by the specified date of 1st November 2007, managing more than 5,000 users in more than 1.500 branches.

LPH VRANOV N/T, SLOVAKIA   51

Finalist; nominated by Technical University of Košice, Slovakia

Nowadays, the implementation of business process management (BPM) modern tools in companies becomes a mater of acceptation of an effective organization management. The effective business process management depends on how well it defines responsibilities and forces an employee to take control of their own performance.

The first ultimate precondition for achieving this goal is a properly structured company. Since we have not been confident whether company's internal and external activities are univocally defined, this reality motivated us to change this situation.

Particularly, in coherence with ISO 9000:2000 our focus had been oriented on gradual transformation of functionally-oriented management to process-oriented business process management. In this effort we went through more developmental periods that are briefly outlined in this study. A concurrent attention had been placed on business process reengineering due to preparing preconditions for smooth implementation of enterprise information system (EIS).

NATUZZI FURNISHING & ACCESSORIES BUSINESS UNIT, ITALY   63

Gold Award; nominated by openwork, Italy

Natuzzi is an international manufacturer of top quality furniture, including sofas, armchairs and living room accessories. Based in Italy, the company's high and growing number of worldwide suppliers from India to Brazil, from Indonesia to Vietnam, required optimization and streamlining of its outdated supply chain processes. By implementing Natuzzi's Suppliers Process Management system (SPMS) we integrated our supply chain both internally and externally, thus maintaining our high customer service standards and improving overall operational efficiency, while meeting or exceeding the projected benefits.

UNIVERSITY HOSPITAL VIRGEN DEL ROCÍO, SPAIN   77

Finalist; nominated by Andalusian Health Service, Spain

Document management is one of the major points of inefficiency in hospitals. Due to the great amount of medical reports that are generated for each patient, and the importance of said reports for the continuity of the patient's care, it's indispensable in the improvement in the generation and management of clinical reports.

This work presents the introduction of speech recognition technology for clinical reports in a healthcare organization in Andalusia (Spain). This technology facilitates a quicker and more secure way for health care professionals to complete patient's reports. The new process reduces possible mistakes in the reports and offers better management of hospital resources. We have used methodology based on Business Process Management to guide the implementation of this speech recognition system.

Section 2: Middle East and Africa

ESKOM, SOUTH AFRICA   91

Gold Award; nominated by ciboodle (formerly Graham Technology)

Eskom, South Africa's state-owned electricity company, operates across six regions. This complicated infrastructure led to an urgent need for a flexible, agile system to drive efficiencies and support the re-routing, escalation and monitoring of work.

The project, named Ubuso (the Zulu word for 'face') provided the means to control routing and monitoring of work over Eskom's vast operational arena and sharing workloads across their regional call centres. GT-X Workflow was also essential for campaign management, segmentation and customer profiling.

Section 3: North America

CONAGUA, MEXICO   105

Finalist; nominated by PECTRA Technology

The CONAGUA—Mexico Water National Commission—in charge of managing and preserving national waters in the Mexican Untied States, optimized Public Work Procurement and Execution Process and also provided access to such information to the community as a whole through the web.

The process called "Management and Development of Hydro-agricultural Infrastructure", the organization's most significant and with the greatest breadth of scope, includes programming, budgeting, procurement, execution follow-up, and project-closing activities aimed at the operation, preservation, maintenance and management of the federal hydro-agricultural infrastructure (drain, roads, levees, water control structures such as sewers and fords, and crossing structures such as bridges, etc.) of the 22 Technified Storm Districts (TSDs). The TSDs are areas in charge of generating and preparing investment projects, establishing the particular characteristics of the works to be performed, each taking into account the peculiarities of its geographical area. These TSDs are located in 9 states, covering a 2.7 million-hectare region and have 115,000 users.

GEISINGER HEALTH SYSTEM, USA   125

Gold Award; nominated by TIBCO, USA

In a move to improve document management and bring greater efficiency to clinical, business and financial processes across its organization, Geisinger Health System undertook a cross-enterprise BPM initiative that has resulted in significant productivity improvements, cost savings and improved customer service. Benefits have included automated document retrieval, faster response on billing and claims inquiries and greatly reduced turn around time on accounts payable processes with resulting cost savings of $1.5 million+ annually.

LOUISIANA SUPREME COURT, USA   131

Silver Award; nominated by BEA Systems, USA

Over the last two years, the Louisiana Supreme Court (LASC) rolled out a business process management system (BPMS) to help bridge the deluge of paperwork and manual processes that underpinned its organization. The solution unifies legal records pulled from several systems in an online portal, enables online collaboration, document sharing, and paper filing, and structures core processes. This has helped make process faster, more convenient, and more transparent.

The BPMS includes BPM, Portal, Collaboration, Content and Document Management, and Search Capabilities. By implementing the BPMS, the Supreme Court of Louisiana automated collaboration, document sharing, and paper filing for the average of 3000 filings per year, making each user process simple, convenient, and transparent. The BPMS significantly increased employee efficiency with robust collaboration and search tools and allows justices and clerks to access court documents and schedules from any Web client. This highly successful system not only enabled the Court to be more efficient and effective in day to day operations, but also enabled it to service and supports its constituents (the public) during and after Hurricane Katrina.

WELLS FARGO FINANCIAL INFORMATION SERVICES, USA — 145

Gold Award; nominated by Lombardi Software

Wells Fargo Financial (WFF) is a division of Wells Fargo & Company (NYSE: WFC) with more than $69 billion in assets. It offers real estate-secured lending, automobile financing and other loan products through their network of stores; offers indirect automobile financing through relationships with more than 18,000 franchised automobile dealers in the U.S., Canada and Puerto Rico; offers consumer and private-label credit cards and commercial services to consumers and businesses. WFF also provides credit cards and lease and other commercial financing. Headquartered in Des Moines, Iowa, it serves 8.8 million customers in the US and internationally. Wells Fargo Financial was challenged with increasingly complex processes that are paper-intensive and have a large number of manual steps and handoffs resulting in errors (for example, in typing, misplaced files, etc.) and inefficiencies. WFF elected to incorporate Business Process Management (BPM) into their architecture to reduce the time and cost between process re-design and re-deployment into production: from >12 months to <4 weeks.

Section 4: Pacific Rim

DAEWOO SHIPBUILDING & MARINE ENGINEERING (DSME), KOREA — 155

Finalist; nominated by DNV Software, Norway

In the business world's race for companies to perform faster, better and cheaper, Business Process Management (BPM) and Workflow have been launched as the "Holy Grail" to success. Many of the BPM vendors are developing templates and frameworks (best practices) covering traditional industry verticals such as finance, manufacturing, telecom, and also government sectors. The marine and offshore industry is faced with the same fierce competition as the rest of the business world and must also continually improve performance. But, best practices from other industry verticals are not readily adapted to this industry segment. The workforce of the marine and offshore industry consists of highly qualified knowledge workers undertaking complex design work spanning a long time frame. Their business processes are typically concurrent, multi-discipline, iterative and highly complex. Such organizations pose severe challenges to process management and workflow implementation supporting their best practices. Korea is the world's largest shipbuilding nations, and the three largest yards in the world are located here. The second largest yard in Korea, Daewoo Shipbuilding and Marine Engineering Ltd. (DSME) has over the past years carried out various attempts to improve performance in design activities. Because of competition from "new" shipbuilding nations like China, it has become a vital issue to increase the efficiency in also the management and execution of the design and engineering processes.

To achieve this goal, an engineering process management system has been developed, named *'DSME Engineering Wizard System'* which aims to accelerate process performance by managing execution, promoting collaboration and maximizing engineering data reusability based on workflow concepts.

MINISTRY OF LABOR, REPUBLIC OF KOREA 167

Finalist; nominated by HandySoft Global Corporation

In the spring of 2005, following three years of government-mandated innovation in knowledge-based administration techniques, the Korean Ministry of Labor faced the daunting task of redefining their knowledge management methodology while substantiating and improving business processes. Exploratory efforts to determine strategic goals, core values, core guidelines, and a methodology for on-the-job knowledge integration revealed an ardent need within the Ministry for implementation of an automated process management solution. Upon review of available solutions, the Ministry of Labor chose HandySoft's *Handy BPM* (known as BizFlow in the U.S.) and *Handy PAL* (Process Asset Library), which were utilized in successfully structuring a Process-based Knowledge Management System (PKMS) for the Ministry between 2005 and 2007.

The fully operational Korean Ministry of Labor PKMS now enforces transparency and responsibilities for administrative action, improves the way in which employees work and share knowledge, enhances on-the-job safety, integrates processes across the Ministry, annually saves millions of dollars in operating costs, and — as the world's first PKMS model introduced for administrative work — has even facilitated government-wide innovation.

MALLESONS STEPHEN JAQUES, AUSTRALIA 181

Silver Award; nominated by Metastorm, USA

Mallesons Stephen Jaques made a strategic business decision to embed BPM into its core technology infrastructure upon which it could develop 'circuit breaker' applications that reduced or removed non-productive and non-billable process overhead from the business.

Mallesons' BPM initiative, known internally as Pulse, is an agent of change. Successfully modifying work culture and practice is rated more highly, and considered of more enduring value to the business, than the efficacy of the BPM tools used to enable this change.

Since 2004 Pulse has delivered demonstrable financial benefits, savings in time, fostered transparency, removed regional differences, improved service quality and delivery, eliminated re-work and duplication, provided consistency, accuracy, and repeatability of processes, assisted enforcement of firm policies and improved managerial oversight and decision making.

SATYAM COMPUTER SERVICES LIMITED, INDIA 191

Finalist; nominated by Satyam Computer Services Limited, India

Satyam has operations spreading across 60 countries, and revenues growing at more than 30% annually. The growth has been possible and can be sustained only if transformational changes are made to the way business processes are managed. We conceived and implemented such a transformational initiative by way of creating an Integrated Service Virtualization platform. We have designed this as a workflow based shared services platform to automate and virtualize business processes. Thereby, we have provided "Agility" to the organization to respond to its business demands. Apart from this, from an organisational strategy viewpoint, we needed to selectively link our external stakeholders to our business processes to gain competitive advantage. In other words, we needed to incorporate these stakeholders into our workflows. Our platform which is innovative, home grown and which leverages the best practices in business process and workflow management achieved these objectives.

A Center of Excellence was created to implement the platform which has developed a proprietary framework for Integrated Service Virtualization. Using this framework, 150 business processes are being managed delivering 9 million service requests annually that range from self service to simple transactional services to complex knowledge services.

SHANGHAI COMMERCIAL AND SAVINGS BANK, TAIWAN   203

Gold Award and International Global Award nominated by Flowring Co. Ltd., Taiwan

In the case study, we present how Shanghai Commercial and Savings Bank (SCSB) operates as the workflow application services provider (workflow ASP) via SCSB's e-Bank portal. Using workflow applications not only in the back-office, SCSB pushes the workflow technology to the customer-side by providing VIP enterprise customers with financial transaction approval workflow services through the e-Bank portal, in which it allows enterprises to define and manage their own workflows and business rules for e-Bank transactions. By initiating the project implementation, SCSB aims to establish better environment and mechanism to enhance both security and services of e-Bank by integrating workflow approval processes with the financial transactions to prevent un-authorized e-Bank transaction that violates the business rules of customer's enterprise.

SCSB benefits from the workflow-integrated e-Bank services to satisfy more VIP enterprise customers by making them happy with their e-Bank transactions more auditable and compliant to enterprise rules.

SCSB was awarded the International Global Award for the most highly-rated submission worldwide.

Section 5: South America

GOVERNMENT OF BERMUDA, FORMS AND TRANSACTION ENGINE PROJECT, BERMUDA   219

Silver Award; nominated by PPC, USA

In 2003, the Government of Bermuda launched its initial on-line presence to In 2003, the Government of Bermuda launched its initial on-line presence to communicate with the island's 60,000 citizens and over 6,000 companies. The initial version of the Bermuda Government Portal focused primarily on disseminating information and providing access to commonly used government forms. In 2006, Bermuda Government sought to expand the portal's capabilities by providing a platform for citizens and business to carry out transactions on the portal. In many cases, these transactions required collaboration and monitoring across numerous government roles, departments, and ministries.

After evaluating various approaches, Bermuda Government settled on Business Process Management (BPM), as both a discipline and a technology, to help facilitate on-line government transactions. An initial slate of government transactions were identified for implementation and deployment to citizens and businesses. Additionally, Bermuda Government established the "Better Process Group" as a BPM Center of Excellence. The "Better Process Group," or BPG, provided governance, education, and a forum for capturing lessons learned. This award submission highlights the initial process project implemented by the Government of Bermuda and the benefits realized by the project.

Finalist; nominated by iProcess, Brazil

This paper describes the evolution of Grupo Pão de Açúcar (GPA), one of the largest retail groups in Brazil, in the implementation of Workflow technology. The company started to use Workflow in 2005, with the Investment Approval Workflow (IAW), which reduced the process completion time in around 80%. Soon after this well-succeeded project, GPA started to expand Workflow technology usage to other business processes.

This paper focuses on the largest Workflow project GPA has implemented, the Travel and Expenses Workflow. Motivated by the need to cut and better control costs, this project has redesigned the travel and expenses processes, achieving relevant financial savings, simplifying the job of thousands of employees and drastically increasing the company's level of control of these processes. The success of this project is now leading GPA to definitively incorporate workflow culture into its operations.

Gold Award; nominated by PECTRA Technology, Inc., USA.

MONEDERO is a leader in means of payment in the segment of micro payments in the Republic of Argentina. Conceived 100% under the logic of processes management, it presently allows the user to pay, with a single prepaid recharge Contact Less card, his/her everyday spending in the public and private transport network, retail chains and shopping malls throughout the country.

Section 6 Appendix

Foreword

Nathaniel Palmer, Executive Director
Workflow Management Coalition (WfMC),
President, Transformation+Innovation

For 18 years the **Global Excellence Awards for BPM and Workflow** have covered virtually every economic environment, from bubble to bust. The first modern process era emerged from the economic downturn of the early 1990s. Then, after years defined by relentless cost-cutting, the new charter for business shifted toward enhancing capacity to address the return of customer demand.

As illustrated in the **Shanghai Commercial and Savings Bank** and **MONEDERO** case studies from industries as diverse as banking and transportation, process management has been the key leverage point to enable rapidly growing business volumes without the corresponding creep of infrastructure complexity seen in years past.

Yet the reality today, and one that is not likely to change soon, is that any competitive enterprise must simultaneously be the low-cost and high-value leader. The realities of a "flat world" mean that firms in every market face not only wage pressure, but increasingly quality-based competition previously prevented by geography. How can firms possibly compete in this new era of globalized competition? Get ready for the new era of process excellence! From **Natuzzi** in Italy to **Daewoo Shipbuilding and Marine Engineering** in Korea, the leverage of process management has delivered the competitive edge needed to survive in industries facing some of the greatest pressures of globalization.

The last decade of innovations and investments in Web technologies (now manifest as "Web 2.0") have resulted in an order of magnitude shift in customer expectations for the businesses that serve them (see the **Louisiana Supreme Court** case study to see how far reaching Web 2.0 has become.) Today any business that does not meet expectations for increasing the value it delivers through each customer interaction faces a real threat of being displaced by a competitor who does. It is a buyers' market. Expect that to change any time soon? Don't hold your breath. Lower switching costs, line extension and horizontal expansion, as well as the greater portability of what previously has been immovable "big iron" infrastructure delivered as virtualized services (see **Eskom** and **Satyam**) all of these combined present unprecedented levels of consumer leverage in every sector. Perhaps the only remaining industry with a captive customer base is the public sector. Yet even there (see the cases studies on the **CONAGAUA, Government of Bermuda** and **Korean Ministry of Labor**) the rise in customer expectations has reached constituent services. There are no more safe harbors for delivering poor service.

This may ultimately be the greatest impact of globalization—the shift from a materials economy where the customer experience begins and end with the delivery of the product, to a service-based economy where products themselves have become increasingly service-oriented. This ultimately leads to "mass customization," defined as delivering mass-produced products custom-built for a single customer. In the same manner, however, service offerings are becoming increasingly productized in the pursuit to consistently deliver repeatable services with predictable quality levels. Examples include the guaranteed turn-around of any mortgage application despite inevitable variables, or ensuring that all patients receive consistent service with predictable results (see **University Hospital Virgen Del Rocío** and **Wells Fargo Financial** case studies.)

In world of nearly limitless access to products, competitive differentiation shifts from "what" to "how" value is delivered. Specifically, firms across all sectors are today increasingly differentiated not by service quality levels and by their ability to serve as a point of sale for a growing set of offerings, rather than by what had been their core product offerings. Consider markets such as banking and telecom, where proprietary differentiation has been all but rooted out from individual products or services in either segment. Today products are largely indistinguishable across banks, and communication quality is essentially equal between carriers. Yet differentiation on price alone is increasingly difficult, if not impossible. There is no way to counter a competitor's "free checking" offer with a lower price point. Rather, the competitive response must be "free checking *plus*." Plus what? As the explosion of customer options now available in banking vividly illustrates, the spectrum of what value-added services can be offered are limited only by imagination and innovation. This shift can be seen vividly in the **Shanghai Commercial and Savings Bank** case study, where BPM is leveraged to deliver VIP products and services through an online portal with the same effort and overhead required for any customer.

For these reasons the measure of "value" will be defined simply in terms of the "cheapest option" for only a handful of firms. For the vast majority it means reducing or at least holding the line on costs while continuously enhancing the variety and quality of services offered. This requires also rethinking the relationship of where business value is created. Productivity-targeted investments made in isolation at the back office run out of steam. As illustrated in the **Geisinger Health System** and **CONAGUA** case studies, realizing competitive advantage today means moving to a model where workflows, business rules and other policies (the elements guiding and defining how work is performed and how decisions are made) are in the hands of those at the front lines of the organization.

Ultimately, it is the imperative for rapid response, in a word "agility," which makes it nearly impossible to overstate the importance of process management. Specifically, it means separating the management of business process from the operation and management of systems and applications. In the last 17 years of BPM and Workflow, we have seen the shift from building closed applications, designed over a period of months and built to last for years. The process-enabled enterprise today is based on an era of agile development where applications are delivered in months and the turn-around on process change is determined by business need rather than the IT backlog. As demonstrated in the case studies on **Mallesons Stephen Jaques** and **infoCaja**, the resulting impact on business is realized through the transfer to business process owners control over the management of business processes. This is the transformational benefit of business process management, as shown at **Technical University of Košice**, where the adoption of BPM is not simply the addition of another application to contend with, but enabling a new (for many unprecedented) level of self-determination, that allows employees to take control of their own performance.

Guest Chapters

Process Measurement and Organizational Performance Redux[1]

Dr. Michael zur Muehlen, Stevens Institute of Technology, USA

Organizational structures and their development are studied by a variety of disciplines, such as sociology, psychology, and economics. The goal of organizational research within the field of business administration is the development of viable and efficient structures for enterprises as self-contained economic units. The term itself *organization* can be viewed through an institutional or an instrumental lens. The institutional view describes an organization as a self-contained entity that has a specific structure. The traditional American organizational literature is dominated by the institutional notion of organization. In contrast, for example, German organizational literature focuses primarily on the instrumental view, i.e. the act of organizing an enterprise.

Much of 20th century organizational research is founded on the works of (Fayol, 1949) and (Taylor, 1947). While Fayol researched the managerial structure of an enterprise, Taylor focused on the operational enactment of tasks and the design of structures that support the efficient execution of these tasks. The ideas devised by Taylor have dominated organizational research until the 1970s and can still be found in many enterprises today. Typical characteristics of tayloristic organizational structures include a high degree of separation between tasks, the functional integration of similar tasks into larger organizational units, and a strong separation between dispositive and operational work. Until the 1970s the functional separation of tasks was appropriate for existing market conditions. Since then, increasing market segmentation and shorter product life-cycles, among other factors, have led both businesses and academia to research organizational structures better suited to adapt to changing market conditions, product portfolios, and enterprise infrastructures. For this purpose, business processes have become a focal point of organizational research.

The alignment of organizational structures with business processes has been discussed in the organizational literature as early as the 1930s (Compare, e. g., (Nordsieck, 1934), p. 76, who defines a process as the treatment of objects). Authors such as (Nordsieck, 1934) and (Henning, 1934) created the distinction between the static structure of the corporate organization (Aufbauorganisation) and the organization's processes (Ablauforganisation). This separation has led to a duality within the field of organizational research, found mainly in the German literature. Among American authors, (Chapple and Sayles, 1961) are the most notable early proponents of process orientation.

Despite this early interest in the topic, the process-oriented structuring of organizations did not gain acceptance in corporate practice until the works of (Porter,

---

[1] An earlier version of this article appeared in: zur Muehlen, M.: Workflow-based Process Controlling. Foundation, Design, and Application of workflow-based Process Information Systems. Logos, Berlin 2004.

1985), (Davenport, 1993), (Harrington, 1991), and most notably (Hammer and Champy, 1993) promised significant efficiency and effectiveness gains through the adherence to process concepts and their implementation. Today, the creation of process-oriented organizational structures is widely seen as a suitable way to overcome coordination problems between functional units, which may result in long cycle times, low product quality, and redundant task fulfillment.

Despite strong interest, implementing process-oriented structures has proven difficult for many companies (for a critical review of reengineering mistakes see, e. g., (Davenport, 1995)). Some of the reasons for these difficulties are established information technology infrastructures, which support functional organizations and hinder the transition toward process-oriented structures. Workflow management systems (also known as Business Process Management Systems (BPMS)) address this problem. They support the execution of business processes through the automated coordination of activities and resources according to a formally defined model of the business process (the workflow model). The use of workflow technology as a central building block of modern information system architectures illustrates the increasing importance of this type of application. Workflow technology leverages the value of existing information system infrastructures and helps enterprises in the transition toward a process-oriented organization.

Implementing process concepts within organizations is only one step toward achieving a corporate process focus. In order to reap ongoing benefits from a process-oriented organization, continuous maintenance and control of the business processes is required. Process management deals with the efficient and effective execution of business processes. It consists of the planning, implementation, enactment and controlling of processes, and forms a life cycle that leads to continuous process improvement. Process management addresses the requirement of companies to stay adaptable to environmental and internal changes. Simultaneously it helps companies realize efficiency gains through the exploitation of cost-effective ways to produce goods and perform services. Notably, process-orientation is not a technical concept, nor does it necessarily involve significant investments in BPM technology.

DEMING CYCLE

Using the Deming Cycle for continuous improvement efforts, the necessary steps to align an organization with its processes can be structured along the four phases *plan*, *do*, *check*, and *act* (Deming, 1992).

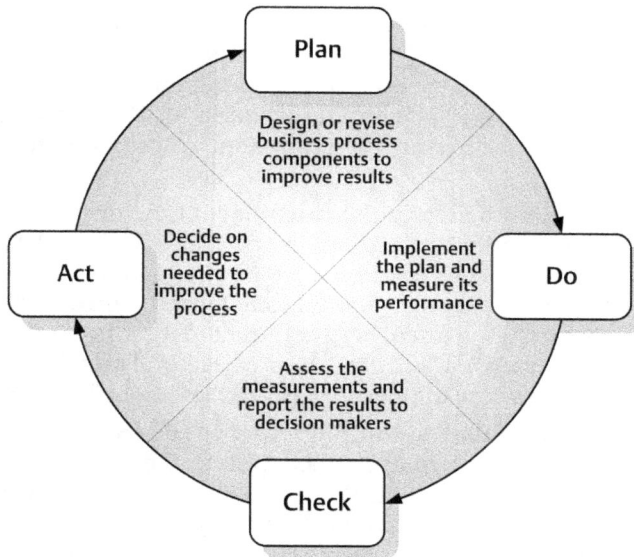

Figure 1: Deming Cycle

Planning Phase (Plan)

Within the planning phase, organizational processes are identified, modeled and optimized. During this phase, various modeling methods can be employed, such as Petri Net-based approaches or Event-driven Process Chains. Most process engineering approaches focus on this phase. These approaches both align and create modification plans for a company's organizational structures and processes, which then lead to reorganization efforts in the execution phase.

Execution Phase (Do)

Throughout the execution phase, processes are implemented and the organizational structure is realigned to fit these processes. Information systems that support individual process steps are implemented, and process participants are trained in the organizational rules and regulations, as well as the use of the supporting infrastructure. Metrics about the process performance are collected during the execution of the new processes.

Evaluation Phase (Check)

Based on the data collected during the execution phase, the effectiveness of the new organization is analyzed in the evaluation phase. Measurements are compared across different processes and organizational units, and relevant results are reported to operative and strategic management units.

Reengineering Phase (Act)

During the reengineering phase, strategic and operative management units review the results of the evaluation phase and analyze the attainment of strategic and operative. Depending on the performance of the organization, adjustments to the underlying goal structure and measures for the improvement of the current situation are used to create alternative plans. One or more of these plans are chosen for implementation and are handed over to the participants of the planning phase as guidelines for their activities.

The Deming Cycle example illustrates that management of process-oriented organizations requires appropriate measurements in order to verify and ensure the effectiveness of an organization's processes. As Michael Hammer puts it "What-ever measures are employed, they must reflect the process as a whole and must be communicated to and used by everyone working on the process. Measures are an enormously important tool for shaping people's attitudes and behaviors; they play a central role in converting unruly groups into disciplined teams." (Hammer, 1996).

Process controlling strives to ensure the rationality of the decision making process by supplying relevant process execution information (Weber, 1997). One of the core tasks of successful process controlling is the installation and maintenance of an infrastructure that validates operational excellence by providing this necessary information. Workflow management systems record events occurring during the execution of process instances and are thus capable of providing detailed infor-mation about the performance of operative processes (McLellan, 1996).

Despite claims by vendors that the introduction of BPMS will foster a more flexi-ble, adaptable organization, there are indications to the contrary (for an early cri-tique compare e.g. (Dourish et al., 1996)). In particular first-generation workflow management systems required specialist knowledge for deployment and mainte-nance, and have often evolved into the next generation legacy infrastructure. In a recent case study, (Royce, 2007) reported that the workflow management system of a large insurance provider was purchased so end-users could change their own processes. This never happened. Instead, end-users submitted change requests to the local IT department, which—for lack of training—had resorted to hard-coding changes around the workflow management system, rather than changing the configuration of the system itself. In Royce's words, "the workflow arteries of the organization were clogged." Recent technological advances, in particular the integration of rules and process technologies suggest that reluctance to adjust-ments may change in the future, but a field evaluation of these advances is still outstanding.

Because the implementation and deployment of workflow-based application sys-tems are complex and therefore time-consuming endeavors, it can be assumed that once this kind of architecture has been successfully deployed, many compa-nies resist the urge to apply changes. The complexity of workflow management projects, however, is only one cause for the reluctant attitude observed toward change. The non-transparency of cause-effect relationships that describe the ef-fects of workflow changes on the organizational, technical, or process level, is a more significant cause for this attitude.

This missing transparency can be attributed to the lack of an integrated infra-structure for the gathering and presentation of performance indicators, which describe the behavior of a workflow-enabled organization. Such an infrastructure would provide guidance on which parameter adjustments might increase an or-ganization's efficiency. A landmark article commonly seen as the origin of modern decision support and management information systems development was the ar-ticle by Leavitt and Whisler "Management in the 1980s", in which the authors argue that decision processes in companies would be automated in the future, leading to a decreasing number of managers (see (Leavitt and Whisler, 1958)). Still, few management decision support systems take the business process per-spective into account. Notable exceptions are management indicator frameworks such as the Balanced Scorecard and Strategy Maps, which explicitly include a perspective for internal business processes (see e.g. (Kaplan and Norton, 1993; Kaplan and Norton, 1996)).

The existing criticism of financial performance indicators and cost controlling approaches does not imply that this information is no longer needed to substantiate managerial decisions. The cost-effective allocation of resources and the efficient use of financial assets are important for the sustainability of any economic entity. Focusing on financial information alone, however, can lead to strategic managerial myopia and—ultimately—the subsequent failure of the organization. The ready availability of process metrics and measurements opens a new front for management by numbers and allows managerial decisions to be more closely aligned with the operational reality of organizations.

REFERENCES

Chapple, E.D. & Sayles, L.R. (1961) The Measure of Management. Designing Organizations for Human Effectiveness. Macmillan, New York (NY).

Davenport, T.H. (1993) Process Innovation. Reengineering Work through Information Technology. Harvard Business School Press, Boston (MA).

Davenport, T.H. (1995) The fad that forgot people. Fast Company, 1, 70.

Deming, W.E. (1992) Out of the Crisis: Quality, Productivity and Competitive Position. Cambridge University Press, Cambridge.

Dourish, P. et al. (1996) Freeflow: Mediating Between Representation and Action in Workflow Systems. Proceedings of the 1996 Conference on Computer Supported Cooperative Work (CSCW '96), 190-198.

Fayol, H. (1949) General and Industrial Management. Pitman & Sons, London.

Hammer, M. (1996) Beyond Reengineering. How the Process-Centered Organization is Changing our Work and our Lives. HarperBusiness, New York (NY).

Hammer, M. & Champy, J. (1993) Reengineering the Corporation: A Manifesto for Business Revolution. HarperBusiness, New York (NY).

Harrington, H.J. (1991) Business Process Improvement. The Breakthrough Strategy for Total Quality, Productivity, and Competitiveness. McGraw-Hill, New York (NY).

Henning, K.W. (1934) Einführung in die betriebswirtschaftliche Organisationslehre. Berlin.

Kaplan, R.S. & Norton, D.P. (1993) Putting the balanced scorecard to work. Harvard Business Review, 71, 134-141.

Kaplan, R.S. & Norton, D.P. (1996) Using the balanced scorecard as a strategic management system. Harvard Business Review, 74, 75-86.

Leavitt, H.J. & Whisler, T.L. (1958) Management in the 1980's. New Information Flows Cut New Organization Channels. Harvard Business Review, 36, 41-48.

McLellan, M. (1996) Workflow Metrics - One of the great benefits of workflow management. In Praxis des Workflow-Management, (Eds, Oesterle, H. & Vogler, P.) Vieweg, Braunschweig, pp. 301-318.

Nordsieck, F. (1934) Grundlagen der Organisationslehre. C. E. Poeschel Verlag, Stuttgart.

Porter, M.E. (1985) Competitive Advantage. Creating and Sustaining Superior Performance. The Free Press, New York (NY).

Royce, G.K. (2007) Integration of a Business Rules Engine to Manage Frequently Changing Workflow: A Case Study of Insurance Underwriting Workflow. Proceedings of the 2007 Americas Conference on Information Systems,

Taylor, F.W. (1947) Scientific Management. Harper & Row, New York (NY).

Weber, J. (1997) Prozeßorientiertes Controlling. WHU Koblenz, Vallendar.

Air Force SOA Enterprise Service Bus C4I Systems Integration Study[1]

Dr. Timothy D. Kehoe, Irene N. Chang, David S. Czulada, Howard Kong, Dr. Dino Konstantopoulos[2] with Linus Chow, Charles Medley[3]

ABSTRACT

Current Air Force (AF) Command, Control, Communication, Computers, and Intelligence (C4I) systems are costly to integrate because they were not initially designed to work together, and many integration efforts still provide point-to-point solutions between tightly coupled systems. The Department of Defense (DoD) is moving toward net-centricity and the AF Air and Space Operations Center (AOC) Enterprise Service Bus (ESB) Risk Reduction Study investigated industry best practices for streamlining the integration process using a Service Oriented Architecture (SOA). The Government study team engaged with three industry vendors and their partners, evaluated ESB interoperability characteristics, explored the business process management workflow orchestration technology, and developed a proof-of-concept prototype for information exchange within the AOC.

1. INTRODUCTION

The AF AOC ESB Risk Reduction Study was an investigation into ESB and workflow orchestration characteristics, and their use in integrating heterogeneous systems. The study focused on three objectives:

- How do standards-based ESBs and other SOA technologies, influence the speed of integration?
- How can business process management (BPM) technology orchestrate the AOC services and mission workflows?
- How can ESB mediation and transformation capabilities ease the pains of connecting heterogeneous C4I systems within an environment such as the AOC?

The study provided insight into both the operational and system engineering benefits of applying ESB and SOA technologies. This was accomplished using industry best practices provided by participating vendors and their partners.

For instance, ESB and SOA technologies can provide automated rapid access to information through stacked services and built-in functions. Previously, this would have been accomplished through manual action by the originator.

---

[1] Approved for Public Release; Distribution Unlimited. Case Number 08-0750; ©2008 The MITRE Corporation. All rights reserved.

[2] Principal System Engineer, Lead System Engineer, Senior Software Engineers MITRE

[3] Principal Consultant, Senior Consultant Oracle Corp.

The study was not a vendor product evaluation exercise. Due to time and re-source constraints, we did neither explore other ESB capabilities (e.g., security, performance, guarantee of delivery, service discovery) nor investigate some ESB related issues like Universal Description Discovery and Integration (UDDI) regis-tries, as well as use of Net-Centric Enterprise Services (NCES) services.

2. STUDY BACKGROUND

Like many other AF C4I systems, the AOC program is in the process of migrating to SOA in order to implement the DoD net-centric vision. The goal is to improve information exchange between loosely coupled systems to address the warfighter needs. The AOC program is considering the enabling of agile integration through use of BPM in combination with a federation strategy that employs SOA at the enterprise level.

The AOC ESB Risk Reduction Study was a proof-of-concept initiative that investi-gated industry best practices in exploiting SOA related technologies. The Gov-ernment engaged with three industry ESB vendors and their partners, evaluated ESB interoperability characteristics, explored BPM workflow orchestration capa-bilities, and developed a prototype system simulating the information exchange within the AOC. The Government and vendor teams successfully integrated six heterogeneous AF systems of record via three different ESB products. The proto-type successfully demonstrated an automated BPM workflow using a notional AOC mission thread.

The AOC mission thread is centered on the production of the Air Tasking Order (ATO). As shown in Figure1, a sequence of strategy, planning, review, and dis-semination activities transforms overall operational concepts into a plan for exe-cution. The focus of this study's mission workflows mainly spans two ATO phases: ATO development and ATO execution.

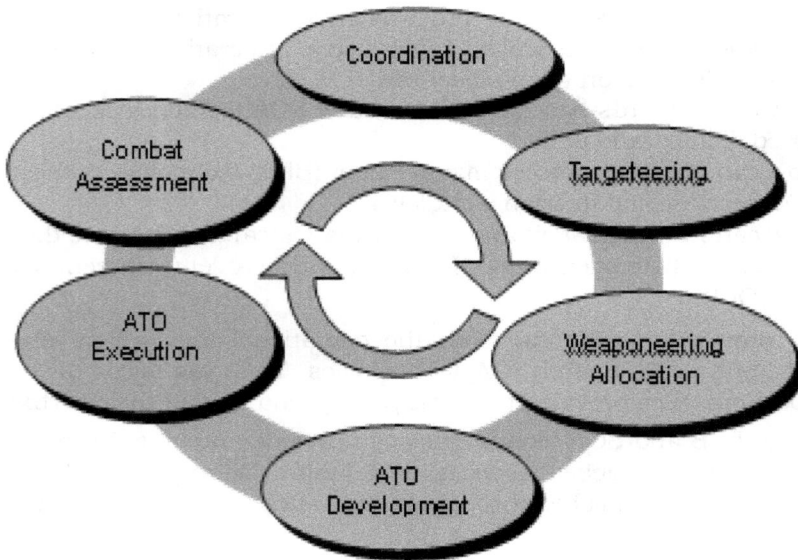

Figure 1. ATO Cycle

3. STUDY METHODOLOGY AND ACTIVITIES

Using ESB and SOA technologies, the study tested the rapid implementation of a proof-of-concept process integrating existing systems. The study sought to determine whether either technologies (ESB or Workflow Orchestration) provided C4I systems with greater visibility, adaptability, control, and agility.

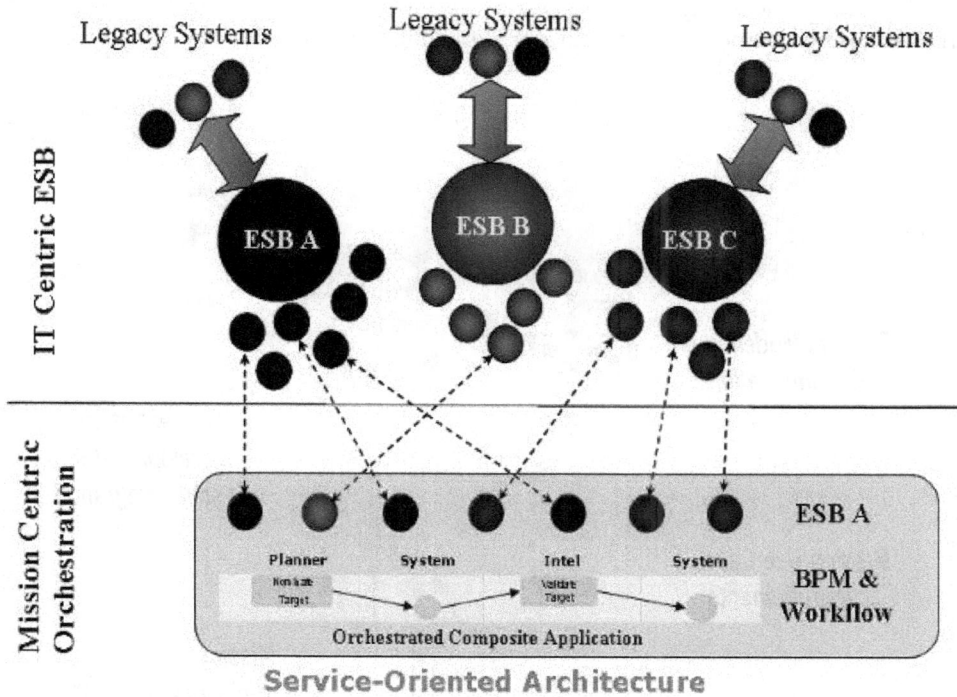

Figure 2. Notional ESB Study Architecture View

As illustrated in Figure 2, three different ESB vendors participated in the study. Each ESB communicated with their assigned AF current systems and other ESB's integration endpoints through emails, SOAP web services, Representational State Transfer (REST)-based RSS services, and legacy flat file data, such as the United States Text Message Format (USMTF) ATO.

Our study encountered some real-life integration challenges such as legacy systems with hardwired proprietary system configurations and differences in data format and message version. These challenges required the vendors to prove that their built-in ESB messaging, mediation, and transformation capabilities could support the integration of C4I systems. Additionally, the study environment required the vendors to demonstrate the ESB interoperability among different ESB products.

During the study we found that the latest BPM technology and methodology provided a level of abstraction of the business logic from the IT centric integration requirements. This abstraction allowed us to rapidly develop user interface components for greater agility of integrating C2 components.

An ESB in conjunction with the use of BPM workflow orchestration presented new integration practices. That included real-time parallel development of small proxy web services to complete the modeling of a business process workflow in the ESB BPM tool. This approach to system integration and business process modeling provided great integration flexibility and could reduce system implementation time. It might improve end-user experiences and allow rapid insight into process and capability changes.

In a short period of time the AOC ESB study team completed at least five iterations of the BPM workflow orchestration development lifecycle. The lifecycle included process modeling, requirements mapping, system integration, orchestration development, and process monitoring as illustrated in Figure 3.

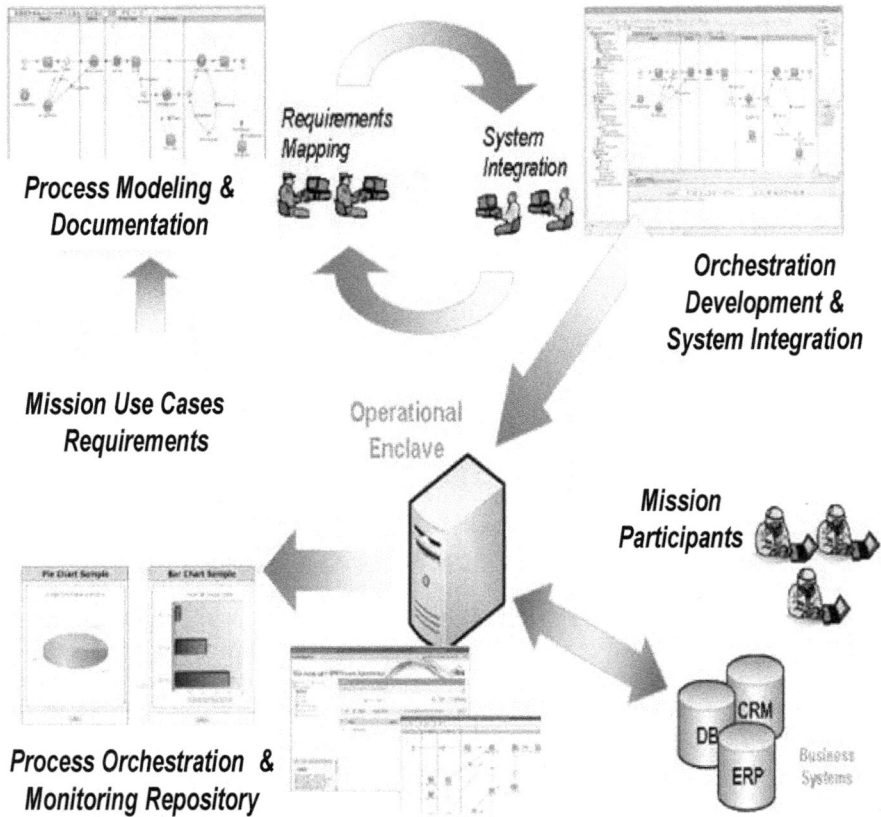

Notional – BPM and Workflow Orchestration Lifecycle

Figure 3. Notional BPM Workflow Orchestration Lifecycle

A notional ATO mission tasking workflow was developed for the ESB study. Illustrated in Figure4, activities in blue icons are system interactions with the ESB, while activities in red icons are human interactions with real-time forms and reports. Note that systems and swim lanes are redacted. Processes and forms are all notional in nature for the study.

Orchestration in the AOC

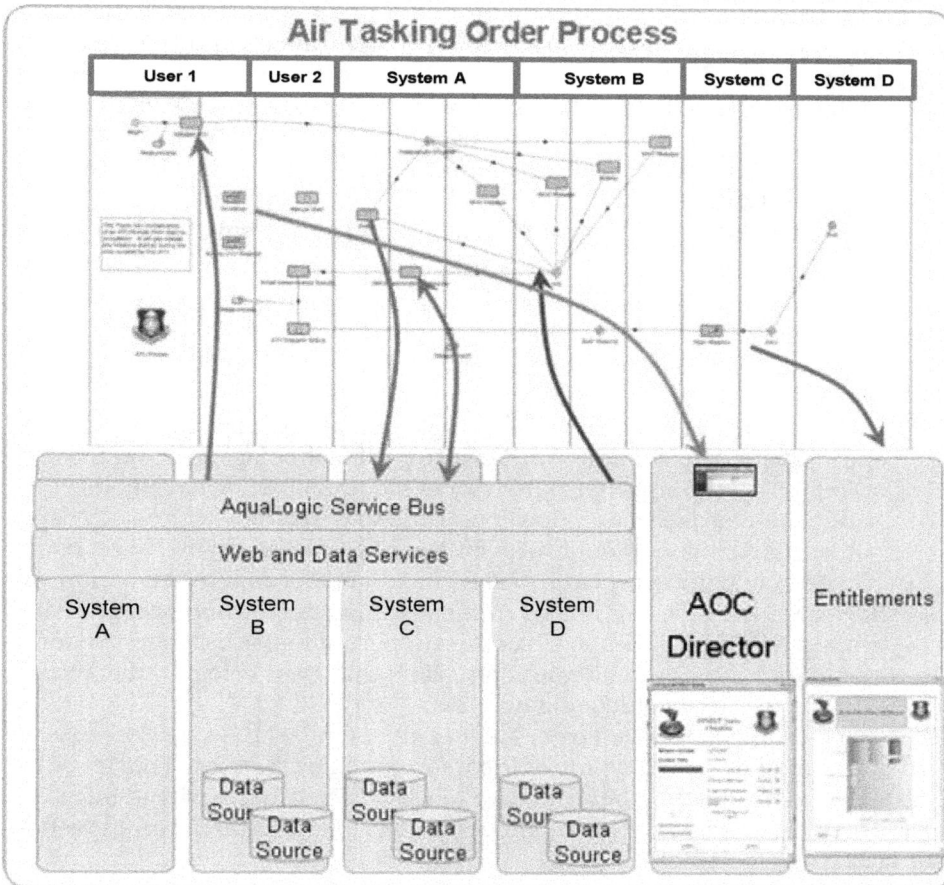

Figure 4. Notional Air Tasking Order Process (Redacted)

4. STUDY RESULTS

Overall the study was successful in producing a working notional system integrated with six AF current systems and three vendor ESBs. The study identified risks and opportunities for SOA interoperability using off-the-shelf ESB products. The use of BPM and workflow orchestration showed the potential for a more agile and rapid development of capabilities.

The AOC ESB Risk Reduction Study demonstrated the following characteristics:

- Increased operator visibility into AOC mission and business processes
- Improved efficiency by automating notification and providing operational status on acknowledgements
- Aggregation of information from different sources
- Automated generation of forms and reports

- Need for Service Level Agreements (SLA) and Quality of Service (QoS) guidelines to control and measure how services are being provided and used at both machine and human interaction levels on the ESB.

Some strengths that the ESB study demonstrated in using the ESB and BPM technologies include:

- Adaptability to changes in integration configurations and business processes
- Ability to model, test, and implement orchestration for operational scenarios
- Interoperability across multiple transports, web services, files, email, RSS feeds, and databases
- Capability for monitoring and reporting gained by using the ESB for inter-system communications

Some challenges that we encountered based on a notional mission scenario include:

- Changing business logic as workflow was reviewed and changed.
- Limited development and short integration time
- Standards are still maturing and implementations may be sensitive to specific versions of standards. Ensuring all technologies are on the same standard is very important. Additionally new technologies may use competing standards. An organization needs to weigh new technology capabilities against operational risks for their specific program. Newer capabilities may not interoperate well with old standards, but the organization may need the new technology capability immediately and accept it on the ground that a new solution has the support of major industry vendors and a large existing customer base. Note that even recognized standards, such as SOAP are still being updated.
- Some established standards, such as the SOAP XML web service standard, require strong typing of the information exchanged. This leads to reduced flexibility in being able to modify the structure of that information at runtime. An evolution towards more flexible standards would be helpful.
- Interoperability requires oversight over various implementation levels (operations, solution, service, and IT asset). For example, the SOAP 1.2 standard may be used but two different versions of the data (schema) are implemented at the IT asset level. A client tries to communicate across both and fails due to incompatible SOAP versions.
- Policy enforcement is the only way to ensure the effectiveness of a governance strategy. For example, if a new capability has side-effects that could cascade through to dependent service consumers, the change must be managed by the people who govern the systems affected.
- Business changes due to mergers and acquisitions of software vendors provide both opportunities as well as risks. In some cases, a merger or acquisition provides more resources and increased scale for product research and development, as well as support. However, if there is product overlap, then there is a risk that one or more technologies will either be discontinued or product support will decrease. It is important to establish what the product roadmap is from the vendor. Note that during this study two of the three product vendors were acquired (Cape Clear was acquired by Workday and BEA was acquired by Oracle).

The study result was the creation of two notional mission processes and several forms and reports along with the integration of six AF current systems through the ESBs.

5. CONCLUSION

The three BPM standards used for this study included Business Process Modeling Notation (BPMN), Business Process Execution Language (BPEL), and XML Process Definition Language (XPDL). As BPM matures, convergence and enhanced support of these standards by vendors continue to develop. Currently, risks are low that BPM standards will diverge due to the general market consensus (Gartner, IDC, Forrester, etc.). BPM is one of the fastest growing technology areas.

The study provided insight into the operational and system engineering benefits of applying ESB and SOA technologies. Advances in product capabilities and improvements in the underlying methodologies create opportunities for more rapid solutions. There is reduced risk during implementation because development spirals are shorter and reusability of approved services is increased. It is important to note that regardless of the technologies selected, organizational and cultural walls will always be a threat to solutions. The organizational challenges grow as these new solutions span both IT infrastructures and mission users.

The study showed that use of ESB and BPM tools to orchestrate workflows can help separate business logic from information providers. This level of separation allows parallel development and integration of small and easy-to-code web services through business process models. This could increase integration flexibility and shorten integration development cycle while reducing risks. This conclusion comes with the premise of a collective effort between business users with a mission focus and information providers with system data expertise. The study also showed that with the appropriate selection of technologies, BPM workflow orchestration capability can automate system interactions, as well as allow humans to participate in the workflow.

Most importantly, the study revealed the need to identify critical information resources and expose them through loosely coupled, reusable, and composable services for successful composition into workflows. Without the basic raw material of workflow, the information consumed by the business process, the ESB will have nothing to glue together and hence the value of ESB orchestration would be severely limited. Without access to information freed of business process presumptions, the recombination of information by the orchestration engine in a new process would be difficult to achieve. Therefore, it is essential for systems to expose quality services that provide access to the information needed to construct workflows with the proper granularity for both current and future transactions.

6. REFERENCES

Organization for the Advancement of Structured Information Standards (OASIS) *http://www.oasis-open.org/home/index.php*

Workflow Management Coalition (WfMC) *http://www.wfmc.org/*

"BPM and Service-Oriented Architecture Teamed Together: a Pathway to Success for an Agile Government," Linus Chow and Charles Medley, "2007 BPM and Workflow Handbook," edited by Layna Fischer, Future Strategies Inc. 2007

"BPM, SOA and Web 2.0 Convergence: Business Transformation or Train wreck?" Linus Chow, Peter Bostrom, 2008 BPM and Workflow Handbook, edited by Layna Fischer, Future Strategies Inc. 2008

Service-Oriented Architecture Concepts, Technology, and Design, Thomas Erl, Prentice Hall, 4th edition, 2006

Section 1

Europe

infoCaja MiFID Client Order Handling Process, Spain

Silver Award, Europe.
Nominated by BizAgi Ltd., UK

ABSTRACT

In view of the challenge to comply with MiFID – Market in Financial Instruments Directive – requirements by November 2007, infoCaja began the process to select a BPM technology so that its affiliate banks could adapt as soon as possible to the regulations. They wanted an agile and efficient business solution which would also support evolution of the guidelines in the long term.

The processes automated with BizAgi at infoCaja, a company that provides shared services for its five affiliate banks (Cajastur, Caja Canarias, Caja Castilla la Mancha, Caja Murcia, y Caixa de Balears), supports the MiFID client order handling process trough a multi-bank, individually administered environment (e.g., each bank can define and modify the tests and their validity).

Thus infoCaja, supported by Pricewaterhouse Coopers and the agility of BizAgi, was able to implement the automation of this process in less than 4 months, and went live by the specified date of 1st November 2007, managing more than 5,000 users in more than 1.500 branches.

The solution is available in 2 languages (Spanish and Catalonian), integrates with the existing financial terminal software, the 5 legacy systems and the document management system, besides providing process services for the Spanish Savings Bank Confederation (CECA).

OVERVIEW

infoCaja is a society established in 2001 by Caja de Ahorros de Asturias (Cajastur) (Asturias Savings Bank), Caja General de Ahorros de Canarias (CajaCanarias) (Canarias General Savings Bank), Caja Castilla La Mancha (Castilla La Mancha Savings Bank), Caja Murcia (Murcia Savings Bank) and "Sa Nostra" Caixa de Balears (Baleares Savings Bank), in response to an agreement aimed at promoting excellence in technological services that it provides for its clients and improving the competitiveness of its associates.

Ever since it was created, infoCaja has allowed its partners to undertake projects together with the aim of obtaining synergies that increase their capacity and effectiveness; this includes sharing the same Data Processing Center and having a common platform for applications, based on high quality technology.

Owing to the consolidation of the European Union and the growth and internationalization of companies trading in financial instruments and their derivatives (Investment Banks, Portfolio Managers, Stock Exchange Commission Agents, Brokers, Finance Corporations, etc.) the European Economic Community and its regulating organizations created the MiFID regulations – Market in Financial Instrument Directive – with the main purpose of unifying and developing a new scheme for trading stocks and shares; with more information, transparency and protection for investors, greater knowledge about the client for whom they are acting as consultants and with mechanisms for more supervision and the prevention of conflicts.

Since the regulations were to be effective from 1st November, 2007, BizAgi were faced with the challenge of helping our partners to adapt quickly to all the guideline requirements, through a Multi-Bank solution (replicable for all the banks) but with individual management of the MiFID Client Order Handling Process.

In order to comply with this objective, InfoCaja created a new operation model based on business and not on technology, seeking to provide our partners with a service that is client focused, compliant with all the guidelines and flexible in sales and marketing in order to benefit from the opportunities that integration has to offer.

After observing and evaluating different technological solutions for obtaining those objectives, InfoCaja selected Pricewaterhouse Coopers and BPM BizAgi, with its Knowledge Module (prefabricated templates adaptable for each organization) for the MiFID Client Order Handling Process. Implementation began in July 2007 and went live on 1st November 2007.

With this implementation in record time (4 months), InfoCaja is at the forefront in Spain in adapting to the guidelines by means of a technological solution.

Likewise, our members have attained an efficient day to day interaction with their clients, whereby, using the database for each one (financial information, suitability, experience, etc.), the client is informed about products or services that each bank offers, transparently, in real time and on the basis of the risk principles contained in the guidelines.

With the BPM system, infoCaja's role as a shared services provider expanded to our associates' business area. It now provides efficient management of processes and monitoring with the possibility of being improved or modified independently in each bank.

Thanks to these results, InfoCaja is planning to apply the solution to new business processes in order to make the most use of the benefits that BPM technology offers within a multi Bank environment.

Key Motivations

With the globalization and consolidation of new free trade agreements between nations, regulations will cease to be national and undergo continuous evolution to create regional regulatory frameworks to protect the consumer.

Every organization has to adapt rapidly and efficiently to the regulations that govern them; manual operations and systems for complying with the regulations lack the flexibility and agility to adapt to this regulatory evolution and demand an enormous effort in time and money on the part of the organizations.

Organizations (shared services) such as infoCaja have an even greater challenge, since they have to find solutions flexible enough to adapt to each members circumstances and specifications, with the information, transactions and other variables that this implies.

In the case of MiFID, infoCaja had to find a system that allowed its 5 associated banks to provide service that complied with the following requirements:

- Consultancy for each client based on their classification (Retailers, Professionals and Peer groups)
- Reliable information about the client: Financial information, marketing experience, business transactions carried out, etc.

- On the basis of this knowledge, evaluation of the client's suitability for the offer of certain products and services with a specific questionnaire (test) for each bank.
- Providing the client with information in real time regarding the service and product options available according to his profile.
- To certify consent and acceptance by the client regarding services or products offered, and if applicable, records of client's responsibility when products not offered are taken.
- Execution of the processes to ensure management of the information on business transactions carried out during the last 5 years.
- Visibility and transparency for auditors and supervisors on the state and execution of business transactions carried out, checking that the rules and regulations were complied with.

With a manual operation execution, it would not be possible to manage and supervise the business operation in real time, with the required level of information, visibility and integration.

Likewise, the solution had to take into account Core processes from beginning to end that affected different areas in each bank and used different host information systems and financial terminal software for their execution. With these considerations infoCaja chose BPM technology to standardize, manage and visualize the MiFID Client Order Handling Process in the 5 banks starting from the client requests a product or service, passing through risk evaluation, experience, etc. till the delivery of a final consultancy result.

The reasons for implementing BPM technology for infoCaja may be summed up as:

- Support in record time for the Guideline: Using the solution to manage and support the process in a minimum lapse of time, with shared application to the 5 banks and individual management of process development.
- Maximum Flexibility for Integration with the Legacy Systems, the document management system and the financial terminal software of infoCaja: Most client information that has to be manipulated and modified to comply with MiFID is found in different types of systems. These systems have to deliver and receive facts on the business consultancy process quickly, in order to keep updating the client information.
- Support the evolution of the regulation through a flexible solution based on processes: Ensuring maximum agility at the moment of modification that supports the evolution of the regulation.
- Management and handling in real time of client information and business transactions that the client has carried out, so as to ensure effective management, control and monitoring throughout the whole operation.
- Better Customer Service with MiFID: On the basis of client knowledge deliver a modernized and efficient business service, able to cope with the consolidation and competition that will result from the integration of the financial instruments market in Europe.

To achieve these objectives we carefully reviewed the BPM solutions available in the market. Our evaluation team gave the best rating to the Knowledge Module for automating the MiFID Client Order Handling Process developed by BizAgi with advice from PriceWaterHouse Coopers. This BPM Module (prefabricated templates adaptable to each organization from beginning to end) permitted delivery of a BPM solution to our associates in record time and achieved the highest rating for the following criteria of evaluation:

- References in the financial sector
- Consistency between the process and the MiFID requirements
- Multi-Bank solution
- Professional staff specialized in financial sector implementations
- Flexible Architecture, whose technologies, such as SOA, Virtualization or Replication of information allowing an agile integration with the proposed platform.
- Solution completely on line, so that there is an effective management, control and monitoring throughout the whole operation.
- BPM platform, agile enough to expand process automation to other areas.

Using a BPM platform, infoCaja was able to adapt more rapidly and easily to the regulations, since it provided all the tools for efficient connection with other systems, and more importantly, it aligned correctly all the staff, resources and information related to the processes so as to comply with the regulations.

Process Innovation For Shared Services

The design of the Knowledge Module for MiFID Client Order Handling process was conceived in order to enable infoCaja to provide a service for its Multibank shareholders and their business. The process is divided into 3 main phases as shown in the following graph:

The process begins with the registration of information phase, that is to say, the moment in which the client requests one or more MiFID services or products and the consultant records the facts through the financial terminal software connected to the BizAgi functionality. In this phase, the consultant located in any of the 5 banks in more than 1500 offices, captures the necessary client information. BizAgi then interprets this information and connects to the legacy system of the corresponding bank (5 hosts) to obtain the information about the client. If it does not exist, the client is created by the solution.

When the client exists, it is possible to see the information recorded from the questionnaire (test) completed when other products were previously requested, and this way the consultant can plan and carry out his/her activities on the basis of the knowledge about the client, thereby increasing productivity and efficiency.

According to the unit and classification of the client, BizAgi automatically generates a list containing the services that can be offered. Once the services have been selected, the MiFID products are listed, so the client can request them.

Datos personales

Tipo de documento

Número Documento   abc

Nombre   abc

Categoría

Perfil de riesgo

Datos de solicitudes

Fecha solicitud desde

Fecha solicitud hasta

Motivo cancelación

Estado del caso   ⊙ Pendiente   ⊙ Cerrado   ⊙ Anulado   ⊙ Todos

Datos del test

Fecha test desde

Fecha test hasta

Fecha caducidad desde

Fecha caducidad hasta

Fecha última modificación Test desde

Fecha última modificación Test hasta

Estado del Test

Tipo de test

Resultado de Test Conveniencia

Resultado de Test Idoneidad

Datos del producto

Familia de Producto

Producto

Client and request Information Registration

Test Information Search

Product Registration

From the moment the client is registered, the consultant may cancel the request either at the client's initiative or that of the organization at any point in the process, and keep a record of this.

Once the requested MiFID services and products have been registered, the second phase of the process is the analysis of the request. This phase establishes whether a questionnaire is required and the type of test to be taken according to the services that have been chosen, the complexity of the products that have been selected and the client's classification.

In order for this section to be managed individually by each one of the 5 banks, the BPM system keeps a database of questions and answers (questionnaire for each bank) for analysis of the request. This data base is executed by the BizAgi Workflow motor, which elects automatically in real time the questionnaire (test) to be completed on the basis of the requested products or services.

The questionnaire (test) may also be modified online by any of the banks in case additional questions are required. In this case, the consultant manager chooses the questions in real time from the data base and BizAgi dynamically changes the questions on the screens according to the modifications.

Using this scheme, BizAgi saves versions of the questionnaires that may be used again, thus considerably increasing customer services and productivity when carrying out the consultancy.

Later, during the analysis of the request, the accuracy of the client's information is certified along with the details of the questionnaire (test) and whether it was previously approved. A service/client evaluation is then made, based on the service/product combination and the client's characteristics.

The BPM Motor makes the validations according to MiFID and delivers automatically the information about the products that are or are not suitable to the consultant, so that recommendations can be made to the client.

Additionally, BizAgi permits identification of the products that were not requested but that are suitable according to the evaluated characteristics. The consultant may personalize the recommendation, adding products that were not requested and yet are suitable according to his/her analysis or eliminate products that, even though they comply with the evaluation, he/she does not consider being adequate. This has increased the flexibility in the processes of each bank and improved standard of customer service.

In cases in which the client decides not to answer the questionnaire (test), the client must sign that he/she accepts the conditions of execution only, and products are recommended by the consultant without their evaluation exactly as indicated by the guideline; these documents are loaded and filed as part of the case history.

Finally, the third Phase of the process establishes Acceptance or Rejection of the Request. In this phase the decision is made regarding the products to be contracted, where the client initially signs the result of the evaluation, showing the products recommended in order to make a decision.

If the client wishes to contract products that have not been recommended, he/she must sign a declaration expressing the wish to contract at his/her own risk. If the client does not accept the conditions, rejection of the client is reported, otherwise, the products are created in the bank's system.

BizAgi allows this based on MiFID execution policies and the banks guidelines.

Time For Compliance And Long Term Flexibility

infoCaja was the first organization to implement a technical solution to handle MiFID because it was able to adapt the BizAgi MiFID Knowledge Module (Process Templates, Structured and Flexible Data Model, User Interface for all human activities, Configurable Business Rules, Interfaces with External Systems, etc.) to the operations of the associated banks, rapidly.

To achieve this, infoCaja worked and provided all its resources 7x24 (infrastructure, test environments, certification, bank managers, etc.) so the solution would be ready by the deadline and they could obtain detailed and in-depth knowledge of the regulations and the solution.

Likewise, to adapt this prefabricated BPM structure correctly, it involved the chief managers of each bank in the process to define and construct the variables for the questionnaires to make the process more flexible and individually compliant. These variables included:

- Months of Validity: Determines the existence of approved tests that are still in effect.
- Complexity of the product: Each one of the products is listed according to complexity.
- Products offered according to the units, the services they provide and the client's classification: Products offered are determined according to established variables such as unit, service, and client classification.

- Fulfillment policy test: The type of questionnaire (test) to be completed is determined according to established variables such as service, product complexity, client classification.

With this strategy, infoCaja acquired the knowledge that positioned it as manager of the solution for its shareholders and were able to implement it in record time.

Integration According To MiFID Compliance

infoCaja is process oriented and decided to integrate SOA and BizAgi according to the existing process scheme. This allowed each bank to interact with its systems at the indicated moment and according to the needs of the process.

Initially, BizAgi displayed its functionality by means of the infoCaja financial terminal software. This terminal is configured by infoCaja to let BizAgi recognize the associate bank and organizes the language, the forms and the data base relative to that bank. When executing the processes, BizAgi connects with the appropriate legacy system through service layer created for this purpose called "Pasarela" and the document management system.

On the other hand, CECA, an organization that provides technological services to the majority of the banks in Spain, requests BizAgi services to carry out some MiFID activities and processes already created for infoCaja.

Using this scheme, infoCaja manages the BPM system efficiently for compliance with MiFID, keeping records of the interactions with each banks legacy system, based on the information previously captured through the finance terminal and supporting document management throughout the process. This business centered service has demonstrated efficiency and productivity to its associates. In the following graph we can see the interaction with the different systems:

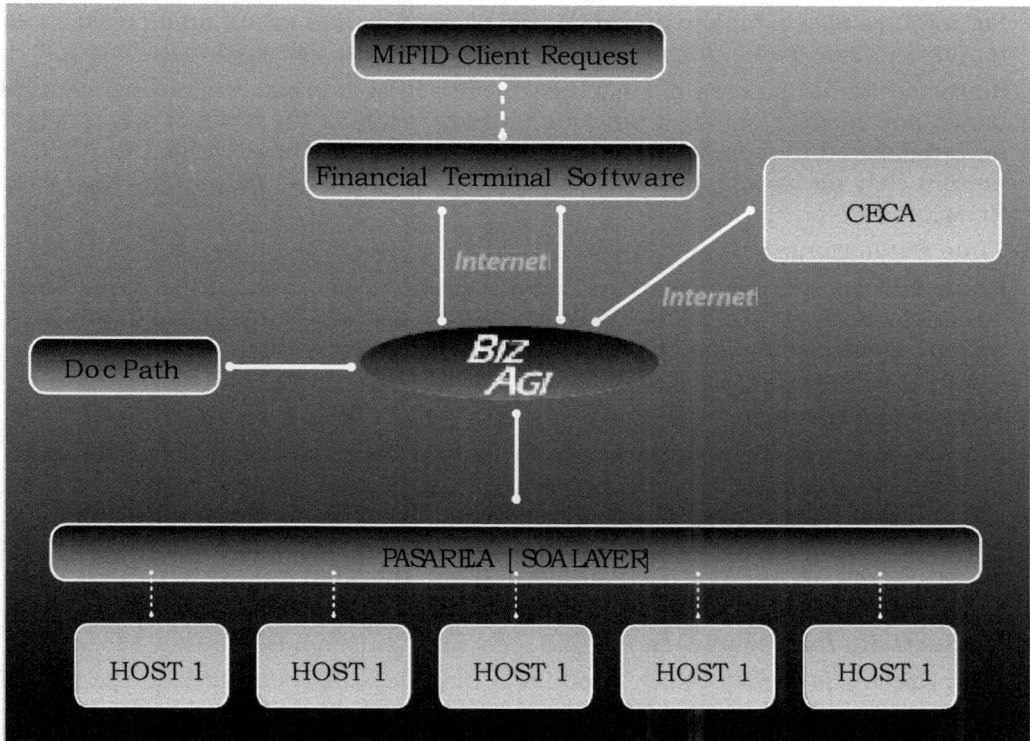

A New Way Of Working For infoCaja And Its Shareholders

The new processes required by MiFID and delivered through the BPM application to the associated banks, changed completely the work habits of its staff.

On the one hand, infoCaja changed the way services were delivered to its associates, previously focused for the most part on technology, (host and data base management). Now its role involves a support to business that calls for greater knowledge of the operation and improvement of shareholders' CORE processes.

Likewise, for the banks, interaction between consultants and clients is now more agile and efficient, but at the same time less proactive and more passive, since, according to MiFID, the client's characteristics are what dictate the services and products that can be recommended.

This change in organizational culture has been a decisive factor in the implementation of BPM at bank level. An important effort was made on the part of the top management to train employees on the regulations and the technological solution.

Benefits Of Complying With BPM

infoCaja, at the moment in which the guideline was issued, made a budget for the implementation of a solution and a commitment to implement by the MiFID deadline. Using the BizAgi MiFID Knowledge Module the compliance process resulted in an investment 80% less than the budget allocated and was achieved in less than 50% of the time.

The main business impact is found in the Time to Compliance of the solution. infoCaja was the first organization in Spain to support technologically the request process of client orders according to the MiFID regulations.

For infoCaja as a company providing shared services this meant an increase in its reputation, image and an increment in the added value delivered to its banks.

Since the MiFID process did not exist before BPM implementation, neither the banks nor infoCaja obtained previous measurements of the costs of this process; nevertheless, the approach has been so important for these companies that at present they are studying several other processes that can be implemented with BizAgi.

Time Reductions

Regulation questionnaire (test) are completed in minutes, so that the consultancy does not interfere with the business pertaining to the sale of financial products, thereby guaranteeing compliance with the regulations without sacrificing opportunities for generating additional income for the banks associated to infoCaja.

Increased Revenues

A better business consultancy before the sale of the product not only reduces legal risks associated with non-compliance of the regulations (these risks can even affect the acknowledgement of losses suffered by a client that has not received the proper advice) but also reduces the risk of a dubious portfolio associated with the financial product that has been supplied. Given the short history of the execution of the system, these savings are not yet quantifiable.

Productivity Improvements

The project was carried out in a total of 4 months with a staff of 5 on the part of the suppliers, which makes it the most efficient project developed so far by infoCaja.

BEST PRACTICES AND LEARNING POINTS WITH COMPLIANCE PROCESSES

The best practices for implementing regulation compliance processes in shared services organizations with BPM are:

- ✓ *To ensure knowledge about the regulations on the part of the suppliers*

- ✓ *Staff 100% engaged with the ability to make quick decisions regarding the design of the process and infrastructure of the solution.*

- ✓ *To start the project with prefabricated Knowledge Modules guaranteeing the scope and cover of the regulations to be automated.*

- ✓ *To centralize the information while decentralizing its management.*

COMPETITIVE ADVANTAGES GAINED

The management of compliance processes in organizations is complex. The lack of information on the laws and processes, the lack of time to adapt to them, and their constant change, does not permit an efficient management under manual operation schemes or inflexible technological solutions.

Our chief competitive advantage when we implement an agile BPM such as BizAgi, is that we are the first organization to adapt to the regulations through a technological solution which allows us to execute, manage and continually improve processes that most of out competition are unable to do.

To have a solution that allows us to monitor and modify in real time the MiFID Client Order Handling process put us one step ahead of our competitors who for the most part carry out their operations manually.

Our approach is different: through the flexibility and agility of BPM we seek opportunities for improvement in the compliance processes which result in business opportunities for our associates. Thanks to this, our banks provide better service to their clients and this advantage can be maintained thanks to the continuous improvement in the processes by using a fulfillment technology based on BPM.

Likewise, with the implemented BPM architecture our services, such as infoCaja expanded significantly; we can now automate new CORE business processes and position ourselves more every day as a strategic partner for our banks, allowing them to optimize the long term operation of their business.

BPM Architecture For Shared Services Compliance

The architecture of the MIFID system basically relies on the following components:

Financial terminal software (TF): An application executed by the terminal staff in each Branch of the 5 banks through which financial operations are carried out.

Website Membership: Allows authentication of users that enter the web portal and offers web services to CECA.

BizAgi WorkPortal: Application where questionnaires (tests) are completed by consultants (suitability, convenience and execution).

"Pasarela" SOA Layer: Intermediate system that solves requests for data of a client, updating the risk profile and results of questionnaires (tests) on the infoCaja central system known as Host.

Host: Legacy System, where the information resides that corresponds to bank clients.

CECA: Invokes via Web Services the main functions of the process modeled on BizAgi, such as tests of suitability, convenience and execution.

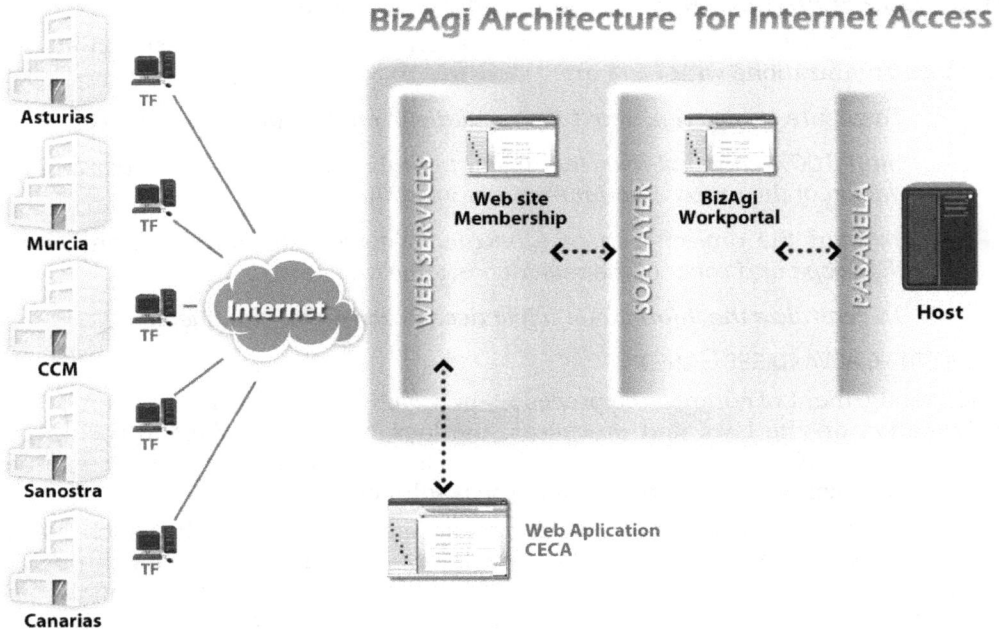

BizAgi Architecture for Internet Access

Using this scheme, each bank that accesses the MiFID services has a Web portal and an independent data base. Just like BizAgi reports functionality to the different banks, this one is available for the CECA Web portal. Likewise, this scheme supports multi languages (Spanish – Catalonian) according to the origin of the consultant that accesses the application, through the values it communicates to the Financial Terminal software.

On the other hand, BizAgi integrates with each host using the "Pasarela" layer to make the various consultations based on the execution of the process and the information captured with the finance terminal. And finally, in order for the different activities of the process to be included in printable reports, integration was made with DocPath.

The configuration of the Basic system includes:

Type	Processor	Hard Disk	RAM	Application to install
1 Server	Xeon 2.4Ghz	80GB	4 GB	Web Server
1 Server	Xeon 2.4Ghz	80GB	4 GB	2 Web Server
1 Server	Xeon 2.4Ghz	120GB	4 GB	Database

In pre-production (development) as well as Production the load balancer is configured which distributes the requests entered to each one of the Web nodes.

TECHNOLOGY AND SERVICE PROVIDERS

BizAgi Ltd.

With a strong foundation in the main European and Latin American financial markets and more than 18 years of study and analysis of organizational processes, BizAgi is the leading BPM solution for automating and improving human processes using the minimum amount of programming. We are 100% dedicated to continuous improvement in the performance of our clients' processes, making them more productive, efficient and agile than their competitors through a unique concept where "The Process IS The Application." BizAgi offers organizations a complete process automation platform designed for supporting corporate trans- formation. BizAgi reduces "time-to-market" for new ideas and business strategies, and facilitates continuous process improvement.

www.BizAgi.com

Pricewaterhouse Coopers

PWC Spain contributed all the knowledge of the MiFID regulations, as well as the management of the project for infoCaja.

Its ample experience in fundamental business processes for the finance sector is the cornerstone of success of any BPM initiative.

LPH Vranov n/T, Slovakia

Finalist, Europe.
Nominated by Technical University of Košice, Slovakia

EXECUTIVE SUMMARY / ABSTRACT

Nowadays, the implementation of business process management (BPM) modern tools in companies becomes a mater of acceptation of an effective organization management. The effective business process management depends on how well it defines responsibilities and forces an employee to take control of their own performance. The first ultimate precondition for achieving this goal is a properly structured company. Since we have not been confident whether company's internal and external activities are univocally defined, this reality motivated us to change this situation.

Particularly, in coherence with ISO 9000:2000 our focus had been oriented on gradual transformation of functionally-oriented management to process-oriented business process management. In this effort we went through more developmental periods that are briefly outlined in this study. A concurrent attention had been placed on business process reengineering due to preparing preconditions for smooth implementation of enterprise information system (EIS).

OVERVIEW

LPH Vranov n/T, injection molding company, has a relatively short history. Established in 1989, LPH purchased their first injection molding machine to make components for electricity meters produced in Slovakia. By 1995, company business had turned into a limited liability company. In this period LPH bought new production hall with 1800 sq m and started closer collaboration with the company Whirlpool Slovakia a. s. in Poprad. Presently, manufacturing plant of LPH Vranov n/T has more than 5000 sq m, and customers now include names like Bosch, Siemens Hausgerate, Xerox, Molex and others. Around 90% of LPH customers are global companies and nowadays they move closer to us, thanks to that, company can deliver the goods to the customer in a shorter time and without unexpected troubles and delays. Especially, automotive sector is the biggest success of the Slovak economic transition. It brings very effective working companies to the country. The Slovak Republic now hosts the third largest volume car producer in Central and Eastern Europe.

The Company pays special attention to the technical innovations by promoting a modern quality management style. For instance, a unique Counterweights Method for Balancing of Mechanisms applied in washing machines was by company's engineers developed. In 2000, LPH Vranov n/T certified its quality management system by ISO 9001:1994. Subsequently in 2002 and 2006 LPH was recertified by ISO 9001:2000. In March 2007, additional quality management system certificate under ISO TS 16 949 has been obtained by the company for the supplies to the automobile industry.

Business Context

Similarly as many other companies, LPH Vranov n/T started with the traditional organizational structure, which is principally organized by objects. Objects are usually represented by divisions, departments or smaller units.

Because a modern organization has to be adjustable to the major or minor changing situation, it is practically constantly transformed. While it is possible to plan retaliations for major change, minor changes may be unnoticed even thought they implicate important functional changes. However, minor organizational changes may pose a serious problem for EIS functionality. Accordingly, organizational structure models might be integral to application architecture of an EIS. The practical problem, from our viewpoint, is lying in an inconsistency of organization transformation and information system (IS) analysis methods. Due to that fact, a choice of suitable business process redesign methodology presents a crucial decision. Based on statistics it is known, that the success or failure of using any of business process redesign methodology is addressed to the issue of company culture or subculture. Company culture or subculture issues, in this sense, are closely related to familiarity of management with applied methodologies. Thus, our approach to the selection of suitable business process redesign methodology was based on respecting this piece of knowledge.

Solving methodological problems requires cooperation between the IS designers that develop and apply tools of business process reengineering and the users that redesign the organization structure. Since the company disposes with its own information technology (IT) department, IT specialists were involved into our team for business process mapping and modeling.

Due to the evident differences between the theories of business processes redesign and information systems development it is important to manage existing semantic gaps. Principally, this phenomenon results from the different subject matters and their theoretical grounds. With aim to overcome this problem the external expert was invited to our project. The rest of our project team consists of company's internal staff members including key managers and quality specialists.

The Key Innovations

The selected method for redesigning business processes described below covers more or less the well known enterprise reengineering tenets to reach process-oriented management attributes. They are:

- Organize around outcomes, not tasks.
- Identify all the processes in an organization and prioritize them in order of redesign urgency.
- Integrate information processing work into the real work that produces the information.
- Treat geographically dispersed resources as though they were centralized.
- Link parallel activities in the workflow instead of just integrating their results.
- Put the decision point where the work is performed, and build control into the process.
- Capture information once and at the source.

Evenly, the eight principles of TQM that have been distilled into ISO 9000:2000 have been taken into consideration, as follows:

- customer-focused organization
- leadership

- involvement of people
- process approach
- system approach to management
- continual improvement
- factual approach to decision making
- mutually beneficial supplier relationships.

From the viewpoint of project objectives, the process approach principle presented the decisive object of interest. By "Guidance on the Concept and Use of the Process Approach for management systems" [1] the process approach introduces horizontal management, where processes are managed as a system, by creating and understanding a network of the processes and their interactions. The example of generic model of a process network shows figure 1.

Business process reengineering (BPR) project and pursuing a quality management effort have dominated management focus on the need to continuously improve processes. Quality specialists tend to focus on incremental change and gradual improvement of processes, while proponents of reengineering often seek radical redesign and significant improvement of processes. The extreme difference between continuous process improvement and business process reengineering evokes a question, when to prefer the first over the second. Since information systems architecting require redesign of business processes, then it could be preferred approach based on BPR in an architectural design of process-oriented management. However, prescriptions of radical changes are criticized on the grounds of practicality and suitability. Therefore, a gradual improvement of processes has to be considered as alternative. In this scope the goal of this study is to present a usability of the mapping and modeling technique for transformation of traditional management to process-oriented business process management.

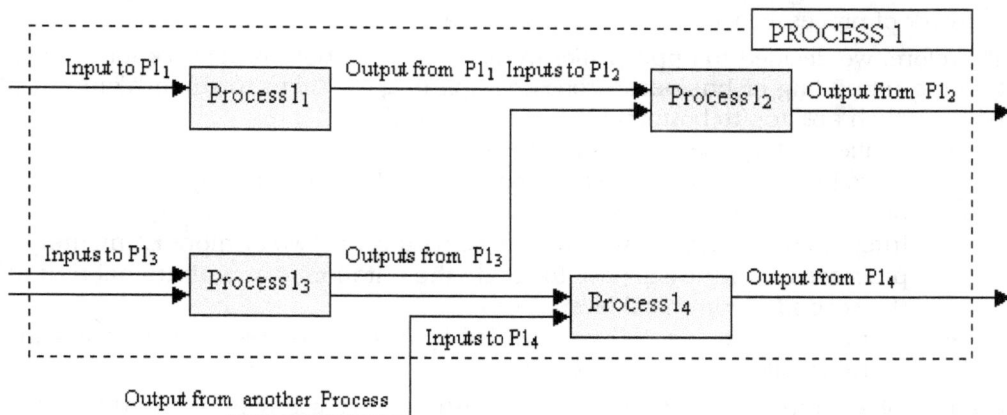

Fig. 1 Network model of the processes and their interactions

Processes before the project

ISO 9000 series standards are building on the basis of "process-based model of quality management system". In coherence with this requirement, company's quality management team, before ISO 9001:1994 certification, prepared so called process-oriented model of organization based on a gradual decomposition, which is shown in figure 2.

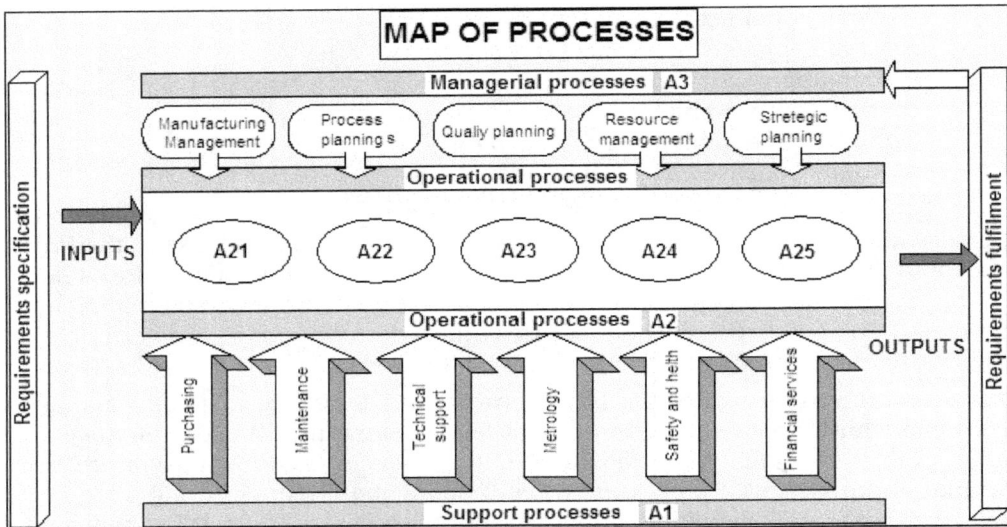

MAP OF PROCESSES

Managerial processes A3

Manufacturing Management | Process plannings | Qualiy planning | Resource management | Stretegic planning

Operational processes

INPUTS

A21 · A22 · A23 · A24 · A25

Operational processes A2

OUTPUTS

Purchasing · Maintenance · Technical support · Metrology · Safety and helth · Financial services

Requirements specification

Requirements fulfilment

Support processes A1

Fig. 2 Process-oriented model of organization

It copies a chronically known approach to the categorization of business processes into operational, support, and managerial processes. The model of process-based quality management system classifies organizational processes into management responsibility processes, product realization processes, resource management processes and measurement, analysis and improvement processes. This classification presents, practically, the areas of conformity assessment with accordance to ISO 9001:2000. One of disadvantages of the first mentioned classification is that it a priory sorts processes by importance. It doesn't help to create network of processes that have to be, essentially, equal.

Therefore, we decided to apply a hierarchical classification framework for the systematic rebuilding of business processes splitting up them to three hierarchical levels, which are (top to bottom) [2]:

- Unified enterprise process (UEP), which consists of one or several integrated processes to the extent that is conditioned by its capability to flexibly and effectively secure customers' requirements.
- Integrated process (IP) which represents a set of two or more Elementary processes with the purpose to create the autonomic organizational unit at the second hierarchical level;
- Elementary process (EP) represented by a set of complex tasks, consisting of the smallest elements- activities;

Smaller objects than elementary processes are hierarchically (top to bottom) classified to two basic classes:

- - Complex Task (CT)
- - Activity (A).

Substantial problem concerning originally applied approach to process-oriented model of organization lied in practical impossibility to create overall network of interaction between connected processes. It was due to a lack of unequivocal methodological rules, as it was recognized later. It was a ground to look for another solution, what resulted in using the following method for business processes mapping and modeling.

Processes after the project

Further described process mapping technique is based on a process decomposition that is resulting in a set of business structure models, which are represented by diagrams in the order given [3]:

- System diagram,
- Context diagrams,
- Commodity flow diagrams of the first and second decomposition stage,
- State transition diagrams of the first and second decomposition stage.

In the sense of the outlined procedure of redesigning business processes, the first step of this method is the creation of a System Diagram. Its purpose is to separate so-called Unified Enterprise Processes (UEP) from the original arrangement of processes. Subsequently, relations between them and the environment of the enterprise are specified. The environment is represented in a System Diagram by External Entities, with which the system communicates, while their content is not a subject of analysis in the following steps. They usually represent the initial source of commodity flows, or their end consumer. In fact it represents the starting base of modelling processes, from which other diagrams are derived using the principle of process decomposition. Based on the transformation of previous process-oriented model of organization the following System diagram has been created (see figure 3).

Prior to a specification of number Unified Enterprise Processes and redefinition of their content the following model of key process clustering was taken into consideration (see fig. 4).

Subsequently are created the context diagrams for each Unified enterprise process depicted in a System diagram. Individual Context diagrams express relations only of the given UEP with its environment. All surrounding elements of the given UEP in Context diagram, irrespective of whether they represent objects outside the enterprise or internal processes, are considered as External entities. Supplier/customers rules might be the same as for external as for internal subjects. An example of the Context diagram of the process A2 is depicted in figure 5.

Consecutively, Commodity Flow Diagrams of the first stage are designed for A1, A2 and A3 process, which describe relations usually between integrated processes. Two of them for the A2 and A3 processes are shown on Fig.6.

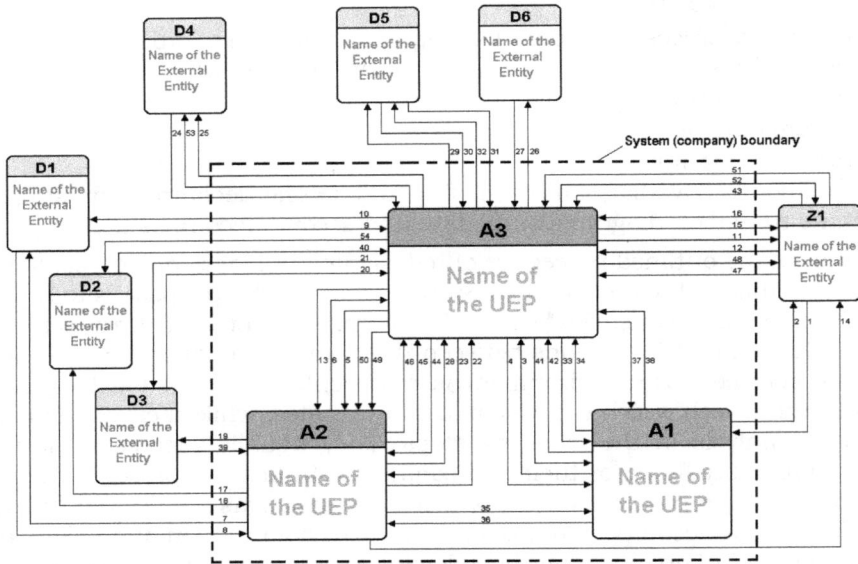

Fig. 3 System diagram

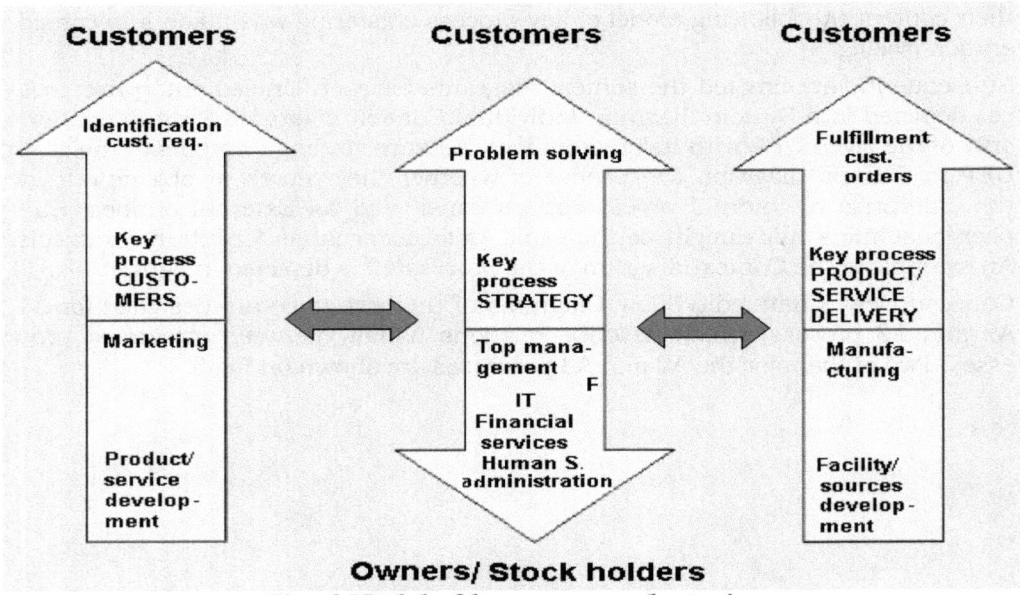

Fig. 4 Model of key process clustering

The purpose of the Commodity flow diagrams is gradual decomposition of UEP, up to the level of so-called elementary processes.

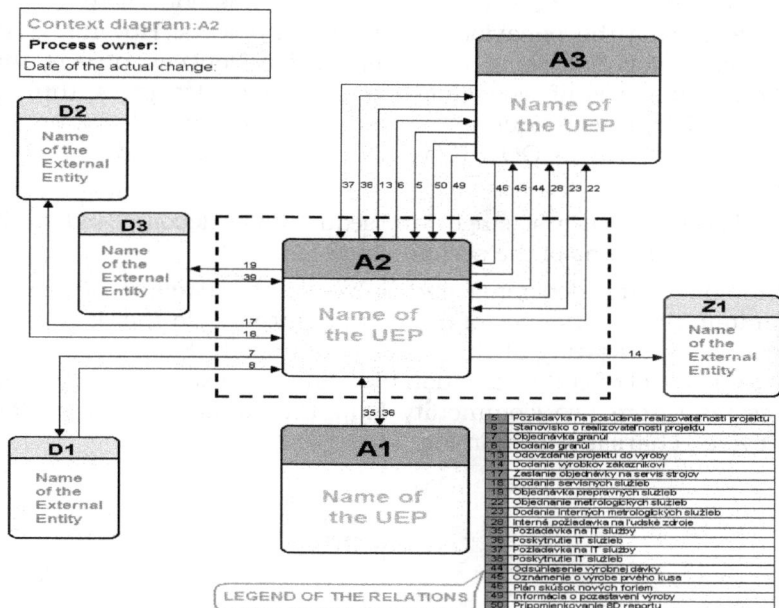

Fig. 5 Context diagram of the process A2

Commodity Flow Diagrams of the second stage are constructed in an analogous way as Commodity Flow Diagrams of the first stage. It is the last stage of Commodity Flow Diagrams because the Elementary processes, which present the objects of modelling, are considered to be the primitive processes.

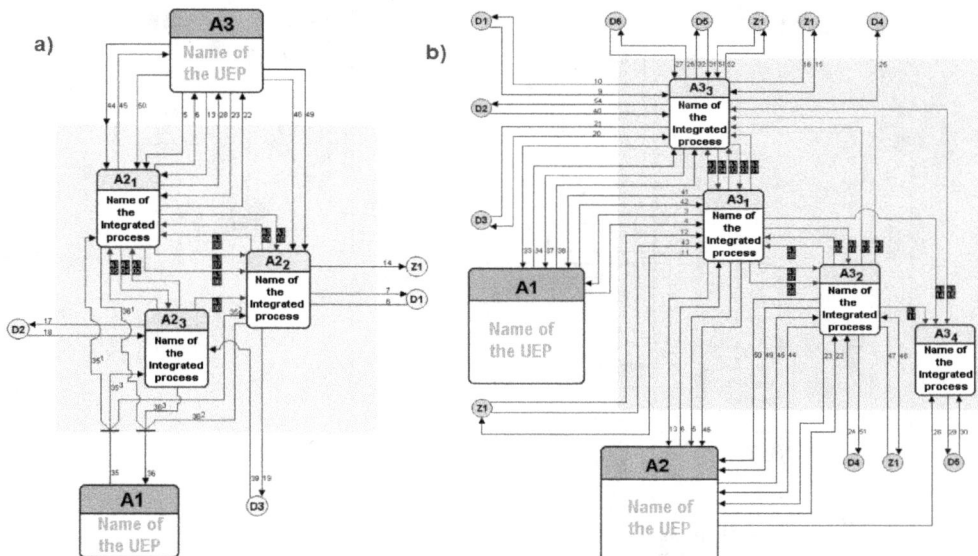

Fig. 6 a) Commodity flow diagram (CFD) for the process A2; b) CFD for the process A3

The objective of the State Transition Diagrams (STDs) is the description of an internal structure and mutual relations of tasks and/or activities of Elementary processes. State Transition Diagrams describe all of the states that an object can have, the events under which an object changes state and the conditions that must be fulfilled before the transition will occur. State Transition Diagrams are basically used for describing the behaviour of individual objects. Hoverer, STDs have limited possibilities for describing the collaboration between objects that cause the transitions. This level of modelling is meant for IS designers, through which proper form modelling technique is selected. The most popular variety of STDs in the programming area of OOD (Object Oriented Design) are the Harel State charts [4].

In analogical way, "STDs of the first stage" are sequentially decomposed to the level of State Transition Diagrams of the second stage.

An important condition in the designing and subsequent modelling of process diagrams is to maintain the consistency of inputs and outputs, so that it is possible to create process maps, starting at the level of Commodity Flow Diagrams of the first stage, up to the level of state transition diagrams. An example of the creation of the process map from two Commodity Flow Diagrams of the first stage specified in the previous chars is shown in Fig. 7.

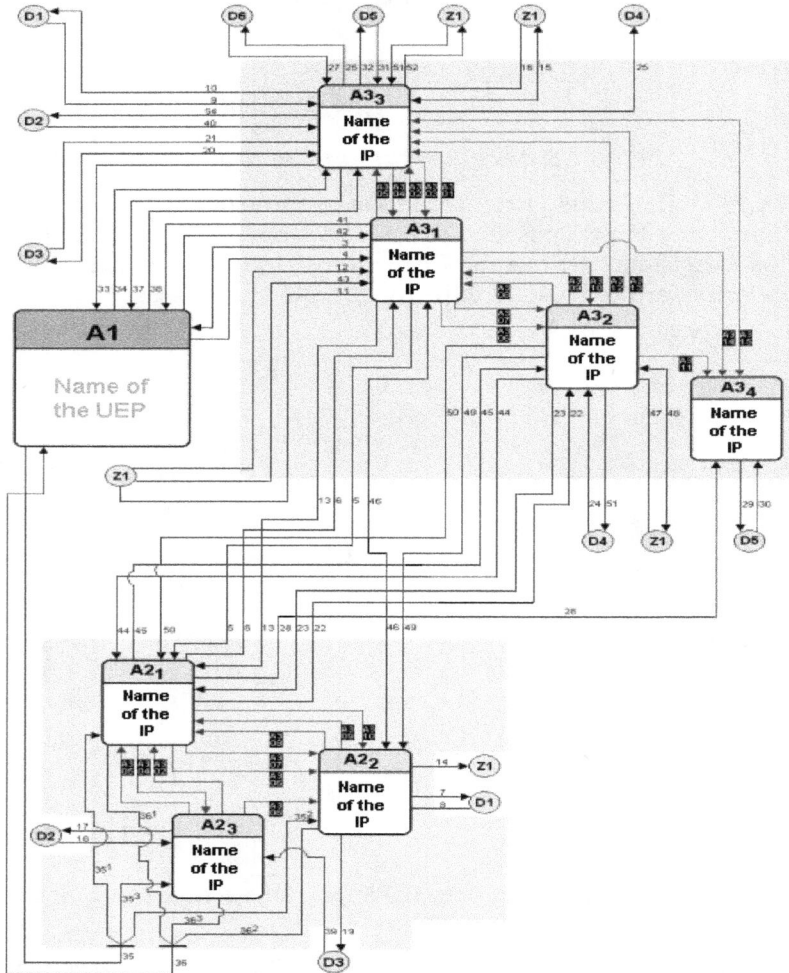

Fig. 7 Process map fragment by the merging of two CFDs at the first level of decomposition.

Making process modeling by QPR software

Competition and changes in the business environment induce the need to constantly adapt and improve the company' business processes. The solution of this problem requires implementing an effective business process modeller tool for visualizing, understanding, analyzing, improving and documenting business processes. For the beginning phase of BPM work it is sufficient to model processes by outlined manner. However, software is obviously a central tool in successfully implementing BPM initiatives.

For this purpose we implemented QPR software that supports all key elements of business processes management - from modelling and documentation, communicating, measurement and analysis, to continuous process management and improvement. It served us to create comprehensive business process models with accordance to the presented approach illustrating the current status of operations. In the first step we modelled the System diagram, in which we used a modified notation of the objects (see figure 8).

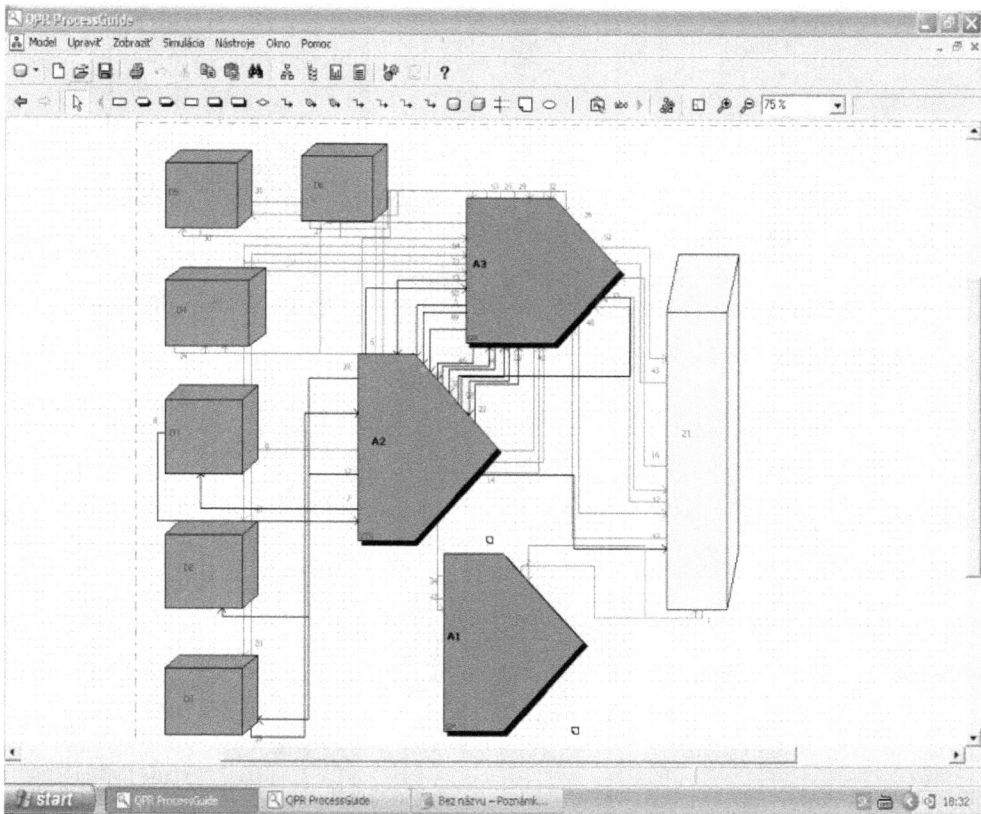

Fig. 8 System diagram modelled by QPR software

Consecutively, it was recognized that Context diagrams, when using QPR software support, are practically redundant. It is because of the ability to infallible transposition of all links from a System diagram to Commodity flow diagram of the first stage.

Two of three Commodity Flow Diagrams of the first stage, designed for Unified enterprise processes A2 and A3, are shown in Figure 9.

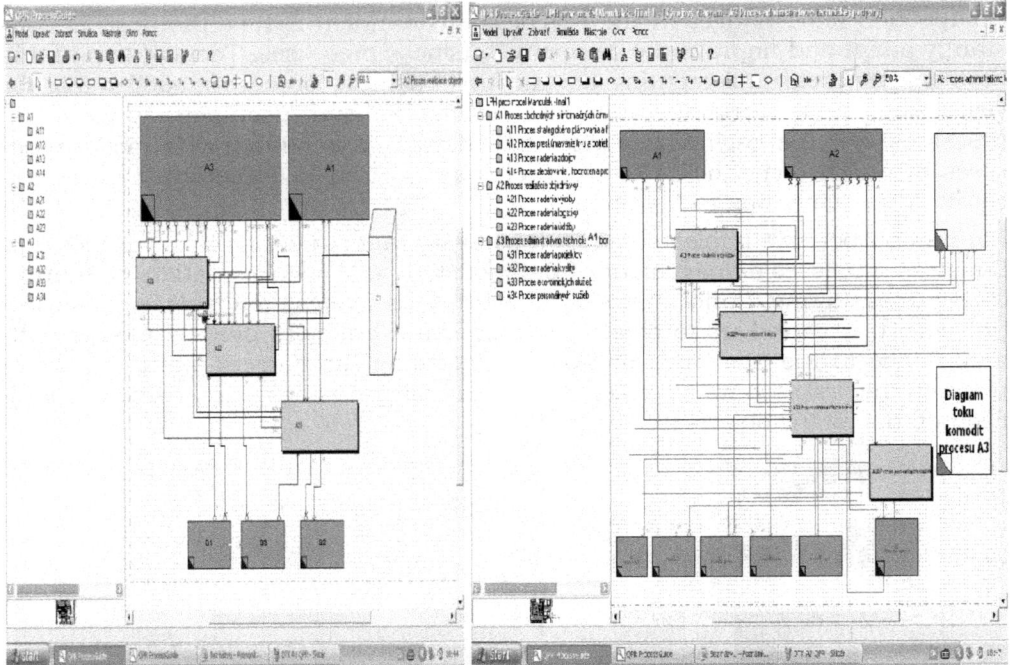

Fig. 9 The examples of CFDs for Unified enterprise processes A2 and A3

Analogically were modelled CFDs of the second stage and State transition diagrams of the first stage. An example of the State diagram of the first stage is depicted in figure 10.

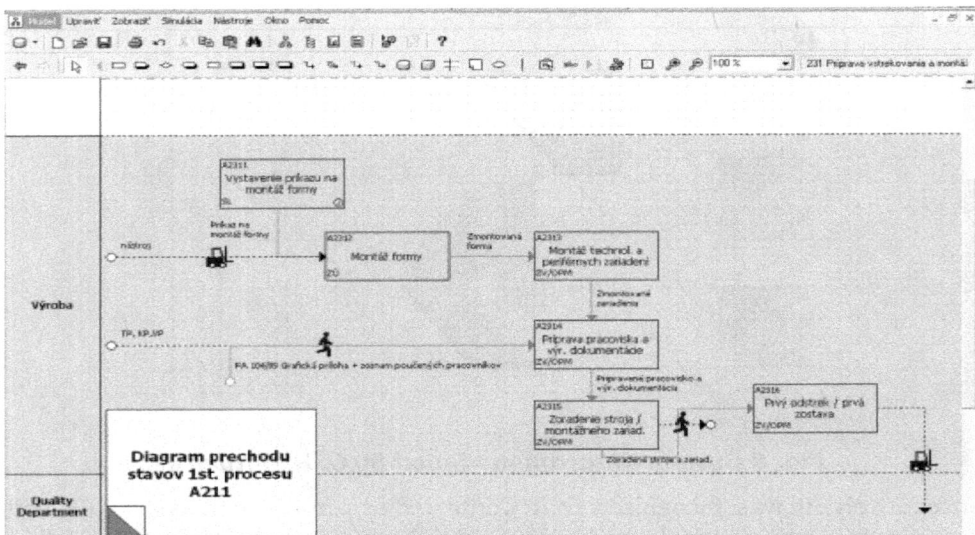

Fig. 10 STD of the first decomposition stage for process A211

Hurdles Overcome

Due to the fact that QPR software enables to generate process maps, equally as was shown in figure 7, we overcame the significant obstacle on the way to modern business process management. It is undoubted that a business process maps present a crucial tool of quality management systems and no less important tool of modern concepts of business process management. Such maps are defining where business process of LPH Vranov n/T starts and ends and identifying the specific activities, which need to be performed by the process owners. From those maps the managers can easily define critical processes and analyze them in detail. This approach evidently differs from the method with which company LPH accomplished requirements of standard for quality management system by ISO 9000:1994. In our opinion, the adjusted present state of process approach conforms to the requirements of ISO 9001:2000.

BENEFITS/FINDINGS

It could be feasible to name explicit or/and implicit effect achieved through this project. Nevertheless, the generic benefits seem to be more important for us than specific ones. The gradual transition to the process-oriented organization envisages a noticeable change in its very existence. That includes the use of potent management tools, such as information systems, which automate business processes by controlling the sequence of activities and by the activation of necessary resources. Now, key managers are not only aware of their role in the specification of requirements on information system functionalities, but they have better understanding of organizational context of information system. Moreover, this form of business process representation also helped the company to reduce complexity and uncertainty in their management practice.

REFERENCES

- 2004, ISO 9000 Introduction and Support Package: Guidance on the Concept and Use of the Process Approach for management systems. http://www.docstoc.com/docs/273282/ISO-9000-Process-Approach.
- Modrák, V. (2005), Business Process Improvement through Optimization of its Structural Properties. In: Fischer, L. (ed.): Workflow Handbook 2005. Future Strategies., Book Division Lighthouse Point, FL, USA, 2005, pp.75-90.
- Modrák, V. (2007), Bridging organizational structure and information system architecture through process. Lecture Notes in Computer Science. Springer Berlin Heidelberg, vol. 4537, pp. 445-455.
- Harel, D. (1987). Statecharts: A Visual Formalism for Complex Systems. Science of Computer Programming 8.
- Manduľák, J. (2006), Generation of Process Model Management in LPH Vranov n/T. Master Diploma Thesis at the Technical University of Košice.

CASE STUDY AUTHORS

Vladimír Modrák and Ján Manduľák

Vladimír Modrák is full professor of Manufacturing Technology at Technical University of Košice in Slovakia. Since 2006 he is also member of staff at University of Perugia in Italy, where he is involved on the course "Corporate Organization for The International Master in Innovation and Business Administration" study branch. In the period 2002-2003 he also was active as visiting lecturer at University of Applied Sciences Wildau in Germany on the course Quality Management. The major areas of his research interest include Business Process Modeling and Analysing, Manufacturing Logistics Optimization and Process Management. Further information: http://modrak.weebly.com

Ján Manduľák received his MSc degree in Manufacturing Management from Technical University of Košice, Faculty of Manufacturing Technologies in 2006. Presently he is in the position of chief executive officer of LPH Vranov n/T.

Natuzzi Furnishing & Accessories Business Unit, Italy

Gold Award, Europe.
Nominated by openwork, Italy

EXECUTIVE SUMMARY / ABSTRACT

Natuzzi is an international manufacturer of top quality furniture, including sofas, armchairs and living room accessories. Based in Italy, the company's high and growing number of worldwide suppliers from India to Brazil, from Indonesia to Vietnam, required optimization and streamlining of its outdated supply chain processes. By implementing Natuzzi's Suppliers Process Management system (SPMS) we integrated our supply chain both internally and externally, thus maintaining our high customer service standards and improving overall operational efficiency, while meeting or exceeding the projected benefits.

OVERVIEW

In such a complex context, involving people using very different systems, tools and devices, the need for a reliable orchestrator clearly emerged: something able to guide, flexibly but rigorously, interactions between Natuzzi and its suppliers. Management chose to adopt a BPM technology not only to solve the specific issue, but also to enter a significant and wider innovation path, re-applicable all over the organization.

Our challenge began with the need for an innovative approach to drive a global business with fast growing volumes involving a high number of suppliers, in order to match customers' shipment deadlines, keeping low inventory and always offering a real-time updated, complete picture for Natuzzi's Furnishing & Accessories Business Unit.

Our measurable successes included an ROI of 100% in much less than 1 year, with a two million Euros increase in revenue, reduction in supplier costs of over 150,000 Euros etc. The resulting combination was a rewarding increase of both supplier and customer satisfaction plus operational efficiency thus ensuring Natuzzi's position at the forefront of the quality furnishings industry.

Natuzzi was founded in 1959 by Pasquale Natuzzi, Chairman and Chief Designer of the Group. It designs, produces and markets sofas, armchairs and living room accessories. Natuzzi is the largest Italian furniture company with a turnover of 735,4 million Euros in 2006 and is world leader in the leather upholstery market. In 1993, Natuzzi became the only foreign furniture company to list on Wall Street (NYSE-NTZ) and is now managed by the Italian headquarter based in Santeramo, Natuzzi Americas located in High Point (North Carolina - USA) and through local Natuzzi subsidiaries in China, Belgium, Germany, Spain, Denmark, Switzerland, UK and Japan.

As of December 30, 2006 the Group employed 8,133 people, in Italy and abroad. Production is vertically integrated through 8 factories in Italy and 5 abroad (two in China, two in Brazil and one in Romania). Raw materials are purchased directly from the primary markets and then finished in the company's facilities, specializing in manufacturing leather, wood and metal frames, foam and finished products. By controlling 92% of raw materials and semi-finished products, the Group guaranteed ultimate quality at most competitive prices.

The Natuzzi products are distributed through nearly 300 Natuzzi Stores in the most important international cities (including Athens, London, Paris, Madrid, Copenhagen, New York, Sidney, Shanghai, Budapest, Melbourne, and Dubai) and over 500 Natuzzi Galleries in partnership with main distribution networks (Selfridges - UK, Sears Roebuck - Canada, Bloomingdales - USA, David Jones - AUS, El Corte Ingles - Spain and Galleries Lafayette - France).

Natuzzi's offering also includes a selection of complementary furniture (wall units, tables, lamps, rugs) and accessories (vases, containers/holders, candles). This part of the business is managed by its Furnishing & Accessories Business Unit: initially simply intended as a complementary part of sofas sales, this area quickly became autonomous with 2006 turnover of 16 million Euros and with a "2 figures growth" currently estimated for 2007.

Furnishing & Accessories was Natuzzi's Business Unit needing support to optimize and streamline interactions with its suppliers while all related procedures used to be manually managed with data and information scattered in different systems.

Management opted for a mid/long term-oriented solution deciding to select and introduce a BPM technology: if at the very beginning this required additional time and attention to train and introduce project members into a new view and approach of business management, this potential perspective very quickly became extremely concrete and worthy.

While on one hand we showed measurable benefits (average order management elapsed timings decreased, customer shipment punctuality increased, business/IT gap significantly decreased, etc.) on the other hand we believe that this project will pay a lot more in the mid-long term as of company's organizational growth and competitiveness' levers in new BPM projects we are working on.

BUSINESS CONTEXT

Natuzzi's Furnishing & Accessories Business Unit activities were always characterized by a significant number of suppliers. This fast growing business required the management to identify the way to optimize and streamline interactions with all its suppliers.

In this context in fact, there were several emerging critical issues that needed to be addressed:
- Organizational process impacting different areas
- Software tools limited to one single area/ environment
- Frequent and rapid organizational changes
- Time-consuming processes
- Process owner not allowed to control activities and related timings
- No real-time supplier performance monitoring
- Unstructured (unreliable) communications

According to those criticalities and in compliance with best practices and management and employees experience, the intervention scope was defined, identifying two main focus points to be orchestrated:
- Purchase Order Management (PO approval, PO notification, Suppliers' PO confirmation, Suppliers' PO deliveries)
- Suppliers' performance management (data collection, monitoring and penalties)

THE KEY INNOVATIONS

Business

The SPMS project had introduced and continues to introduce relevant and new elements and positive effects for several fundamental company's stakeholder groups:

- Shareholders: the company is listed on Wall Street (NYSE-NTZ) and as a consequence it is always very careful about compliance and internal controls. Natuzzi's dedicated internal audit team (known as "SOX Group"), responsible to supervise all related aspects, has examined and validated the process and the way it is now managed using a BPM technology, highlighting it perfectly fits laws requirements, contributing to Risk Management improvement, a concrete asset for Natuzzi's shareholders. In fact, among all other benefits, the company is now able to trace everything about purchase order management and find out WHO did WHAT and WHEN immediately or even months later.

- Customers: as mentioned in Natuzzi's values statement "we understand people's needs, wherever they are in the world". This means in the company everybody must pay maximum attention to every detail in the production process (materials, design, colors, etc.) but also in all other steps that bring Natuzzi's products to customers. This first BPM project had a very important impact on that: as customer orders are shipped only when the delivery is complete, in the past the company used to often suffer situations like this: we weren't able to ship a "two sofas + three armchairs + one wood table + one table lamp" customer order, simply because "the lamp was out of stock" due to a supplier delay we were not aware of! Those new BPM tools have helped to drastically reduce these cases. All this of course doesn't only positively impact Natuzzi's Furnishing & Accessories BU business, but whole company's business, generally increasing customer satisfaction. In fact, once customers have ordered their own and special "sofa + armchairs + accessories" combination, they want it in their living room as soon as possible and will hate any delay, no matter what could causes it. Removing roadblocks like the "out of stock" example above, is strongly helping Natuzzi to get punctual deliveries... and happy customers!

- Suppliers: the manual way previously used to manage suppliers orders simply generated "tons" of separated puzzle pieces of information very difficult to handle and very difficult to put together when needed. Consequent problems did not affect exclusively Natuzzi's organization but also suppliers' ones (continuous alignment phone calls, fax re-sending, unreliable data, etc.). Suppliers immediately verified what the new approach and tool introduced end even if most of them had never heard about BPM (and may be some continue to ignore what BPM stands for)... they loved it! Now mistakes are drastically reduced on both sides allowing suppliers to work better and more efficiently. On top of that, in case of any problem, Natuzzi's Suppliers Program Management operators are now able to immediately share related order info and documents with suppliers in order to fairly clarify what happened. One clear example of those suppliers' benefits is the process step called "production early check": when 80% of the scheduled and agreed time for production delivery has passed (e.g. after 4 days for a 5 day production) the process alerts the supplier requesting a confirmation that everything is proceeding on time or details in case of any issue. Suppliers appreciate this improvement support very much and it increases their trust in Natuzzi as a company.

- Natuzzi's employees (Furnishing & Accessories BU - Suppliers Program Management Office): they considered software as a very static set of tools, very difficult to modify or adapt according to changing business needs. This generated employees' frustration as they frequently detected what could improve the business management, but knew it would take months to get software updated... often not even getting exactly what they wanted. Once they discovered, with SPMS system, the key elements of BPM and their completely different approach, they realized they were now able to significantly control software application logics definition and get them changed much easier than before. This was fundamental to "open their minds" and let out concrete proposals for process optimization. Definition of specific process activities in this project ("notification receipt check" and "delivery check" first of all) benefit of this effect: all because of the growing trust that new ideas may now quickly be transformed into new operating procedures supported by BPM. This may boost agility into the company, a key factor in global competition.

Process

According to known best practices plus management and employees experience, the most important focus points that needed to be orchestrated for Natuzzi's Furnishing & Accessories Business Unit were Purchase Order Management and Suppliers' Performance Management.

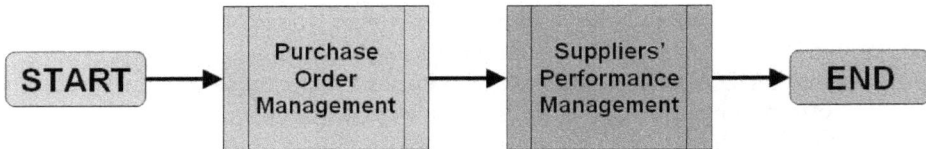

Picture 1 - Macro processes: focus point to be orchestrated

BEFORE BPM

Before the introduction of a BPM technology with SPMS system, Furnishing & Accessories Business Unit main activities related to Purchase Order and Suppliers' Performance Management were triggered by replenishment planning tool (DPM) creating a new PO in the ERP system (custom AS/400) and triggering the following activities:

	Activity	Tool	Trigger
0	New Purchase Order detection	ERP (custom AS/400 application)	PULL
1	Purchase Order approval	Paper + ERP (custom AS/400 application)	PULL
2	Purchase Order notification	FAX machine	PULL
3	Purchase Order notification receipt check	FAX machine + MS Excel sheet (manually updated)	PULL
4	Purchase Order	MS Excel sheet (manually up-	PULL

		confirmation	dated)	
5		Purchase Order delivery check	MS Excel sheet (manually up-dated)	PULL
6		Supplier perform-ance monitoring	MS Excel sheet (manually up-dated)	PULL
7		Supplier penalties management	MS Excel sheet (manually up-dated)	PULL

Table 1 – BEFORE BPM: process main steps

Main issues were not related to process and activities structure and logics: main issues came from the way the process was executed / driven and the tools used.

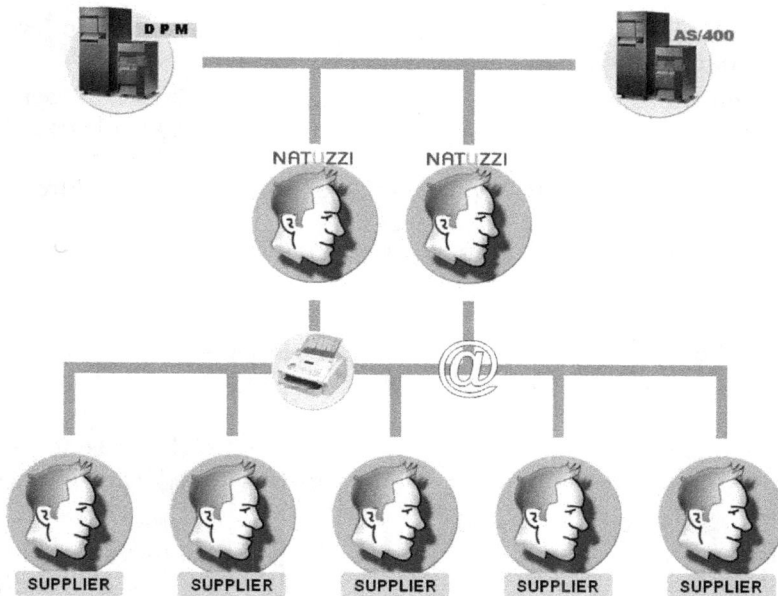

Picture 2 – People and Systems involved

In fact to improve this behaviour Natuzzi, desiring the whole procedure to be completed on time, respecting all deadlines and adding the possibility to trace and verify each step, "simply" needed to approach some relevant criticalities that had to be examined and solved:

- Organizational process impacting different areas: the managed process involved people from different Business Unit areas not always "perfectly trained" to work together as a team, but sometimes letting an old fash-ioned functional silos approach emerge.
- Software tools limited to one single area / environment: in most (if not all) cases human also act as system to system interfaces with consequent high risk of inaccuracy.
- Frequent and rapid organizational changes: irrespective of the approach and/or tool adopted, it must allow operations agility and ability to change very quickly, otherwise it will not be a long time solution.
- Time-consuming process: most activity steps can be automated and for others human performed, time-lag reduced.

- Process owner not allowed to control activities and related timings: most (if not all) procedure steps are pull-driven: operators have to manually check event occurrence to trigger further actions, with no automatic alerts or notifications support.
- No real-time supplier performance monitoring: of course, no opportunities to verify activities status and/or measure service levels.
- Unstructured (unreliable) communications: all the actors of the process communicate with each other exclusively with an unstructured approach (e-mail, manual fax, phone calls) increasing management complexity and making extremely difficult any data tracing (path to be manually "re-built" for every single case).

The final motivation that triggered the change program was the impossibility, for Furnishing & Accessories Business Unit, to get the desired service level due to repeated warehouse stock-out.

Despite a careful "Sales and Operations Planning" activity this used to happen not only as a consequence of suppliers' late deliveries, but also because we discovered that quite often:

- It could happen (and it actually happened) we forgot to fax Purchase Orders to Suppliers.
- Delivery dates that Suppliers confirmed, different from the ones we requested, had not been properly updated, propagated and processed in the MRP.

All this was not due to employee skills but more reasonably because we were not using the most appropriate tool and most of all because we were not using the most appropriate approach.

A very high number of simple, low added-value but crucial and sensible process elements, were exclusively entrusted to very powerful but fallible "devices": human brains.

WITH BPM INTRO

At the very beginning we were going to simply solve the issue we had, just like many others in the past, that is in a functional perspective, "simply" searching for the right software solution to solve the issue.

But when we investigated BPM as one of the potential solution to adopt, we immediately had the clear feeling this could be an innovative solution for many more and much wider organizational issues in our company and may be a completely different approach with benefits and potential that seemed to worth the way for exploring. Company's traditional sensibility on quality aspects, also related to ISO certifications (ISO 9001, ISO 14001) did the rest and we decided to go for a BPM technology.

Starting from the way Purchase Order and Suppliers' Performance processes were managed we set up a team essentially made of:

- Process Analyst (openwork - BPM vendor consultancy)
- Process Owner (Natuzzi)
- Process Key Users (Natuzzi) – daily skilled about Suppliers' needs
- IT manager (Natuzzi)

At the very beginning of the analysis, we proceeded slowly, maybe even slower than our worst expectations, but we held on and in fact we discovered later on that it was only due to the introduction of project members into a new business management perspective and approach.

Even in a well prepared organization where quality programs and ISO certifications are a must, process definition is normally something that remains on paper and that are then used to be re-interpreted (more or less faithfully) during real-life operations.

So it has not been trivial and immediate to get introduced (and to believe) to an environment like the BPM suite we experienced, where drawing a process also means defining logics of the actual software that will drive users daily operations.

Key concepts and focus drivers we referred to during the work the project team performed are:

- **System vs. Human**: split process into basic activities separating ones requiring human intervention form others that may be automated.
- **Orchestration**: assemble basic activities in an automated process to guide people and system in compliance with organizational rules.
- **Evolution**: agility and ability to apply changes to processes from an organizational (model) and a technological (execute) point of view at the same time.
- **Push vs. Pull**: procedure has to be an active element guiding, reminding and pressing process actors instead of waiting for their intervention.
- **SLA**: alerts related to process deadlines have to be introduced to measure service level.

After less than three months the complete structure of the process (and related sub-processes) was defined and the BPM solution released in production environment.

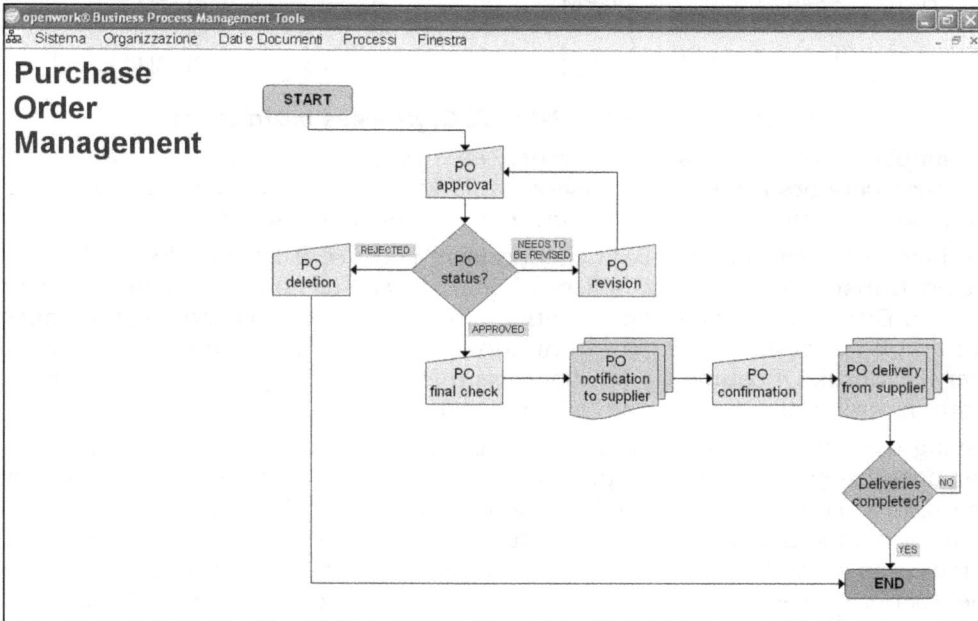

Picture 3 – Purchase Order Management process (simplified)

Activities description and content is only slightly changed, but many of those activities have been automated, including BPM integration with the ERP system (custom AS/400 application) and FAX software application. Replenishment planning (DPM) triggers the process generating a new PO in the ERP system (custom AS/400 application) and this is automatically detected by the BPM that submits the PO to the appropriate user for approval. Then the whole process is completely orchestrated by the BPM technology itself, requesting activities to humans (and checking each completes its own on time alerting for any risk of delay) and transferring data among the different systems involved when needed (avoiding any operator to do this manually).

	Activity	Tool	Trigger
0	New Purchase Order detection	BPM – automatic (integrated with ERP - custom AS/400 application)	PUSH
1	Purchase Order approval	BPM	PUSH
2	Purchase Order notification	BPM – automatic (integrated with FAX application)	PUSH
3	Purchase Order notification receipt check	BPM – automatic (integrated with FAX application)	PUSH
4	Purchase Order confirmation	BPM	PUSH
5	Purchase Order delivery check	BPM – automatic (integrated with ERP - custom AS/400 application)	PUSH
6	Supplier performance monitoring	BPM	PUSH
7	Supplier penalties management	BPM	PUSH

Table 2 – AFTER BPM INTRO: process main steps

To simplify context and start-up issues, as a project decision we chose to let all Natuzzi operators become BPM users, while we let all suppliers continue to work with tools and methodology (fax, e-mails, etc.) they were used to.

We have been very happy about this decision because it let this change be completely transparent for our suppliers while it allowed us concentrate and familiarize with BPM tools and concepts limiting project scope and postponing the impact of the roll-out of an application to hundreds of remote external users located all over the world. Of course we will not miss this part of the project, but simply roll it out in a separate phase we already planned.

Saying that "this change [has been] completely transparent for our suppliers" is not completely true. In fact they very quickly discovered that something had changed while they noticed we became much more efficient in pushing them to deliver on time and generally supporting them with feedback to let them better serve us as a customer. They appreciated that also because this let them improve their performance and reduce the amount of penalties due for late deliveries.

A great operational support to this part came from the Business Activity Monitoring tool integrated with the BPM technology we used: this allows us to get in real-time what is happening with our suppliers' Purchase Orders.

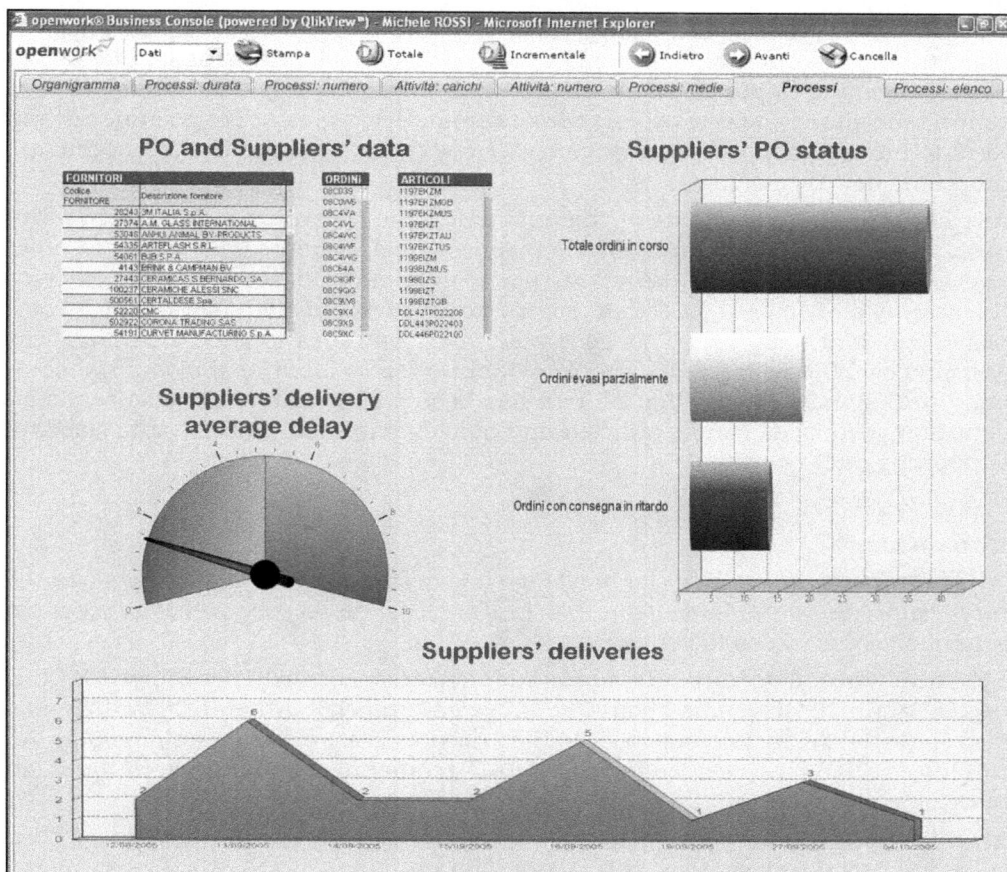

Picture 4 – Business Activity Monitoring Tool

Most immediate and relevant facts we noticed since a few weeks after our first BPM project was completed and live were:

- users know what to do even when not knowing (partially or totally) the process,
- users understand what is happening in the process thanks to e-mail, reminders, alerts helping the process to advance,
- users are now monitored and traced during activities execution.

While the BPM solution delivered fully satisfied our requirements on the GO LIVE project date, of course our needs are not static.

We are now able to easily let our processes evolve, working on process models drawings and immediately getting as a result the same change on the corresponding software application for all future related cases. On top of this, we also experienced the opportunity to act not only on process models, but also on single process instances. This means that we are able to change the way a specific PO has to be handled (e.g. in case of an exception) simply modifying graphically its process instance and letting unchanged the way all other PO's will be processed (graphical exception management).

ORGANIZATION

Natuzzi's operators immediately benefitted from BPM introduction with SPMS, simply because their lives became easier. In fact they started saving all the (physical and psychological) energy needed to keep all PO deadlines and details in mind (or on unstructured, personal notes): definitely all non-added value activities contributing to put them under pressure. Now operators have energy to concentrate on much more relevant tasks: examine and validate PO documents and work to improve suppliers' performances, having time to listen to their needs and proposing new type of partnership.

Another very positive impact of this project on the organization is about awareness. Supporting the evolution of the business model and being involved in process and related software definition, users were able to see improvements for themselves and, most of all, they started to understand the potential of a completely different approach. This generated, and continues to generate, new ideas and proposals from business people side in order to improve the way the company works and it seems that all this has been triggered as they now feel confident that good ideas can be adopted and quickly reflected, via BPM, into software supporting daily operations.

HURDLES OVERCOME

Management

While on the business side the challenge has seemed quite stimulating since the very beginning, some elements in the classical, traditional schemas of a company, generated some issues to be managed.

Specifically in a company a business requirements normally describes WHAT is needed and not HOW this should be provided, especially when the "WHAT" is a piece of software. In fact in this case IT is used to more or less autonomously decide the "HOW" part respecting the "WHAT" requirements coming from the business part.

As BPM puts together this two aspects (business + software), there have been some internal discussions with IT about who had to define HOW to solve the existing issue and this caused some delays in the project until it was clarified that the adoption of the BPM approach was a business decision while the technological validation of the right BPM tool was of course in the hands of IT.

Business

The main challenge related to Natuzzi's operators involved in the project, was strictly related to the awareness opportunity it offered. In fact it was immediately clear that management was going to know, with plenty of details, workloads, execution timings, etc.

At the beginning this was not "appreciated very much" by users as they saw it as a menace for their autonomy at work. It only took a few weeks for operators to understand that now they have the opportunity to be correctly evaluated with an objective tool and in compliance with the real quality of the task they complete. Today personal KPI taken from the BPM solution for PO management are included in the Management by Objective (MBO) program.

Organization Adoption

Getting an organization to change its mind and way of thinking is not an easy task and maybe this is the most important strategy driver the management immediately focused on. It may be less or more difficult depending on the company history, structure, business, etc. but introducing BPM in a company is not straightforward.

This complexity awareness has helped a lot the whole project team to think about and manage this aspect and it certainly allowed to avoid underestimations. These may in fact occur when very innovative tools, like many BPM suites, are seen for the first time, generating fast enthusiasm that is absolutely essential for process success but we were able to manage expectations to avoid unmotivated and faster disillusions.

BENEFITS

Project Duration and Continuous Improvement
- project KICK-OFF = March 2006
- project GO LIVE = May 2006

This time period is related to the first implementation of our BPM system for Purchase Order and Suppliers' Performance Management. It's fundamental to underline that not only the project was delivered in a very short time, but also that a continuous improvement of processes was set up and now we regularly collect suggestion and modify processes on a monthly basis, in tune with our changing business needs.

Project Users

Over **150 users** including Natuzzi's operators (12) and Suppliers (over 140 located all over the world).

As previously mentioned, to simplify project start-up we chose to let all suppliers continue to work with unchanged tools and methodology (fax, e-mails, etc.) even if now communications are completely and transparently driven by the BPM solution adopted. We have already planned a new project phase with the target of involving all Suppliers as direct BPM solution users (see paragraph "4.2 Process – With BPM Intro" for details).

PURCHASE ORDER PROCESSING

The current number of Purchase Order processed via the BPM solution is:

> **2.000 PO/year** (> 40 PO/week).

The average number of processes simultaneously processed is:

> **100 Purchase Orders**.

COST SAVINGS

Average Reduction of Supplier Management Resources

50K €/year: 30% average reduction of supplier management resources calculated at 2006 business volumes. The key point is that even in 2007 the same staff has been able to support a rapidly growing business volume and even future volume increase would not need additional resources.

Supplier Penalties Amount

50K €/year: Supplier penalties amount. In the past we were not even able to calculate and request such penalties to our suppliers, but most of all they knew we were not able to properly monitor their performance. Now we have shown suppliers that we can demonstrate with facts when and how they had late deliveries: along with BPM solution early alerts they receive this is helping them to improve and reduce delays concentrating them to the lowest 10% penalty belt of the existing three. In fact the Supplier penalties amount value is decreasing month after month as suppliers performance is getting better and better and we look forward to a "0 € penalties target" that would mean 100% timely deliveries.

Time Reductions

The average Purchase Order management time delay decreased from **28** to **13** calendar days 10 months after project went live.

Increased Revenues

Only measuring Furnishing & Accessories Business Unit effects (but the advantages extend to the whole business) the 10% increase for the SLA related to ability to ship orders keeping unchanged stock levels caused a **2M €** increase in revenues.

BEST PRACTICES, LEARNING POINTS AND PITFALLS

Best Practices

✓ **Get sponsorship**: *get appropriate sponsorship and set up a well structured project team including at least Business Unit manager, IT manager (CIO where applicable), Line of Business users.*

✓ **Process-oriented awareness**: *in order to maximize, especially strategic benefits, plan and invest to create a Business Process vision, thinking and culture within the project team and the whole company.*

✓ **Start small, than extend**: *it was very important and helpful to have a clear mid/long term perspective, but to demonstrate a proof of concept with first BPM project, it was essential to define a reasonably small project scope.*

✓ **Improvement cycle**: *set up an internal process to collect suggestions and proposals for process improvement and reiterate it continuously.*

✓ **Measures**: *measure KPI (especially before BPM introduction) to be able to highlight improvements.*

Pitfalls

✗ *Targets sharing: considering the implicit streamlining and monitoring nature of BPM projects, sometimes employees may feel it as a potential menace for their jobs. An accurate and early communication of actual project and BPM targets and benefits should not be missed.*

✗ *Planning Big Bangs: the positive enthusiasm that BPM may generate can sometimes exceed into huge project scope that management believes will solve everything in one shot. BPM can help to reach great results but, as it also implies a cultural change impacting first of all people, it has to be introduced at a reasonable speed to avoid rejection.*

✗ *Technology choice: for sure BPM is also made of technology but there's a lot more. Before selecting the right technology or technologies for this "trip" be sure you identified where you want to go tomorrow and in the future: this may impact your technology choices.*

COMPETITIVE ADVANTAGES

The company needs to accumulate additional BPM experience to get a final confirmation, but it seems Natuzzi has identified and started to roll-out a strategic approach and thinking that, properly supported by the right technology, could provide great benefits in the high competitive market arena.

As a global manufacturer Natuzzi has always needed efficient tools to work and interact with external suppliers. But in a fast-changing world the real challenge is: how can I improve the way the business is managed with quick response time and reasonable costs? The answer doesn't impact exclusively suppliers management, but the whole business.

Our ability to react nearly real-time to market new demands is crucial for the company to reach and keep reaching its competitive advantages and BPM will certainly help in such a context.

TECHNOLOGY

Once we generally investigated BPM and decided to go for SPMS, we had to identify the software product to adopt: we finally chose openwork (www.openworkBPM.com) a web BPM suite, Service Oriented Architecture (SOA) XML-based using Web Services plus other standard technologies (HTML, XML, XSL, Javascript).

Here are the essential technical data of the server system installed for the project while all users simply needed Internet browsers on their clients.

Category	Model	Version
Operating System	Microsoft Windows	2003 server
Database	Microsoft SQL server	2000
BPM system	openwork	5.4.1

openwork offered the most original combination of the key factors we took into consideration for the selection and some of the most important ones are listed here below.

- **Filling Business/IT gap**: we needed a BPM tool actually business-oriented and able to represent and manage strategic and daily contexts and rules: no need for IT knowledge to define application logics but a powerful technological framework where needed for integration and other relevant aspects.

  This element has been fundamental to ease line of business involvement in project and process construction: all have been able to contribute to organization chart, forms and process flows design decreasing the time needed for requirements definition and functional analysis even when initial specifications were not completely clear and well defined.

- **Light approach, but solid architecture:** we needed a BPM Tool easy to be understood by line of business people, not needing too many resources to be driven, able to deliver solutions in weeks and not months or years at reasonable prices. In compliance with BPM philosophical agility, we wanted something scalable and able to support company's growth with BPM from every point of view.

  Despite some initial doubts, rolling out this first project and the improvement steps that followed, concretely demonstrated that a BPM tool may actually support business agility far beyond easy advertising.

- **Powerful organizational rules**: we needed a BPM tool able to represent and manage even very complex organizational structure and business relationships (hierarchical and horizontal ones) and not only IT-oriented users and groups.

  The simple business-oriented but powerful functionalities in this area were very important when, during both functional analysis and improvement steps, decisions changed several times. Working at business-level instead of IT-level helped a lot as, immediately after changes, we could check software application new behaviour in real time.

- **DMS**: we needed a BPM tool including (like openwork) or seamlessly integrating a Document Management System. In fact documents were a critical issue not only for this first project, but also for our general needs and purposes. On this specific point we appreciated the flexibility of openwork forms very much.

One single environment to define not only organization structure and process flows but also forms classification and layout was a very daily support for the project team. Specifically the ability to define, at business-level without code writings, WHO can see/modify/should fill/etc. WHAT and WHEN for every form element, including attachments, was really helpful and relevant for project evolution.

- **Business Activity Monitoring**: we needed a BPM tool able to collect, organize and present all the relevant and valuable business data related to process execution. This was a project must for both daily operations monitoring and mid-long term data analysis for process re-engineering.

As a direct consequence of using the delivered BPM system to manage processes, we got a real-time updated status of all Purchase Orders, and are able to evaluate both specific supplier performance on a single PO or global supplier averages for strategic analysis.

THE TECHNOLOGY & SERVICE PROVIDERS

For such a delicate first experience with BPM, once we selected openwork as the preferred technology, we requested the software vendor to directly support project delivery along with our IT department. Their high quality business process and technological experience have certainly been very important.

openwork is an Italian Independent Software Vendor that concentrates all its efforts exclusively on the homonymous Business Process Management (BPM) suite, designed to represent and manage organizations, data, documents and business processes. The company has been operating on the market for 10 years through an indirect business model based on a channel of specialized partners, made up of IT consulting and organizational companies, and independent Vendors.

University Hospital Virgen del Rocío, Spain

Finalist, Europe.
Nominated by Andalusian Health Service, Spain

EXECUTIVE SUMMARY / ABSTRACT

Document management is one of the major points of inefficiency in hospitals. Due to the great amount of medical reports that are generated for each patient, and the importance of said reports for the continuity of the patient's care, it's indispensable for the improvement in the generation and management of clinical reports.

This work presents the introduction of speech recognition technology for clinical reports in a healthcare organization in Andalusia (Spain). This technology facilitates a quicker and more secure way for health care professionals to complete patient's reports. The new process reduces possible mistakes in the reports and offers better management of hospital resources. We have used methodology based on Business Process Management to guide the implementation of this speech recognition system.

OVERVIEW

It is well-known that healthcare practices produce large amounts of documentation. Research conducted by the American Medical Industry Transcription Association in 2006 and by the Giga Information Group in 2004, estimates that around 12.000 million dollars a year are spent on medical report transcription in the USA alone. The process of dictating and transcribing these reports and delivering them throughout the hospital and to patients is a slow and troublesome task. Today, the most generalized way to complete these reports is the following: the doctor records an audio tape that it is transcribed by administrative staff. The transcript is then reviewed by the doctor, who makes revisions if needed or signs it. This way, the process can take several days to complete medical reports, which delays a patients' treatment. To solve this problem, speech recognition systems have been proposed as new technology, able to automate capturing the information, thus allowing its distribution nearly immediately. These systems can eliminate problems derived from transcription, verbal communication, or communication through manuscript notes between professionals. It implies an important reorganization of hospital resources, as it serves to reduce or eliminate subcontracting external services and release the internal administrative staff of the tedious task of typing.

This work describes the development of VOZENEC (VOZ EN Estación Clínica – Voice in a Clinical Station) Project. This project consists in the deployment and integration of a speech recognition system that converts speech into text within the "Virgen del Rocío" University Hospitals, the largest hospital in Andalusia. Several pilot Units were selected for the project: Diagnostic Units (Radiology and Pathological Anatomy), Surgical Units (Respiratory Diseases Unit, and Plastic and Reconstructive Surgery Unit) and Clinical Units (Endocrinology and Nutrition Unit).

In order to efficiently keep the organizational change required by the implementation of such a system, we have applied Business Process Management (BPM) techniques. BPM methodology serves to ease the deployment of the system by 1)Involving the clinical staff in the implementation process, 2)Providing the IT professionals with a description of the process and its requirements, 3)Assessing the advantages and disadvantages of the speech recognition system, as well as its impact in the organization, and 4) Helping reorganize the healthcare process before implementing the technology, in order to identify how this technology can improve the overall objective of the organization.

The use of this speech recognition system to register medical information has brought numerous benefits for patients, professionals and the healthcare organization. It permits a natural and direct EHR (Electronic Health Record)-healthcare professional interaction, to reduce time during registration, and to avoid intermediaries that can increase mistakes, costs and invested time. Therefore, as for healthcare quality, the use of this technology allows professionals to reduce the time in registering the information.

BUSINESS CONTEXT

"Virgen del Rocío" University Hospitals (HHUUVR), as part of the Andalusian Public Health Service (Servicio Sanitario Público de Andalucía, SSPA) and Andalusian Health Service (Servicio Andaluz de Salud, SAS), must be integrated in the line of evolution of this organization, specially with Information Technology projects and Systems development. Due to its facilities, HHUUVR is an excellent proof station to develop all kinds of projects, assuring success in other hospitals.

The HHUUVR is one of the most popular hospitals of SAS, thanks to its special develop features, capacity and structure. Its large numbers in 2006 are very significant: 54.367 asylum internment, 310.5422 emergencies attended, 62.046 surgical procedures performed, (15.955 Ambulatory Major Surgical), 1.441.616 Medical Records in "SIDCA" (the EHR System in the HHUUVR), 9.231 New Medical Records monthly, and about eight thousand professionals. The infrastructure of this hospital, which is composed of 16 hospital centers, compels to seek technological solutions in order to encourage clinical information sharing in a secure, fast and efficient way.

Today, medical report production is one of the hospital's main costs. The dictation process, sending it to an external transcription building, transcription, report recovery and delivery to patients, are very slow and tricky processes. It's possible that several days are needed to create a medical report and a patient's treatment is delayed unnecessary. With speech recognition, doctors and hospitals will be able to access new technologies that do these tasks in an efficient way, reducing costs and improving the quality of care that the patient receives.

Report generation in HHUUVR, at first was accomplished in three ways: registration information was handwritten, registration taped- transcription by administrative staff - doctor validation, and PC registration through keyboard. These processes implied: a delay in the availability of a digitalized report and in the report generation process (e.g. laboratory tests, diagnosis, etc); errors or lack of information in transcribed report: correction/validation; transcription costs; time spent by professionals checking over transcribed reports, etc.

In this project, we have tried to solve this problem in an integral and interoperable way, making a multi-modal channel (keyboard and voice) in report generation.

THE KEY INNOVATIONS

Business

The final goal of the work performed in hospitals is to provide quality health care to the sanitary system's clients (patients).

Population aging in developed countries, increase of chronic illnesses and dependent people have increased the need for more attention and services in hospitals and sanitary centres (more tests, treatments, reports, etc.). It is necessary to adjust to this new situation. This is one of the reasons why report generation has increased; because of this, the use of ICTs (Information and Communication Technologies) appears to be a good alternative to ease both report generation and accessibility.

The introduction of new technologies and information systems in the health care field to improve the assistance quality and hospitals efficiency, is subordinated to the way of implantation. Until now, it was made in a very little programmed way, only considering local determining factors and not taking into account the whole hospital or the global assistance process. In this sense, it is of vital importance, and supposes an innovation, to introduce Business Process Management (BPM) techniques and tools in a complex and diverse world like health care. These BPM techniques allow to analyse activities involved and to plan them in an optimum way, taking time restrictions, resources and specialists' availability and costs data into account. Also, these BPM techniques give value and consistence in both, the redesign and re-engineering processes and software development.

Today, the different sanitary institutions are encouraging their different departments to use BPM. This makes professionals more interested in learning techniques and tools to facilitate this kind of management. This interest is really positive because in BPM it is essential hospital professionals' implication in different levels: managerial, operative and functional, as well as the providers' and other external agent's implication.

Process

The methodology adopted to define the process is ARIS (ARchitecture of Integrated Systems), which uses a graphic notation to describe processes named EPC (Event-driven Process Chain).

In the following figure, the before proces state (As-Is Process) and after (To-Be process) are described:

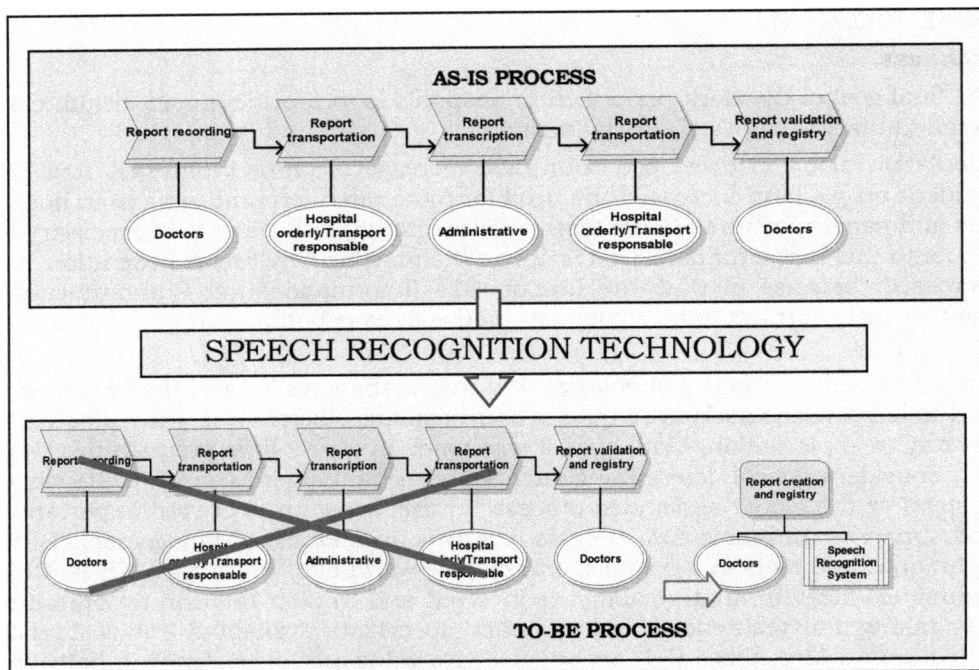

Figure 1. As-is & To-be Processes

One of the report generation processes that caused the most delays and implied higher costs was tape recording.

The report generation As-IS and To-Be models of three clinical units (Medical-Surgical Unit of Respiratory diseases, Endocrinology and Plastic and Reconstructive Surgery) and two diagnosis services (Radiology and Pathological Anatomy) were modeled.

The modeling and simulation were made with ARIS Toolset. To have operative models and all with similar scope, it was established to use at the most four or five levels. Beside, a glossary of terms is being accomplished in order to ease the models comprehension and to define common concepts in all the models, facilitating this way the transfer of knowledge. The following figure depicts an example with the first level of detail in the report generation process "As-Is" model in the Respiratory Unit.

ORGANIZATION

The project's development requires a joint work effort of external and internal hospital professionals (managers, doctors, administrative personal, engineers, technicians, etc.). In the HHUUVR, there already existed this kind of collaborative experience. In 2003 was created at a national level the "Cooperative research thematic network about new models of provision of healthcare services using telemedicine", and the HHUUVR participated in it. A technological group composed of doctors, an economist and several organization engineers participated. This previous experience together with the later development of other R+D projects in different areas (systems interoperability, Virtual Reality tools, Process Management, etc.), and with the incorporation of new professionals (telecommunication and industrial engineers, medical practitioners from others assistance units, etc.) had generated an environment of knowledge and background in BPM techniques. Because of that, it was only necessary to extend these techniques to the professionals from the clinical units who didn't know them and to the external vendors and software development companies. This project developed a process modelling methodology to identify the roles of the different participants and to ease communication channels within the entity.

In regard to the way the project's development affected the professionals' way of working:

1. The sanitary personnel had to prioritise its daily assistance work, which stayed the same, as well as make an effort to elicit requirements.

2. Doctors involved in report generation had to learn how to use the speech recognition tool and change their wording and validating reports.

3. Couriers and other staff in charge of delivering recorded tapes and reports, stopped doing so. Etc.

HURDLES OVERCOME

Management

One of the main challenges in innovation which faces ICTs find in the health care area is to provide simple and natural gateways between the health care professionals to the services and applications of the Hospital Information Systems constructed on the base of knowledge technologies. Hereby, different international media have recently concluded that the assistance activity of health care professionals is suffering significantly from the need to dedicate more time to the interaction with the information systems, to the detriment of the dedication to doctor - patient relation and other activities of a diverse nature.

For health care institutions, a basic need is to start with solutions that facilitate the day to day work of the professionals and that are a real time saver at the moment the information is introduced into the systems.

The creation of the medical records can be delayed several days, delaying without need, a patient's treatment. Thanks to speech recognition, doctors and hospitals can offer patient's higher quality attention, reducing costs and increasing its efficiency. Using the speech recognition system, there is an improvement in the report generation process. An increase of the efficiency and a 50 % reduction of the cost can be reached.

Therefore it is necessary to direct large efforts in the development of interface technologies, which offer manners of simple and natural interaction between man - machine, that includes intelligent strategies of adjustment for the users and natural access with capacity interaction through the voice response to different stimulus.

Business

Hospital Information Systems or Primary care have numerous challenges in front of them, many of them have already been met, such as the improvement of user interface, the electronic signature, the automatic codification, management of laboratory tests, etc. Nevertheless, there are very few health information systems that integrate speech recognition systems, though little by little the integration is obtained progressively. That way, medical institutions will be able with the help of speech recognition to increase its productivity and to reduce its administrative costs.

ORGANIZATION ADOPTION

In spite of the evident improvements in Speech Recognition Systems , the utilization in the medical sector is still scarce, largely due to two important reasons: The distrust of new technologies, especially this technology, and that the development companies do not implement these functions in its Sanitary Information Systems.

Today, in HHUUVR this is integrated in different hospital information systems (RIS and EHR). The interaction of the speech recognition system allows us to improve the report creation process, and reduce wait time for doctors and patients to receive the finished report. In general, the use of speech recognition systems integrated in the clinical Station facilitates and maximizes the creation of medical and clinical reports.

The utilization of Business Process Management techniques allows the ideal design of the integration process of speech recognition system in the clinical station for transcription reports and application management. This is the best possible alternative at the moment a hospital could implement as a solution. The use of these technologies will facilitate the final evaluation of the implemented solution in terms of cost and time.

BENEFITS

It is well-known that healthcare practices produce large amounts of documentation. The process of dictating and transcribing these reports and delivering them throughout the hospital and to patients is a slow and troublesome task. Today, the most generalized way to do these reports is the following: the doctor records an audio tape that it is transcribed by administrative staff. The output of this transcription is then examined by the doctor, who revises and signs it. This way, it can take several days to complete the medical reports, which may delay a patients' treatment. To solve this problem, speech recognition systems have been proposed as new technology able to automate capturing the information, thus allowing its distribution nearly immediately. Speech recognition systems can eliminate problems derived from transcriptions, verbal communication, or communication through manuscript notes between professionals.

In order to fulfill the requirements, we suggest applying Business Process Management (BPM) techniques. The overall objective of BPM is to improve the efficiency of a system by means of systematic management of the business process. BPM considers the different activities of an organization from a customer viewpoint, not limiting itself to a specific organizational (functional) unit. I.e.: the focus of BPM is on global improvement rather than local (functional) improvements. By modeling and analyzing the activities and processes, we obtain a better understanding of the process and establish the foundations for its improvement. In industry, BPM is regarded as a very efficient tool, ensuring the success in a high percentage of the companies and organizations where it has been used. However, there are not much evidence of its success in health care. Indeed, there are authors claiming that hospitals lack the necessary conditions to BPM, although they specifically refer to 'radical change' or 're engineering', which is just one possibility among the different options offered by BPM.

Several advantages have been identified by driving the deployment of the speech recognition system by the BPM methodology. First, by involving the key staff within each unit in the modeling process, they have a clearer picture of the all relevant processes within the unit, not only of those under their direct responsibility. As a result, they gain more knowledge of the clinical practice in their units and they are able to detect points for future improvement that they were not previously aware of. This is a widely-discussed characteristic of BPM of particular interest in the health care sector, as the strong specialization of the clinical staff has lead to the fragmentation of the health care process into smaller areas of responsibility where (local) improvements may not be reflected in the (global) process. As a result, some practices have changed in view of the implementation of the speech recognition system. For instance, in the Pathological Anatomy Service, the macroscopic report was sent to the pathologist's consulting room while waiting for the laboratory's results. In the new process, the report is sent to the laboratory together with the specimens. When the results are obtained from the laboratory, then both the report and the results are sent to the corresponding pathologist for diagnosis. With this organizational change, administrative (non-value added) time has been saved with respect to the previous situation.

On the other hand, process modeling has eased the deployment of the speech recognition system in the different Units, such as the process of documentation and analysis gained through process modeling have made the IT professionals in charge of implementing the speech recognition system know exactly which requirements and daily practices of each medical practitioner, thus reducing both deployment time and its degree of failure. In addition, the BPM methodology employed here has served to make an *a priori* assessment of the technology to be implemented regarding both time and cost.

Therefore, we can say that the implementation of the speech recognition technology will suppose the following benefits:

- Benefits for the patient:
  - To accelerate the health care
  - Better quality health care
- Benefits for the health care staff:
  - Reduction of time in the execution of the reports
  - Habits of more flexible work
  - More reliability in the distributed information
  - Automation and centralization of the process of documentation generation, which in turn facilitates the use of the Electronic Health Records
- Benefits for health care organization:
  - An important reorganization of the resources in the hospital, which implies a reduction or elimination of subcontracting external services and to release the internal administrative staff of the tedious tasks of typing.
  - Increase productivity and quality.
  - Costs saving

COSTS SAVING

Costs saving is associated with the redesign of the report generation process:

- External administrative staff contracted by the hospital exclusively for the transcription of these reports.
- Time of internal hospital administrative staff dedicated to the transcription of these reports.
- Time used by the doctor for the validation of transcribed reports compared to time that will be saved in correcting a report generated by the speech recognition tool.

Cost reduction has been associated to the processes modification, this reduction is necessary to the cost-benefit estimation. This estimate has been done specifically in the Endocrinology and Nutrition Unit the reports where sent to an external building to be transcribed. With the obtained data, the calculation is as follows:

Unitary cost by transcribed report: 1.42€*

- *Billing costs of external transcription company.

Data obtained from the simulation: 996 reports per month in consulting rooms situated in the Diagnostic and Treatment Centre:

- 465 forthwith → No computed in the transcription.
- 531 were sent to transcribed.

Therefore:

- Savings = 531 report/month x 1.42 €/report = 744, 02 €/month.

TIME REDUCTIONS

In order to compile the time reduction study both kinds of models, "as is" and "to be" models, were used in the simulation. With the result obtained from both processes we analyzed and compared the results.

By simulating the processes and analyzing the output, important time reduction with regard to document generation has been anticipated. For instance, the time reduction in document generation was estimated to be around 89% with respect to the previous situation in the Endocrinology and Nutrition Unit, and about 75% in the Respiratory Diseases Unit. These estimations proved to be fairly accurate, as well as the cost reductions estimated by the simulation of the documented processes.

Today, the data from the "as-is" model is being compared to the pilot scheme.

INCREASED REVENUES

As "Virgen del Rocío" Hospital is a public hospital that belongs to the Public Health Network in Andalusia (SAS), its main goal is not to increase benefits but to improve the healthcare quality of its patients

PRODUCTIVITY IMPROVEMENTS

With the implementation of this technology, we expect that in the near future every patient will leave the consult with a report in hand. The report will be done instantly and when the results of the tests come back another report will be generated including the results. This will suppose an increase in report generation.

BEST PRACTICES, LEARNING POINTS AND PITFALLS

Best Practices

As best practices adopted from the beginning of the project, we can indicate the use of standard methodology like: METRICS v3 (developed by Spanish Ministry of Public Administration) and PMBOK for project management.

During the modelling phases of the process and implantation of the technology, we were able to identify critical points that impeded the suitable development of the project and allowed us to extract "Learning Points" and carry out Best Practices.

Process Modelling:

From the learning points, a "best practices" model for process modelling was established. In the following phases of the project and in other projects with BPM work methodology was defined to detect critical points.

Some of the most important aspects are:

1. To establish modelling objectives that are always aligned with project objectives, and to make a Development Work Plan. The Committee Project Director and Modelling Group will make these decisions.

This is a very important point. Modelling must be orientated to the objectives that need to be managed, therefore, it is very important to identify them clearly, and not modify them during the project.

2. One of the most difficult points for modelling is the reluctance of the key people in the process to facilitate information. This can be due to several factors:
   - A data gap about the project, the purpose of modelling and its responsibility and participation in the same.
   - Reluctance to change.
   - Fear of criticism of the work or suffering changes in the same.
   - Etc.

To avoid this, it is necessary to have informative reunions between the Committee Director, the Modelling Group and group leaders in charge of the different groups in the process. It is necessary that each group leader inform their participants before the modelling process of what is their part in this process.

3. To establish a common glossary of terms for all the modellers. The glossary of terms is created in consensus with all the participants, since they are the experts in their domain. This is another project result, and must be available to all the modellers and people that will use the model.

Implanting Technology:

1. To establish an implantation project coordinator
2. To inform the personnel implied of any changes that the process will suffer, and to inform them the degree of their implication in this process.
3. To respect the steps defined in To Be models.

If there are some circumstances that have not been modelled, project director will agree on the solution with the committee, and will receive documents if necessary.

4. To realize implantation planning, including task contemplation, budgeting, resources and time costs.

PITFALLS

The difficulties of the project are as follows:

- Requirements of high bandwidth, this system can't be used with thin client technology. Thus, the need for an important investment in a total renovation arises. Another option would consist of assuming a limited deployment of only those working places that fulfill the mentioned requirements.

- The training period for the professionals must be under an intensive support and supervision program, during this period the risk of rejection is high. Incorrect training reduces the credibility of the recognition. This supposes a cost to consider.

- A large number of documents are generated from models which only need to incorporate some of the concrete data. Vozenec currently does not respond to this need in an optimum way. It is a new area of development.

COMPETITIVE ADVANTAGES

The development of this project started by "Virgen del Rocío" University Hospitals has caught the interest and is supported by Andalusian regional government's Ministry of Health, that of which has financed it for two years. If the project is successful, the technology used could spread to other hospitals within this autonomous region.

This project permits technology pilots and system pilots that also allow interoperability with EHR which are shared throughout Andalusia. In addition, a dictionary has been created (MultiMedSSPA) which contains medical terminology to be used by professionals to write reports, to have greater precision and speed during the speech recognition process. The Creation of this dictionary and thesaurus will facilitate correct information coding. Technology integration with EHR and the development of the MultiMedSSPA dictionary are the most important competitive advantages of the project in Andalusia.

If the project extends to other hospitals, BPM tools and the knowledge generated would provide a great value, and contribute to the implementation of the same (best practices).

Because we are of a public nature, our business interest is only to reserve possible patent and copyright rights associated to the project.

TECHNOLOGY

The methodology is adapted from ARIS (ARchitecture of Integrated Systems) methodology, which uses a graphic notation to describe processes called EPC. The choice of the ARIS methodology has been based on a previous analysis of the existing methodologies for business process modelling, this being the methodology that covers the needs presented in the healthcare processes. Among them, it is worth noting, that it allows the description of both the process that specify each activity and the underlying process structure, and the flow of objects and its relations.

ARIS is the architecture created to develop business process models, which contain all the basic features to describe this process. A model is normally complex, ARIS divides it into individual views to make their understanding easier. Owing to this division, the content of the individual views can be described by special methods for each view without considering the relations and interrelations with the others and represents the healthcare processes giving a overall vision of the same, integrating all the elements that make it up (including human resources, administrative processes, and all the processes support that contributes added value to the process).

The views are:

- Organization View: it is formed by the staff that intervenes in the process: doctors, nurses, patients, administrative, etc.
- Functions View: it is formed by the functions (activities) that are realized in a certain process.
- Data View: it is formed by the objects that are generated and use in the process, as the documents, the patient history, the reports, etc.
- Control View: it is the view that relates each view and gives temporary form to the process, this way we know who does each function and the objects generated at every moment. In this view we find a kind of graph that describes the process by means of a Process Chain guided by Events (EPC), the EPC has perspectives, and in addition it fulfils the previously

mentioned requirements, doing that it is the ideal skill for business processes modelling.

The EPCs fulfil the fundamental requirement for the modelling processes, simplicity and easy comprehension by not expert users. Since it is based on the Petri's Network, the resultant models are, in a certain way, compatible with the models of Petri's Networks.

The use of this model methodology has allowed:

- To describe the process' mission in a clear manner.
- To permit assigning responsibility for the completion of the process objective.
- To be flexible to incorporate changes.
- To identify and to evaluate the impact of the above mentioned changes.
- To use as analysis guide of requirements.

The core of the methodology consists on the following phases:

1. Process definition: In this phase, the healthcare processes to be studied are established together with a definition of its limits, inputs and outputs, Units involved in the execution of the processes, selection of the staff in charge of assisting during the modelling process and in the validation of the models.

2. Generation of "as-is" models: The output of the phase is a detailed graphical representation (in terms of EPCs) of the current state of the processes. In our project, this refers to the processes before the implementation of the speech recognition system. The "as-is" models have been obtained through an iterative process of: design, verification and corrections, and until their validation by the staff in the different Units.

3. Gathering simulation data for the "as-is" models: By extracting data from the Hospital Information Systems as well as data provided by the staff in the different Units, the dynamic "as-is" models designed have been fed and simulated.

4. Simulation Analysis: The statistical data resulting from the simulation of the "as-is" models are analysed for its interpretation.

5. Building the "to-be" models: In our case, it consists on the expected final state with the implementation of the speech recognition tool. The collaboration of the system's technical software developer is essential for this phase.

6. Simulation of the "to-be" model, analysis and comparison of results: Once the "to be" models is simulated and the information obtained, the models are compared.

THE TECHNOLOGY & SERVICE PROVIDERS

Andalusian Health Service: The Andalusian Health Service (AHS) is an autonomous organism attached to the ministry of health of the Andalusian regional government. It belongs to Andalusian public health service (APHS). Its mission is to give medical attention to Andalusian citizens, offering quality public health service. http://www.sas.junta-andalucia.es/principal/

"Virgen del Rocío" University Hospitals: This hospital belongs to Andalusian Health Service where the project has been carried out. Participants: Technology group R+D, Information Technologies Service, Advanced Clinical Documentation

Centre and Clinical Units (Respiratory, Endocrinology, Plastic surgery and major burns, Radiology, Pathological anatomy). http://www.huvr.org/

Everis: A multinational consultant which offers overall business solutions. Its participation has entailed the implementation and integration of the speech recognition process with information system of Electronic Health Records (EHR) in the hospital, and future thesaurus integration and databases involved in the automatic encoding process. http://www.everis.es

Philips: Royal Philips Electronics (NYSE: PHG, AEX: PHI) is a global leader in healthcare, lighting and consumer lifestyle, delivering people-centric, innovative products, services and solutions through the brand promise of "sense and simplicity". In this project, Philips is the provider of SpeechMagic, featuring industrial-grade speech recognition technology, and is also taking part in thesaurus elaboration. http://www.philips.com/speechrecognition

NewDoor: Company associated with Philips, it's specialized and certified in SpeechMagic (speech recognition technology chosen to develop the project) integration, deployment and maintenance. http://www.new-doors.net/

Section 2

Middle East-Africa

Eskom, South Africa

Gold Award, Middle East and Africa.
Nominated by ciboodle, UK

EXECUTIVE SUMMARY / ABSTRACT

Eskom, South Africa's state-owned electricity company, operates across six regions. This complicated infrastructure led to an urgent need for a flexible, agile system to drive efficiencies and support the re-routing, escalation and monitoring of work.

The project, named Ubuso (the Zulu word for 'face') provided the means to control routing and monitoring of work over Eskom's vast operational arena and sharing workloads across their regional call centres. GT-X Workflow was also essential for campaign management, segmentation and customer profiling.

OVERVIEW

Eskom, South Africa's state-owned electricity company is in the top 13 utilities in the world in terms of generation capacity, and ninth in terms of sales. The utility company, whose revenue stands at ZAR 44,448 million (US $5,756m), serves more than 4.1 million customers throughout South Africa. This vertically integrated utility generates 95% of the electricity used in South Africa and generates over 45% of the total electricity produced in Africa, making Eskom by far the continent's largest utility company.

Prior to 1988, Eskom supplied electricity principally to large customers, such as mines and municipalities. This placed them as one of the largest electricity generators in the world, with only 120,000 customers! However, in 1988, Eskom developed its "Electricity for All" concept and began to supply electricity directly to millions of domestic customers.

Eskom operates across six regions. This complicated infrastructure led to an urgent need for a flexible, agile system to drive efficiencies and support the re-routing, escalation and monitoring of work.

However, as with many utilities, efficiency was hampered by inconsistencies in the handling and recording of customer issues, and out-of-date information increased the potential for further customer dissatisfaction. The organisation's principal pain was its legacy technology, which was limiting operations in several core areas, including self-service, integration and automated workflow. The result was longer call-handing times with limited routing and self-help abilities. This led to repeated call backs from customers and significantly increased the overall call load. Inefficiencies were compounded by having very limited integration with other systems, such as the billing system.

Work began to extend Eskom's virtual contact centre philosophy in January 2004. The company overhauled and refurbished their existing contact centre infrastructure, creating seven state-of-the-art contact centre sites serving its six regions and providing 24 hour customer service.

Eskom's CRM systems traditionally consisted of non-integrated, predominantly manual processes, which were constraining the company by preventing automated workflow. The implementation of ciboodle's (formerly Graham Technology) workflow solution provided the means to control routing and monitoring of work over Eskom's vast operational arena, sharing workloads across their seven call centre sites. GT-X Workflow was also essential for campaign management, segmentation and customer profiling. The implementation of a campaign management system enabled the company to give customers proactive notification of power outages in localised areas, which previously led to regional contact centres being inundated with fault calls.

Eskom highlighted customer segmentation as being particularly important, in order to identify 'sensitive' or VIP customers (e.g. hospitals).

Graham Technology ensured that tasks are now executed according to priority, with GT-X Contact History supporting this through a 'single customer view'. The presentation of information has been simplified by a central repository, which accesses customer details across multiple back-end sources. An electronic 'contact trail' of every customer now exists, and this capability provides efficient segmentation and targeting.

BUSINESS CONTEXT

In terms of technology issues, Eskom lacked an enterprise workflow management system. They had limited use of Calling Line Identity (CLI), no Computer Telephony Integration (CTI) and no automated outbound dialler. There was also no unified queue management for calls, faxes or emails.

A vital aspect sought from the project was the provision of a unified agent desktop providing the ability to manage customer information, all interactions and interaction history via one single interface. Eskom also required the ability to manage cases from opening of a request through to its closure. In addition, back office operations needed to be consolidated to achieve economies of scale.

Due to the lack of single customer view, staff competence and experience gaps were aggravated and staffing levels in the organisation were high compared to best practices.

As a result of the project, cases can now be tracked from opening, through to closure, rather than them disappearing off management's radar. Thus, a single customer view has been achieved. Agents and Managers can view all interactions that the organisation has had with the customer through one single interface.

Through the Ubuso project and the implementation of a CRM system, the customer experience was enhanced and customer service improved. The new system enabled overheads to be lowered as staffing costs reduced. Previously, the majorities of processes were non-integrated and were handled manually, therefore, training costs were extremely high.

THE KEY INNOVATIONS

Business

The project has had a major impact on the way Eskom does business with its customers. Previously, telephoning the Call Centre or visiting a Walk-in Centre were the only options available to the customer to make any enquiries about their account. However, now choice has been given back to the customers as they can select their preferred channel of interaction with the organisation, across phone, web, email and mobile. This means that the customer can now track their own cases from opening to closure, in the convenience of their own homes or offices.

Employees now have access to all the necessary information at their fingertips. As a result, agents have become more empowered to meet the needs of the customers. They are also dealing with more interesting tasks as low value cases are dealt with by the customers themselves over the web, which also reduces costs. Higher value cases are put through to the most knowledgeable agents, allowing segmentation of customers and improved job satisfaction.

The contact centre is now able to track resources through analytics and allocate resource where it is needed most. This also has the benefit of ensuring no employees are left idle when there is work to be done. Similarly, agents with a large workload are not left struggling to cope.

Process

Prior to the project, the processes did not provide customer satisfaction. In order to improve the customer experience, the processes were developed to deliver a single point of contact, ownership of requests, feedback and closure and skills based routing. In terms of multimedia channels, the previous processes could simply cope with voice. They now enable interactions via voice, email, fax, SMS and Internet. In terms of architectural position, Eskom previously ran with islanded, individual call centres. They have now been moved to a distributed contact centre with shared software as a result of the Ubuso project.

The previous point-to-point integration methodology was changed to Enterprise Application Integration and the Implementation approach moved on from being a build approach to using Best-of-Breed commercially available packages.

Finally, Internet presence, which previously was purely informational, moved past transactional and became interactive. The service delivered to customers became more integrated into production systems, managed by workflow and with all interactions logged to provide an integrated view of customers and a consolidated data view.

As the company conducts its operations through multiple channels, a high quality service had to be delivered across all channels as standard. This introduced a more convenient way of working at a lower cost and also built in the ability for customers to self-serve.

Customer service segmentation was also achieved across all channels, allowing prioritisation of customer queuing, and differentiated service standards. It means that customers can be served through their preferred channel and resource can be allocated accordingly.

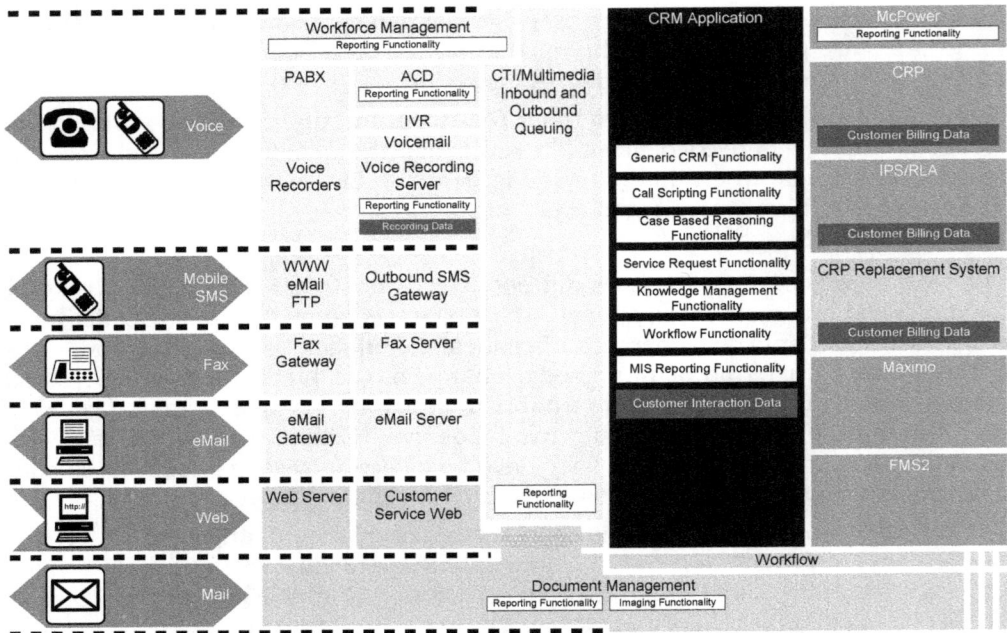

The above diagram is the technology architecture that was achieved for Eskom's Ubuso project. This technology architecture provides Eskom with a centralised platform for the contact centres in the various regions.

The the left hand column of the diagram shows the multiple channels (voice, mobile SMS, email, wed and mail) which can be utilised by Eskom customers to get in touch with the contact centres. The second, third and fourth columns show the technologies that enable communication via these channels.

The fifth column represents GT-X and the functionality that it has provided, such as workflow.

Back end applications that provide the integration data required by the call centre agents are represented in the last column.

Organisation

Eskom's managers have now gained the power of visibility and control. Every work item received is dealt with by a common set of business processes. This consistency means that it is simple to compare performance across its regions.

Eskom has increased the flexibility of its business processes, which is critical to reaching their internal targets and especially for increasing their 'one call to complete' resolution rate.

The company has an internal committee, the OCI (Optimise Customer Interactions) Value Chain committee, which decides SLAs and expected resolution dates. These targets are now achievable.

GT-X has provided this huge and complex organisation with the ability to quickly understand any one of millions of customers' situations; to communicate in an informed, prompt manner; initiate the appropriate action; and to cater for each customer's needs.

Finally, additional benefits gleaned by Eskom through working with Graham Technology were as follows:

- ownership and ease of customization as a consequence of the intuitive GT-X development environment;
- the flexibility of GT-X deployed Eskom business processes; and
- the GT knowledge transfer approach to allow for self-reliance upon roll-out.

The GT-X solution was implemented, on time and on budget, at all seven call centre sites, in the back office and at regional customer service area offices. Eskom's total number of users has reached in excess of 2000; the legacy system has been decommissioned; and all users have been brought on line. The GT-X solution is highly scalable and offers room for significant growth, as Eskom's business needs demand.

Employees are now empowered with all the information they need, available at their fingertips. Customer service levels are higher. Through the introduction of the web channel, employees are challenged through dealing with more complex interactions and more repetitive tasks are met by customers themselves.

Graham Technology also had a full technical team on site, completely focused on Eskom and resolving any issues as they arose across each of the dispersed locations.

> "Superior customer service is seen as a 'win-win' situation: Eskom is now easier to do business with, at a realistic cost to Eskom."

> Kevin von Berg, Corporate Specialist (Customer Service), Eskom

HURDLES OVERCOME

Management

The main hurdle overcome in this project was the improving the collaboration between business and IT within the organisation. This was a major cultural change as change was previously handled by a typical 'waterfall' method where a concept was raised then went through a change management process before it was put into effect.

As a result of the new technology adoption, Eskom have been able to introduce a change champion culture to ensure buy in from key individuals throughout the process.

Business

In order to ensure the project had a successful go-live, extensive training was provided to all employees. As Eskom employees were previously working with manual processes, technical training was a hurdle that had to be overcome at this stage.

A hurdle, often evident in this sort of project, is that buy in from all areas of the business can be difficult to achieve. In order to overcome this challenge, focus groups were held with stakeholders from all areas of the business. This was an opportunity to gauge attitude to the change and gather any specific requirements.

Organization Adoption

Graham Technology has been able to provide support and guidance throughout the implementation process as we have implemented similar projects with large organisations in the past. Graham Technology has worked closely with key stakeholders in both the business and IT communities at each of the key project milestones to ensure there were no unexpected issues or surprises along the way.

As well as providing technical training to all employees, focus groups were held to gather requirements prior to the implementation. A soft go-live took place before the launch to test the system, identify any problems and resolve any issues.

BENEFITS

> "We wanted the best system: one that had proved itself globally; had the flexibility to meet Eskom's requirements; and had all the features we wanted to deliver on our Customer Service vision."
>
> Hugh McGibbon, Divisional Customer Service Manager, Eskom Distribution

COST SAVINGS

A significant number of cost savings have been made as a result of Graham Technology's implementation:

- Reduction in training costs – Graham Technology's CRM System Solution has enabled agents to focus on customer service, rather than the system. Due to the process-centric nature of the CRM System Solution and the ability to provide an intuitive process-driven front-end, the agents are led through the process rather than presented with a wide variety of fields where they have to learn to input the information, or worse, switch between applications. The CRM System Solution consolidates all existing front-end systems, therefore, there is only one system to learn. All processes can be completed using the same look and feel, thus eliminating the need to be trained in other applications.
- Costs are lower for people skills because a single front-end, results in only one skill-set being required. Graham Technology's CRM Software Solution conforms to industry standards, therefore, these skill-sets are easy to find (e.g. JavaScript).
- Reduced cost per customer interaction

EFFICIENCY IMPROVEMENT

The implementation of the Graham Technology solution at Eskom has also delivered a number of benefits with regard to Efficiency:

- Efficiency from Reduction in Average Call Handling Time. The CRM solution is process driven and front ends all the relevant processes, pulling information from any system to enable the call to be handled from a common front-end. This means that the agent does not need to navigate between different systems. By having this information more readily available, the call time is reduced.
- Efficiency from First Call Resolution (reduction in despatched items) - All calls that do not need to involve a separate point of contact can be handled on first resolution. This includes a wide variety of call types and agents are able to handle a wider variety of calls following implementation of the CRM software solution because it can integrate to all relevant systems and can present these in an easy-to-use process.
- Efficiency from One Call Resolution (reduction in repeat calls) – Handling the call right first time means fewer repeat calls as the customer is served – and satisfied – at the outset and has no need to call back to chase up his request.

COST SAVINGS

There have been a number of significant cost savings since the implementation of the Ubuso project. Staff training and support has seen key cost reductions. Website interactions have also served to reduce costs as customers are able to self-serve.

Some of the specific Returns on Investment are detailed below.

Item	Benefit over 5 years (US $)
Efficiency from self service channels	$1,653,158
Efficiency from first call resolution (reduction in despatched items)	$3,725,891
Efficiency from one call resolution (reduction of repeat calls)	$1,293,980
Efficiency resulting from decreased AHT	$2,976,155
Efficiency from improved Case Management	$15,092,016
Reduction in training costs	$209,931
Efficiency from flexibility for process changes	$1,452,977
Total Estimated Savings	$26,412,219

Financial quantification

There are a number of strategic and tactical benefits that will be realised through the implementation of the CRM System Solution. These benefits cannot be quantified, but will have an impact on Eskom's strategic readiness for future industry changes as well as improved customer services.

The table below indicates the benefits that can be financially quantified and related to the eight key benefits that have been identified:

	2005	2006	2007	2008	2009
Benefits	$2,004,597	$4,825,872	$5,587,177	$6,480,784	$7,527,201
Accumulated benefits	$2,005,170	$6,827,897	$12,417,422	$18,901,758	$26,427,332

Productivity Improvements

- Efficiency from Flexibility for Process Changes - The CRM System Solution will significantly enhance the ability to change, modify or delete processes. This flexibility is attributed to the architecture of the CRM System Solution framework where processes are mapped into a 'flow-chart' used in the CRM System Solution software. Each process can be dragged and dropped to change process flow, incorporate new processes or delete redundant ones. This increased flexibility offered by the CRM System Solution is particularly noticeable for organisations that have previously experienced 'hard-coded' packages.
- Efficiency from self-service channels
- Efficiency from improved Case Management - This is all be handled through the Workflow system. There have been significant efficiencies gained by automating the Case Management Process. By making it more effective, customer service has clearly been increased by cutting out the need for various people to check things have been done and passing work around in an inefficient manner. The CRM Software Solution automates

all this, based on the specific procedures that best suit Eskom. Again, these processes can be improved through time to continually increase efficiency.

- Real-time updates customer requests for front-line agents significantly reducing volume of process handoffs
- Integrated eight business-critical systems into a single view for agents, providing real-time access to details of customer interactions
- Allowed prompt, accessible and cost-effective self-service access channels, such as Web and IVR systems, to deal with simple tasks, such as account balances and automated fault reporting

BEST PRACTICES, LEARNING POINTS AND PITFALLS

Best Practices

✓ *Training Academy – Full training provided to all employees in advance of go-live*

✓ *Inclusion of key stakeholders in the organisation in planning stages to ensure all requirements are met by the implementation. It was essential to have complete buy in from both Business and IT within the organisation for successful implementation.*

✓ *Create internal committees to manage the change effectively. For example, at Eskom, The OCI (Optimise Customer Interactions) Value Chain governance committee was tasked to decide Service Level Agreements (SLAs) and ensure targets are achieved*

Pitfalls

✗ *A potential pitfall could result from cultural differences around the world with regard to technology. In South Africa, the majority of citizens have mobile phones, however, a much smaller proportion have access to the Internet. As a result, more focus was placed on the mobile channel. Web may be considered more important in other regions.*

✗ *Implementing a solution without business wide consultation to ensure buy in from all stakeholders*

COMPETITIVE ADVANTAGES

Business Process Management software manages processes; Graham Technology manages customer interaction processes. These are very specialised types of processes and require a platform designed to deliver capabilities such as high volume concurrency running to tens of thousands of agents. Rich process composition is accessed through a unified interface, and collaboration features promote the best use of knowledge and personnel. Presentation capabilities allow processes to be accessed by all known channels and devices.

The Graham Technology Process Modelling Toolkit can be changed dependent on organisational need. Changes to processes can be done within the business community, or the IT community to give the user control of the change. A suitable user is able to update a process, insert new steps and decision points and rules. The process can be re-saved, the version incremented and the change fully audited. The changed process is then exposed across all channels. The change can be piloted prior to deployment using the simulation tool. This could be used to check the process, the cost of the change and discover any bottlenecks that may exist. The product is built for change, is adaptable to the business context and is information rich.

TECHNOLOGY

This following figure shows the Workflow Model and its various components:

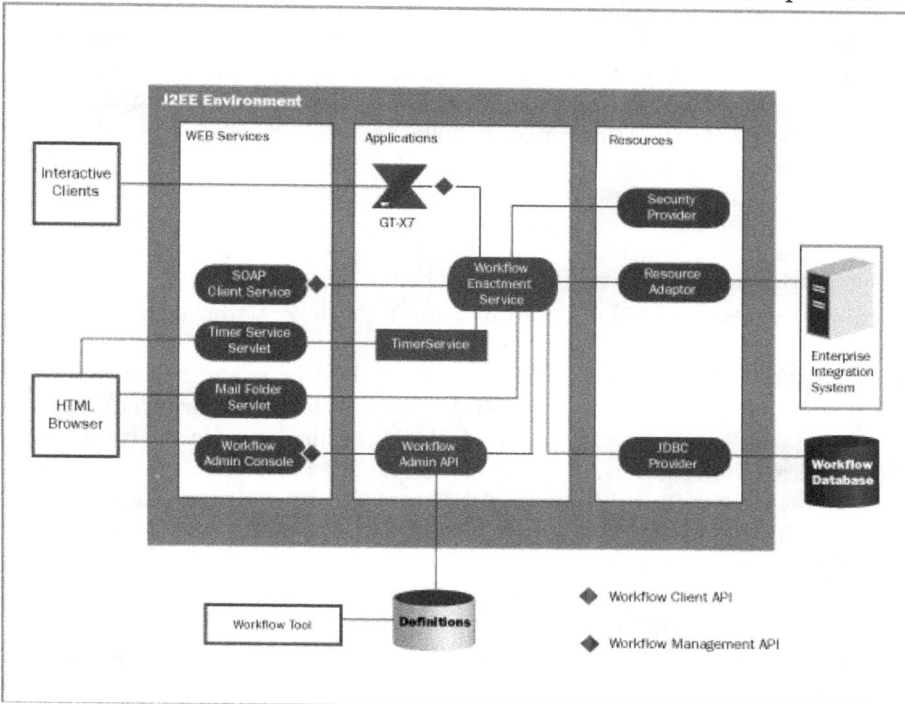

The components of the Workflow Model are as follows:

- **Workflow Enactment Service (Workflow Kernel)**: The Workflow Administration API interprets the Workflow definition, and controls how Workflows are instantiated and Activities are sequenced. It adds work items to the user and role work lists, maintains internal data, and invokes applications and tools as necessary.
- **Workflow Tool**: The Workflow Tool is used to create the Workflow description, which is written as an XML definition file, based on the GT-X7 definitions.
- **Definitions**: The Workflow definition, once loaded, is stored in the Workflow database, and contains all necessary information to allow the Workflow Kernel to execute the Workflow, which includes:
  - Completion conditions
  - Activities and rules for navigating between completion conditions
  - Tasks for users to undertake
  - Any required field definitions
  - Set of permitted users and roles
- **Workflow Database**: The Workflow Kernel maintains a persistent state which controls:
  - Data the system uses to manage system state (for example, the names and locations of Workflow definitions).
  - Internal state information associated with the various Workflow sessions and Activityinstances that are being executed.

All this information is stored in a database, used by the Workflow Kernel, and only accessed by a GT-X7 Administrator.

- **Workflow Administration API**: The Workflow Administration API provides a number of supervisory operations. These operations enable the supervisor to identify and modify participants for a specific role, to track Workflow sessions, to trace the history of a particular Workflow session, and to enquire about incomplete work and other statistics. The administrator uses the Workflow Administration Console to access the state of the Workflow system. This console allows you to:
  - Load a Workflow
  - Delete a Workflow
  - Terminate or suspend a Workflow
  - Resume a Workflow
  - Add, delete and modify system properties.

You can access the Workflow Administration Console using any standard Web browser.

- **Clients**: A client can be either a single user or a participant in an organisational role. The client logs on the Workflow system and then can request the list of all available work that matches the client's roles, or just the next scheduled item of work. The GT-X7 Process Kernel communicates with the Workflow Kernel via the Workflow Client API. The GTWClient Object allows GT-X7 Processes to gain access to the client API.
- **SOAP Client Service**: If you want to use Workflow functionality without using a GT-X7 client, you can access the Workflow Kernel using a SOAP client service, which permits access to the Workflow client API.
- **Timer Service**: The Workflow Kernel has many functions that are time-critical. For this reason, the GT Workflow model uses a custom-built timer service to handle all time-dependant functions. The timer service creates and stores all timers used to drive the Kernel. The administrator uses the timer service servlet to monitor timers from the database. You can access the Timer Service Servlet using any standard Web browser.
- **Security Provider**: J2EE environments have standard built-in security features. In addition, the Workflow system also allows connections to GT-X7 Security Providers, and to custom Security Providers as required.
- **Resource Adapter:** J2EE environments use resource adapters to connect to back-end systems. You can also add resource adapters to the Workflow service to allow connections to other systems. For example, a resource adapter can be used to run JavaBeans.
- **JDBC Provider**: All connections to databases are performed using the J2EE JDBC providers. This offers built-in transaction support, allowing greater stability and recovery from errors.
- **Workflow Monitoring**: You can use Workflow monitoring to record the values of Workflow fields at specified stages in the Navigation. GT-X7 provides a default monitor class, but you can also use a custom monitor.
- **Gateways**: The Gateway through which work is submitted creates a Workflow message to encapsulate each piece of work. The Gateway appends the target Workflow to the Workflow message. So, when a Workflow is instantiated the Workflow Kernel knows which messages to pass it. When a Workflow Session is started, the Workflow Kernel will pass it the appropriate Workflow messages.

THE TECHNOLOGY & SERVICE PROVIDERS
- ciboodle (www.ciboodle.com)

ciboodle, formerly Graham Technology, is a wholly owned subsidiary of Sword Group. Specialists in process centric customer interaction software for contact centres, our unique approach to customer interaction gives agents a comprehensive view of customer data across multiple channels, and is the only enterprise scale BPM based CRM product to focus exclusively on contact centres.

ciboodle helps large organisations across North America, EMEA and Asia Pacific drive operational efficiency and improve customer experience.

Headquartered in the UK, ciboodle has offices in Australia, Indonesia, South Africa and North America.

Customer References: Vodafone, Standard Bank, Eskom, BT, ScottishPower, Friends Provident, Pacificorp, Ergon Energy, Pacificorp.

- Accenture (www.accenture.com)

Section 3

North America

CONAGUA, Mexico

Finalist, North America.
Nominated by PECTRA Technology, Inc., USA.

EXECUTIVE SUMMARY

The CONAGUA – Mexico Water National Commission (www.conagua.gob.mx) - in charge of managing and preserving national waters in the Mexican Untied States, optimized Public Work Procurement and Execution Process by implementing PECTRA BPM Suite, also providing access to such information to the community as a whole through the web.

The process called "Management and Development of Hydro-agricultural Infrastructure", the organization's most significant and with the greatest breadth of scope, includes programming, budgeting, procurement, execution follow-up, and project-closing activities aimed at the operation, preservation, maintenance and management of the federal hydro-agricultural infrastructure (drain, roads, levees, water control structures such as sewers and fords, and crossing structures such as bridges, etc.) of the 22 Technified Storm Districts (TSDs). The TSDs are areas in charge of generating and preparing investment projects, establishing the particular characteristics of the works to be performed, each taking into account the peculiarities of its geographical area. These TSDs are located in 9 states, covering a 2.7 million-hectare region and have 115,000 users. By implementing this system, CONAGUA complied with two important national acts, to which it adheres:

1. Act of Public Works and Related Services enacted by the Congress on January 4th, 2000. The purpose of this act is to regulate actions involving planning, scheduling, budgeting, procurement, expenditure, performance, and control of public works as well as of their related services.

2. Act of Transparency and Access to Governmental Public information made effective by the National Government on June 12th, 2002. This act establishes a number of duties to sort and preserve documentation included in files belonging to entities and departments of the Federal Public Administration (FPA), with the aim to foster transparency in public management, accountability, and access by individuals to information held by the State.

The outcome being that CONAGUA was awarded an Honorable Mention in the 2005 Transparency Annual Prize organized by the National Institute of Public Administration and the Department of Internal Affairs. That same year, CONAGUA also obtained the Innova recognition from President Vicente Fox, an incentive to successful innovative practices created by the 2000-2006 Administration, as the system is considered to have a favorable impact on the Six Strategies of Good Government. Additionally, the Department of Internal Affairs included the System in its catalog of good practices as to regulatory improvement, which can be replicated in other Government institutions.

"The implementation of PECTRA BPM Suite meant a superb achievement for the institution, taking into consideration the demands of the Mexican community to governmental entities and organisms, favoring greater control of tasks, processes and actions carried out by their officers and employees", highlights Mr. Juan Carlos Garcés del Ángel, Operating Coordinator of Hydro-agricultural Management

System based on PECTRA BPM Suite, belonging to the Department of TSDs, CONAGUA.

"An honest and effective administration that provides more and better services to citizens is the goal of governments. The implementation of PECTRA BPM Suite allowed us to design a system to digitally administer operations, ensuring citizens full access to information and a better control of the tasks performed by governmental entities, their officers and employees", says Mr. Isidro Gaytán Arvizu, System Director, Manager of TSDs, CONAGUA.

OVERVIEW

The mission of CONAGUA, an autonomous division of the Department of Environment and Natural Resources of Mexico, is to manage and preserve national waters with the participation of the community to attain the sustainable use of said resource.

Management is carried out by 22 TSDs, whose functions are:
- To restore the infrastructure built in order to transfer its regular preservation to users.
- To provide infrastructure users with technical advisory aiming at the technical, administrative and financial autonomy of their organizations.
- To foster water management and soil preservation with the purpose of achieving sustainable development of resources.

These activities are carried out by means of public-work and related-services contracts. Additionally, machinery and equipment is procured in the districts in order to hand them over to users as a means of preserving and operating the constructed infrastructure. "There was the internal need to sort out management in order to increase the efficiency and productivity of a substantive technical-administrative process, such as public work, taking into consideration the opinion of different users at different levels –national, regional, and state- to connect the various operational, IT, and documentary systems", mentioned Mr. Gaytán Arvizu. "The challenge was defined. Therefore, we had to obtain the best tool in the market place to satisfy our needs, that would adapt quickly and easily to what the Government requested from us", he concludes.

The implementation of PECTRA BPM Suite allowed CONAGUA the standardization, control, and improvement of administrative and management processes related to the Management and Development of Hydro-agricultural Infrastructure, complying with two important goals:
- To optimize the Investment Scheduling, Procurement and Execution process of Public Work.
- To provide access to relevant information to the community as a whole for control and assessment of public management by means of simple procedures.
- In this way, CONAGUA got two important benefits:
- To attain successful results as to compliance with national laws and rules.
- To dramatically improve efficiency in resource management, achieving:
- Time optimization.
- Cost reductions.
- Error reduction
- Increased response capacity.
- Increased positive perception on the side of the community.

BUSINESS CONTEXT

As many other Latin-American countries, Mexico lacks transparency in the actions and services that the Government provides its citizens with. The national annual survey on citizen's perceptions and attitudes, prepared by the Department of Internal Affairs confirms that 94% of Mexicans believe that citizens ought to participate to combat such lack of transparency, and 75% considers that existing lack of governmental transparency is a shared responsibility1. The Survey of the Program Federal Open and Participatory Government 2001 shows that Public Works and Construction is the activity lacking the most transparency in Mexico.

Activity	Rate*
Public Works/ Construction.	1.3
Weapons and Defense.	1.9
Oil and Gas.	2.7
Real Estate/ Properties.	3.5
Telecommunications.	3.7
Power Generation and Transmission.	3.7
Mining/ Transport.	4.0
Storage.	4.3
Pharmaceuticals.	4.3
Heavy Industry.	4.5
Banking and Finance.	4.9
Forestry.	5.1

Scale from 0-10, where 0 indicates very high corruption levels and 10 no corruption.

Managing federal resources allocated to public works is considered to be a critical process, in which diversion can take place. These irregular –and likely to happen– conducts for recording work assessments and payments for non-performed works, have triggered the Government's general decision to tackle matters related to transparency. These issues have a clear reason, though not always all outcomes have been measured. Consequently, the Mexican Government issued two Acts identified as the key factors that prompted the CONAGUA to implement a solution such the above-mentioned one.

- Act of Public Works and Related Services.
- Act of Transparency and Access to Governmental Public information.

The latter is considered to be a significant step forward in the government-transparency process, as it allows users to request any entity within the federal public administration the information that concerns them. Among the specific purposes of this act, we can mention that:

- Anybody can have access to information by means of simple procedures.
- Citizens can have a better understanding of public management performance.
- To ease user search, this Act defines the minimum information that government agencies must include in their web sites. With both acts effective,

---

[1] Survey on Corruption and Citizens' Attitudes. Department of Internal Affairs. Mexico 2004.

and a new way to manage public administration, early in 2004 the CONAGUA began to look for a technology tool that would be instrumental to such strategy. The CONAGUA identified the need to automate the process of "Management and Development of Hydro-agricultural Infrastructure" as to Public Work Procurement and Execution follow-up.

Hydro-agricultural Infrastructure

"In our country the region of the humid tropic encompasses the Gulf of Mexico and Southeast strip. Its population represents 23% of the overall national population and is mostly made up of mestizos, even though it concentrates 60% of the indigenous population in the country. Rainfalls and floods are typical of this region and account for one of the most significant restrictions for its agricultural and livestock development, even threatening the life of its inhabitants", says Mr. Garcés while introducing us to the problem.

"This region covers 23 per cent of the national territory, that is to say 46 million hectares, of which 7.5 million have a high farming potential. The region concentrates 70 per cent of land with medium and high farming potential in the country, and for centuries its development has been limited by numerous problems related to its topography with low slopes, high rainfall levels, and average temperatures of 24° Centigrade –that can reach 40° C during certain periods in the year-, humidity excess, and complex and frail ecological systems seriously damaged", adds Mr. Juan Carlos Garcés.

At a national level, the Technified Storm Hydro-agricultural infrastructure is made up of: road network: 5,117 km; drainage network: 3,192 km; levees: 536 km; and Water-control and vehicle and foot-crossing structures: 7,069 structures. For management purposes, the CONAGUA divided the country in 13 hydro-agricultural administrative regions. This coverage makes it essential to attain the goal of information centralization, not only regarding contents, but also the format in which such information is delivered.

Historical Background

"Government intervention in these areas has been constant, with successes and failures, but the demands for support from the population settled there has been growing. During the 70s the first governmental interventions took place around integrated development projects, whose main component was the construction of hydro-agricultural infrastructure. As of 1991 the Department of TSDs was created with the purpose of prompting water control and check by means of the operation of the hydro-agricultural infrastructure built, allowing production increase and diversification, a sensible use of resources, and the improvement of living conditions for producers and their families. In 1996 the policy of transferring the infrastructure built by the federal government to organized users, was set in motion. The same applied to machinery and equipment for preservation purposes so that users with their own resources would take over conservation and administration of such infrastructure", explains Mr. Garcés.

THE KEY INNOVATIONS

Business

"The fulfillment of the central goal of standardizing and controlling administrative and budgetary resource-management processes by means of an on-line system, available for public consultation, has been an innovative move for the CONAGUA", says Mr. Sergio Soto Priante, General Assistant Director of Hydro-agricultural Infrastructure of CONAGUA. "The implementation of PECTRA BPM

Suite implied a dramatic transformation of methods for detailed follow up on final use of budgetary resources of the federal government", mentions Mr. Soto Priante, confirming the results achieved.

Garcés del Ángel also adds: "we systematized the direct capture of each stage of the juridical and administrative norms on public works and machinery acquisition. This has resulted in standardization of activities and a reduction in tasks that created no value, which, together with the control of processes, has modernized governmental management in a field that traditionally lagged behind but today assures efficiency and effectiveness within a framework of transparency. Thus, society's confidence in the system gets strengthened. The above-mentioned resulted in a direct and positive impact on the Mission of the General Subdirectorate of Hydro-agricultural Infrastructure: 'To manage and develop hydro-agricultural infrastructure jointly with the community to attain sustainable use of water".

Today, the system displays a high level of innovation promoting that all staff know key processes, in turn motivating and encouraging an efficient operation and, as it is available in the Internet, fostering users active participation", points out Juan Carlos Garcés.

"With PECTRA BPM Suite, operations go beyond the boundaries of our Headquarters, linking branches of Regional and State Departments as well as the operating staff in 22 TSDs, located in 9 states in the country, with a 2.7 million-hectare and a 115,000-user coverage. All connected in a simple manner, through the Internet. With this system, investment resources from the federal government for a total amount of US$ 35 million have been managed jointly with user organizations from 2003 to 2007", mentions Mr. Gaytán.

"We have undergone an important transformation as to management methods and task organization, for the application of the solution has allowed overcoming geographical dispersion, format diversity, and report-delivery times", Mr. Gaytán points out.

Likewise, the following are the main achievements:
- A thorough knowledge of all activities performed in each TSDs.
- The national standardization of activities, eliminating those that do not create value.
- A detailed follow up on resources allocated to public works in a technological platform
- Work means availability, online and through the Internet, open to public consultation.

"As a complement, all the benefits obtained have further importance as they impact and affect the six items of Good Government set by the 2000-2006 Administration, in a National Development Plan launched during 2007 with the current Administration, designed so that, from the very beginning, the Federal Government can follow the route towards a good government, capable of replacing old bureaucratic structures for innovative systems that allow to strengthen institutions that are agile, efficient, honest, and transparent, in accordance with the demands of the society, with clear and permanent accountability", says Mr. Garcés.

The Mexican government is carrying out a profound transformation in the area of Public Administration, not only in the manner in which the institutions work, but also in the attitude of those working for them. The process approach, transparency in resource management, and the opening to public consultation of all the information, are key factors that define tasks under the new system, essentially cooperating with these new rules.

The new vision of the Government is expressed in the year 2000's Presidential Agenda for a Good Government through its six action lines[2]:

- An honest and transparent Government: that promotes civil servants' probity, the firm and upfront fight against corruption, as well as transparency in public management, in order to regain society's trust in their government.

- A professional Government: to attract and retain the most skilled men and women in public service, sustained in human resources development schemes completely separated form political positions, in order to make sure that public administration moves forward in management changes, in the least traumatic and most efficient possible manner.

- A quality Government: that day after day improves products and services supplied to society, satisfying and even excelling citizens' expectations.

- A digital Government: that, by means of the optimal use of new information and communication technologies, makes citizens' access to government services more agile, providing better timing, quality, and efficiency, thus contributing to fight corruption and fostering transparency in public function.

- A Government with regulatory improvement: that removes burdensome paperwork, keeps costs related to citizens' compliance with laws, norms and administrative requirements to the minimum, guaranteeing swiftness and certainty, as a factor to promote general competitiveness.

- A less costly Government: that multiplies the quantity and quality of services rendered to the community, by means or restructuring public expenditure, reducing expenses that do not add value, while increasing resource allocation to areas that offer the community better and more benefits.

The implementation of Process Management directly contributed to each of these action lines. The system -applied at a national level with direct effects, both internally (staff involved in the processes) and externally- is currently being analyzed to be replicated in every entity within the scope of the Department of Internal Affairs performing public works.

PROCESS

A process now in the past:

"From 2001 on, the Government of Mexico implemented the Quality and Innovation Program in order to make public expenditure more efficient and effective and to promote citizens' participation in the supervision of public resources. Said program asked for the setting up of a management system to make possible the development of technical processes so as to increase efficiency and productivity, to ease awareness of citizens' needs, and to ensure administration transparency", states Gaytán Arvizu.

Before the implementation of PECTRA BPM Suite, the process of "Management and Development of Hydro-agricultural Infrastructure" was carried out by means of written documents. That meant management delays and less control, with the

---

[2] Governmental Innovation and Quality. Presidency of the Republic. Government of Mexico. Mexico 2000.

added difficulty that the information provided to citizens was limited and not always reliable.

The manual follow-up of process activities was long and tedious, and it brought about indirect costs such as information collection, validation, transmission, and sending. "The process was carried out by means of paper-written documents, as well as the reports on the progress of activities", explains Gaytán Arvizu. "Information was processed in a craft-made way since everyone sent it in any way, with any format, through any means available: telephone, fax, courier, e-mail or whichever. Gathering and decoding that information was a too expensive task in terms of time, resources and money", he adds.

"The concept of process was not considered for technical-administrative activities. Everything was understood as watertight compartments, with a strong vertical structure, which made operation difficult as each district fulfilled its functions in a different way", Garcés adds. "Coordinating and managing the different activities carried out represented a great challenge", he remembers.

In turn, Gaytán expresses that "the use of non-standardized formats and methodologies and, above all, the lack of knowledge about relevant aspects of processes and procedures did not allow making an efficient public work execution follow-up. Neither was it considered the means to keep the Districts' users informed, nor the citizens in general.

On the other hand, the importance of the staff's functions was left aside due to the magnitude of tasks related to documents and reports, thus significantly discouraging human resources specialized in technical tasks. Spending half of the working day with a secondary activity such as producing reports summarizes the problem faced by CONAGUA. The agricultural producers' dissatisfaction with the institution's staff, which carried out more and more office and less fieldwork, was constant. The existence of said problems was due to:

- Reports based on estimated data, thus being difficult to articulate due to their partiality and diversity.
- Incongruity in the physical and financial progress of works, without reports on the destination of resources.
- Inaccurate information transmission, which increased the administration costs.

Also, the agricultural producers had a general lack of information regarding the annual investment amount in each District, the programmed and developed activities, the moment when works were started, the service-provider companies that were awarded the biddings and the progress and conclusion of activities, among others.

Thus, the General Sub-directorate of Hydro-agricultural Infrastructure of the Water National Commission decided to implement the System of Hydro-agricultural Infrastructure Processes Management, with PECTRA BPM Suite", Gaytán Arvizu declares.

First stage: Selection & Design

"In a first stage, the Department of TSDs was selected for the system operation, in a strategy framework that allows to move from what is simple to what is complex, in a down to up dynamics, starting from local needs. It was about the design of a system that could profit from the initiative capacity of institutional representatives and local population, and that could be used in other fields of the General Sub-directorate of Water National Commission and the Federal Public Administration", Gaytán Arvizu further states.

The system's performance scale is that of the minimum administrative unit to which budgetary resources are allocated, that is to say, the Management (its equivalent is the General Directorate of State Departments). The processes are practically based on the budgetary program structure set up by the Treasury Department and Public Credit and they are a regulatory improvement proposal expressed in public policy processes derived from the main laws and norms that regulate them.

During the gathering stage, guides, general criteria, and observation and control mechanisms were established to generate in the institution's staff a culture of transparency and accountability as well as a favorable perception among the contractors and external participants of the processes.

Second stage: Integration

The integration of PECTRA BPM Suite with the existing IT systems in the CONAGUA provided inter-connectivity to the entity, favoring the flow of processes and with that, the quality of products and services.

First, PECTRA BPM Suite was integrated into the system's back-office used by the Mexican Government for governmental procurements named: Compranet. Compranet allows the government's purchasing units to make known, by means of the Internet, their requirements of goods, services, leases, and public works. In this way, suppliers and contractors have access to that information and can submit, through the same means, their bids and follow up the whole process until the good or service is provided. In Compranet the bidding processes of more than 6,500 purchasing and public work units are concentrated, both from APF (Federal Public Administration), and state and municipal governments, with more than 45 thousand companies consulting data, obtaining bidding conditions and generating bank payment formats. Compranet's web page registers an average of 22,500 searches a day. Every year, more than 27,000 biddings are published in the system; about 45% of them are made by electronic means and represent 60% of the amount awarded by that means.

Besides, some applications of suite Microsoft Office such as Word, Excel, Outlook, among others, were integrated. Behavior and responsibility frameworks were established and performance indicators were incorporated for the management's monitoring of organization processes in order to detect bottlenecks and justify decision-makings.

The integration with the Commission's web portal has allowed the creation of a strong database, with budgetary figures form previous fiscal years, and the internal and external users' possibility of retrieving information. The graphics provided by PECTRA BAM tools (Business Activity Monitoring) allow the community to get to know the moves of substantive information flow.

Third Stage: Implementation

The process that the Department of TSDs carries out with public resources is called: Management and Development of Hydro-agricultural Infrastructure, in complete consistency with the Mission of the General Sub-directorate of Hydro-agricultural Infrastructure: "To manage and develop hydro-agricultural infrastructure with the participation of the community in order to achieve water sustainable use".

Before the implementation of PECTRA BPM Suite, it was impossible to see and value the investments made by the TSDs. Today, the information presented through the Transparency Portal for public and open consultation is organized according to three sub-processes: Programming and Budgeting; Bidding and Procurement; and Executing and Supervising.

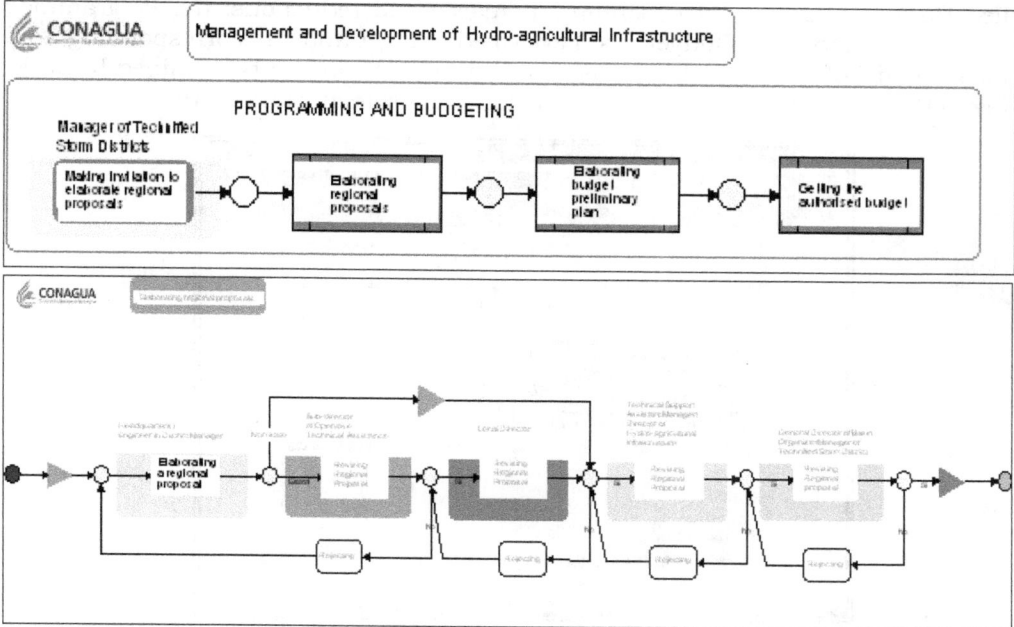

Access: Transparency Web Portal

The Transparency Web Portal is the access point – via Internet – in which users can make consultations by selecting the fiscal period or year they refer to.

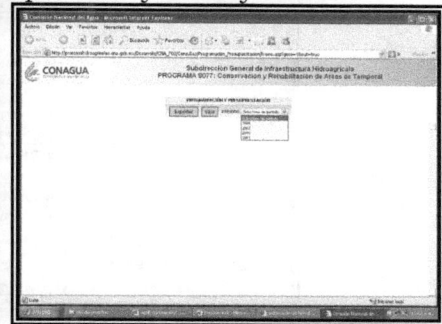

The information is classified according to the Administrative Hydro-agricultural Region it belongs to. At this level, sub-programs are differentiated: infrastructure restoration; water handling and soil preservation; technical consultancy and training; machinery and equipment acquisition; and work supervision according to contract.

Programming and Budgeting

The information of these sub-programs refers to the budget allocated to investment. In addition, there is a sub-program called "indirects" and is assigned for current expenses. Investment programs come up from local needs, ending in the issue of the Investment Release Letter. Through the portal, it is possible to have access to information about budgets: Regional Proposal (or project portfolio); Budget Preliminary Plan; and Authorized Budget. Moreover, it includes the Modified Budget, with the corresponding increases and reductions; the Programmed Budget, the Procured Budget, the Performed Budget and the corresponding Savings. Details of the regional proposal or project portfolio can be obtained by clicking in the underlined sub-program. The following screen will then be seen:

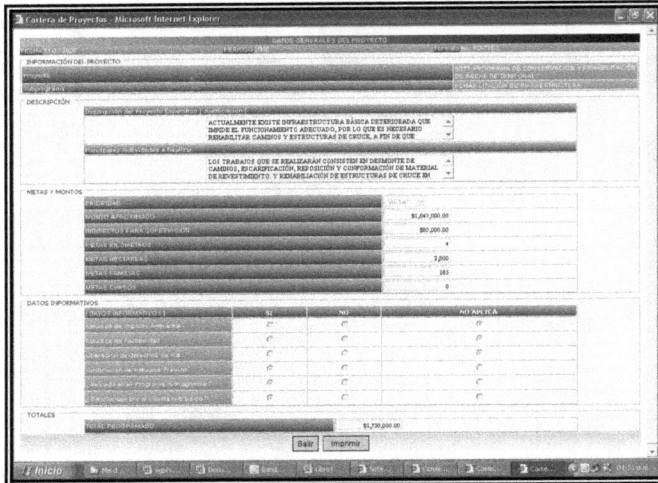

Bidding and Procurement

Again, click to have access to the second sub-process, and the following screen will appear:

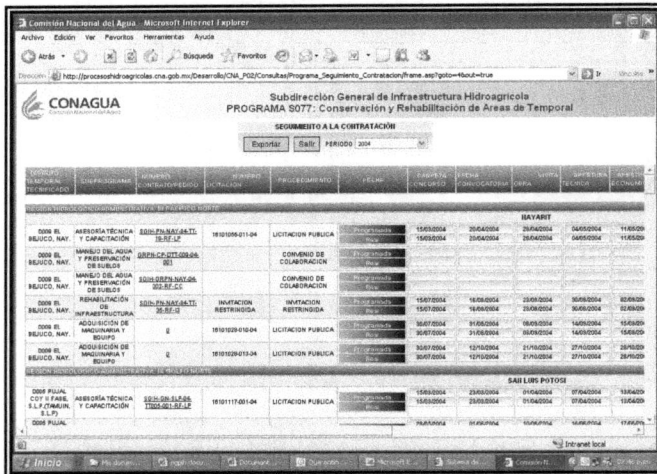

This sub-process starts with the amounts authorized in the OLI and starts the bidding program, which is carried out in a parallel and complementary way to the process developed through Compranet Web Page, (http://compranet.gob.mx) for all the public administration entities. This sub-process finishes with the contract signed between CONAGUA and a contractor company to carry out the tasks requested by the institution. Every contract has a technical-economic proposal for the tasks and is monthly scheduled.

In this sub-process, the system makes the information transparent according to the contract or order number, and the bidding number. On these grounds, the bidding procedure is stated and the bidding scheduled and real dates are established. In the bidding, the dates are associated to: the elaboration of the bidding file, notification, work visit, technical opening, economic opening, decision, contract signing, contract starting, contract ending. All this information is generated during the above described sub-process, but the transparency portal also includes the programming, the work handing over and reception dates, as well as settlement, rights termination and hidden defect bail release dates.

Executing and supervising

The process starts when the economic proposal is uploaded in the system and the institution representative supervises the carrying out of the works, and finishes with the acts of handing over, settlement, and termination of rights and duties, associated to each contract.

Just like the other sub-processes, this one can be visualized in the following way:

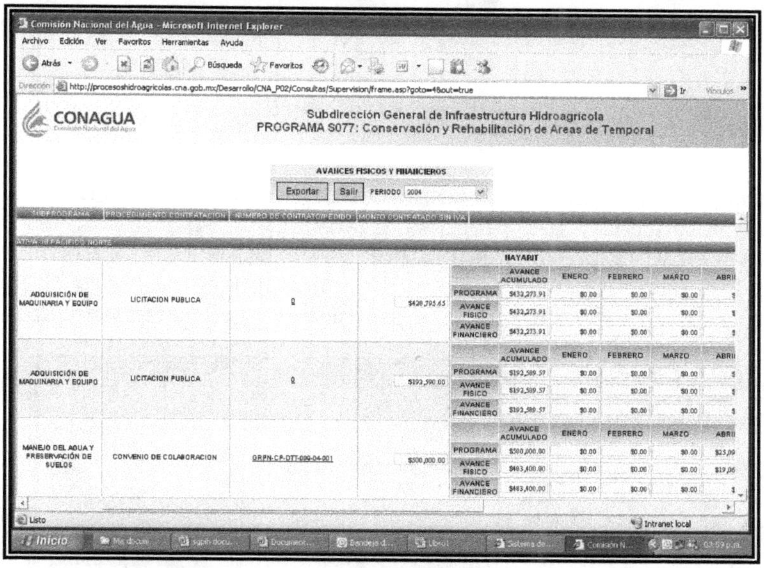

For each contract, the screen shows the bidding method, the order or contract number, a summary of the budgetary resources measured in Mexican pesos, monthly scheduled and based on the technical-economic proposal of the procured company, and the corresponding space to show the physical and financial progresses. For details of the contract, click the underlined contract number and the following screen will appear:

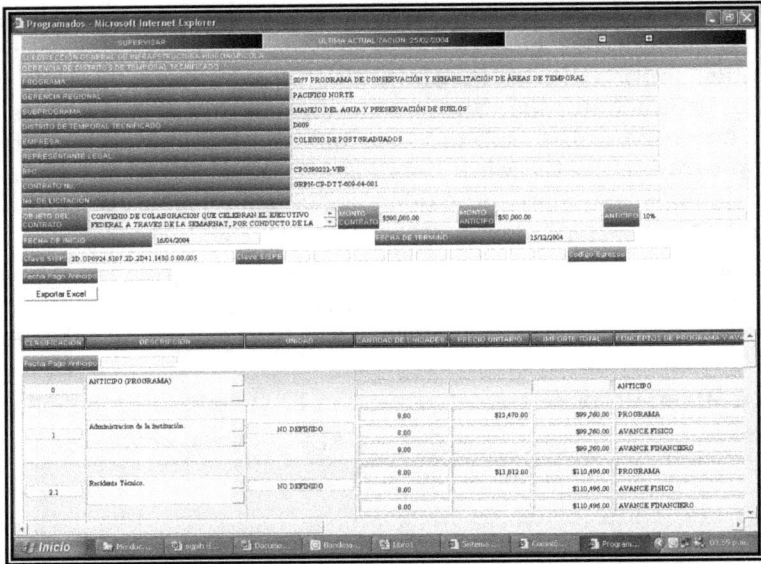

It is also possible to have access to data about the contract, the contracting parties' names, the purpose, the progress if any, the budgetary codes and the monthly scheduled work program submitted by the contractor, with the details of every cost. In this case the system allows the possibility of capturing the information on physical and financial progress as they are generated and immediately

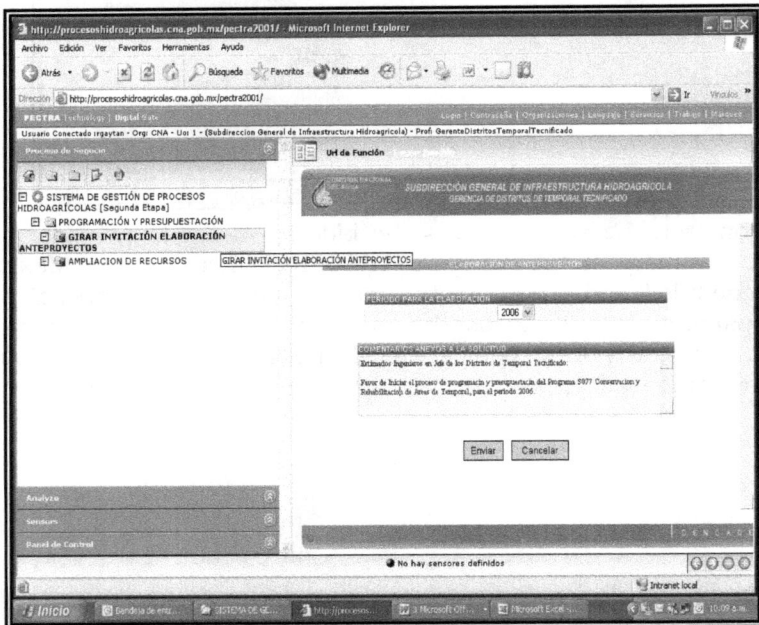

made transparent in the transparency portal.

Here iis the screen to start capturing information. The process name and stages it is going through are on the left. In the same left column, downwards, there is an information multi-factor analyzer, a system control panel and there are also monitoring censors. The first capture screen is on the right. It is about the invitation made by the National Manager of TSDs to elaborate the project portfolio or regional proposal. Once the invitation has been made, by clicking the send button, the instruction is distributed to the 21 District chief engineers, to the Regional and State Managers, to the Regional and State Assistant Managers of 5 Regional Departments involved in the operation of the country's TSDs. In the system's language, this activity is called "releasing the instance". Every process is organized in a group of activities that give rise to a product. With the automation, the activities communicate among them through the instance that is a kind of baton. In this way, the user, according to his/her profile, carries out the activity, captures data and then "releases the instance" or passes the baton for the second activity.

For example, this screen corresponds to the District Authority's profile. The profile, on the left column, has the detail of the process' different stages in which he/she takes part. Notice the fact that his/ her activities within the process are different from the ones seen before and that belong to the profile of the Manager of TSDs. In this case, the District Authority has already passed the stage of elaborating the portfolio and continues with the stage of elaborating tender packages and programs.

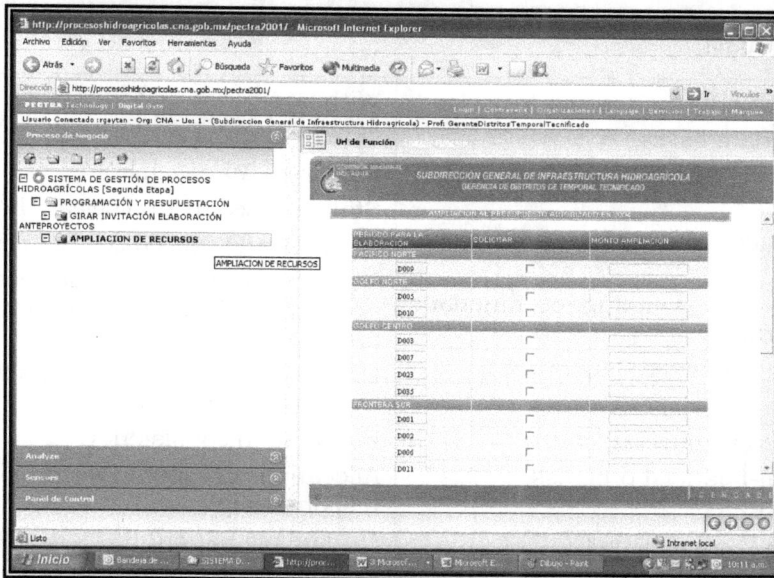

The system also has a screen for the users who have profile and capture license to be able to express their comments and suggestions regarding the system's efficiency. Those opinions are the base to carry out improvement actions.

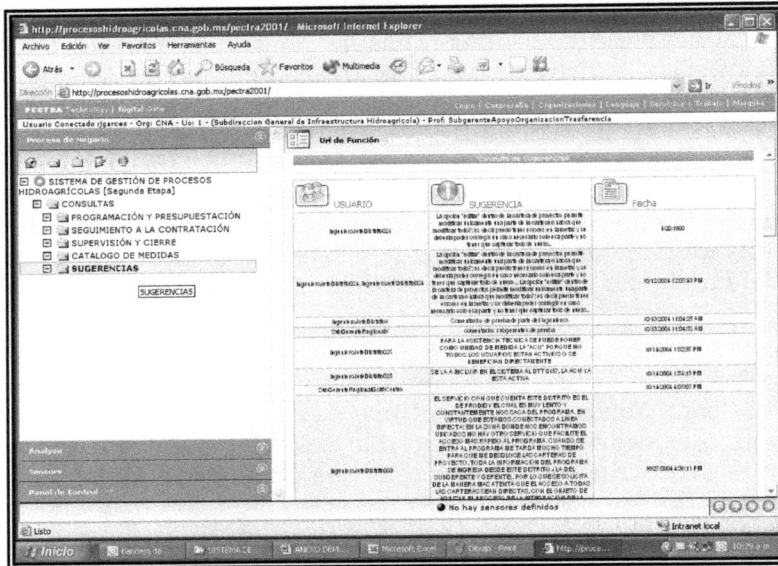

BEFORE AND AFTER

Without BPM	With BPM
Different data bases.	Overall data base.
No determination of client/supplier activities.	Processes Management.
	Standardised technological platform.
Heterogeneity of formats and procedures.	Formats and procedures' standards.
Diversity and doubling of functions and reports.	Unique and equal activities with criteria and guidelines standardised at national level.
Generally estimated data and figures.	On-line and real time information transmission and capture.
Delays and incongruity in the physical-financial progress information.	Information consistency.
	Allocation of operation profiles and responsibility.
	On-line regulation.
Lack of process global view	Remote accessibility via Internet under a transparency pattern.
Lack of standardised guidelines and criteria about information handling.	On-line interaction of all the process participation stages.

After the implementation of PECTRA BPM Suite, CONAGUA dramatically changed the way of working by offering users access to the system in a remote way via the Internet to upload data from any place, being the sending of documents and data carried out exactly as stipulated in the main process. Since the pattern, which prioritizes transparency, is on-line and available for public consultation, it contributed to the modernization of public entity's performance, eliminating the above-mentioned factors that hindered an efficient management.

Today, the system makes it possible the monitoring of all the stages in each work, from its bidding to the handing over, under a systematic and permanent record. Said record contributes to the unification and formalization of criteria for the control and monitoring of public work process under the terms of the Law, and thus becoming an innovative practice completely based on processes management.

ORGANIZATION

"The TSDs staff in the whole country has achieved an important skill development through specialized training not only in administrative procedures and processes but also in equipment handling", emphasizes Garcés.

The process redesign and implementation had the active participation of all the staff related to TSDs, from the directors to the operating staff, to attend to the following stages:

- Process preliminary redesign: 5 regional teams.
- IT and Telecommunications: 1 multi-regional team.
- Redesign analysis, validation and implementation: 1 multi-regional and multi-disciplinary team.
- System Operation: 1 team per Regional Department and 1 team per State Department.

The involved areas that work nowadays include:

- At Central and Regulatory Level:
- 1 National Manager of the TSDs
- 3 Assistant Managers.
- 3 Project Managers.
- 1 System Coordinator.
- At Regional Level:
- 5 Departments: South Border, Yucatán Peninsula, North Pacific, North Gulf and Center Gulf.
- 5 Under departments.
- 5 Coordinations of Irrigation and Storm.

At State Level:

- 5 Departments: Nayarit, Tabasco, Campeche, San Luís Potosí, Quintana Roo.
- 5 Under departments.

At District level:

- 22 Technified storm district headquarters that interact with 33 non-profit associations which include more than 115,000 beneficiary users.

HURDLES OVERCOME

In general terms there were no important hurdles when implementing PECTRA BPM Suite, "mainly due to the great job carried out by PECTRA Technology's consultancy area as regards Change Management, key aspect, in my view, for the incorporation of such technologies into an organization", sums up Garcés.

"It was a necessary work since people were used to defining all the activities in very long stages, so that fact obliged us to summarize the tasks and activities each one carried out. This was the most tortuous part of the implementation", Gaytán says.

"The practice was designed from a processes perspective, thus in a first stage a multi-disciplinary and inter-functional group was created, including suppliers and internal clients of the public work process, in order to update and change the technified storm districts' administrative methods and operation", he confirms.

However, the cultural transformation to carry out a shared view among the headquarters and the offices located in rural areas has made it necessary to establish ways of rewarding staff taking part. National and regional systematic meetings are held twice a year to share experiences with the aim to keep contact at a personal and not just virtual level, creating in this way an intellectual synergy.

Besides, training diplomas and certifications are given to all the participants as well as recognition in different fields: participation, consistency and improvement contributions.

BENEFITS

The implementation of PECTRA BPM Suite provided important benefits to CONAGUA. Said benefits are related not only to the observance of laws and rules (due to its Governance character) but also to aspects concerning the efficient resource administration and the improvement of the community's perception of the organism's image.

On-line and real time information is available at site http://sgh.cna.gob.mx/PECTRA2001 and it offers a complete panorama about aspects of public work programming, budgeting, procurement, follow-up and investment closing, thus giving complete transparency to investment management and use.

In this way, it is possible to have access from any place to the information about: investments; contract awards; suppliers; goals; follow-up of public work's physical-financial progress in all the districts, contract closing and management indicators.

With this implementation CONAGUA has succeeded in:
- Standardizing processes and local, regional, and state technology.
- Maximizing the performance of the existing technological systems.
- Defining, designing, and monitoring processes with a digital system and recording them on- line.
- Measuring, analyzing and creating processes' statistics.
- Improving processes' efficiency and having an Integral Information System.
- Having management indicators for decision-making.
- Reducing time and cost of information processing, capture and analysis.
- Reducing duplicities and improvisations in the execution of activities.
- Having clear process guidelines, shared at all levels.

As a result, CONAGUA has achieved the following proposed goals:
- Centralizing the information from entities and organisms, making easier the administrative procedures and reducing the associated costs.
- Adhering to the agreement for control, accountability and verification of the transparent management of federal public resources.
- Strengthening the transparency of governmental procurement by implementing a mechanism of community's participation, by means of which the processes of governmental performance are assessed, making known the way in which all and each of the procurement stages took place.
- Promoting, through the study, analysis and debate about the corruption phenomenon, the observance of some recommendations derived from commitments undertaken by Mexico at international level and directly related to fighting corruption.

- Strengthening the development of a service, honesty, ethics, accountability, precaution and corruption-fighting culture.
- Improving public function by promoting the exercise of the right to information and citizens' participation.
- Encouraging co-responsibility.
- Promoting citizens' participation to improve the governmental policies and programs, by generating the interchange of successful experiences among states, municipalities and Federation

CONAGUA has also obtained successful results concerning operative efficiency:

- Time Optimization: The hours spent by the district authorities to elaborate reports were reduced from 50% to 5%, and that time was better spent improving the supervision of works and increasing the time for intellectual work related to technical consultancy, assessment, analysis and prospecting work.

The integration with existing information systems made it possible to accelerate 40% the involved processes.

Cost reduction:

- Of labor-hours spent in the report-making activity.
- Of data transmission.
- Of postal messenger and fax.
- Of supplies used for the elaboration of reports (paper, equipment, etc).
- Opportunity costs, due to non-performing substantive activities.

Activities	Benefits
Report-making time.	Time reduction from 50 to 5%.
Reports prepared.	150% reduction
Telephone calls	60% reduction
Courier.	Total reduction.

Return on Investment (ROI)

The **payback period** of the total investment was 18 months (in US$).

Total investment in 4 years:	137,319
Annual total investment	34,329
SAVINGS	
Stationery:	12,484
Telephone and fax:	18,171
Courier:	9,158
Man-hours to generate reports:	25,640
Opportunity cost:	6,023
Materials and supplies:	12,821
Annual total reduction:	84,297
Total reduction in 4 years:	337,188
Annual saving:	49,968
Saving in 4 years:	199,872

Additionally, there were year savings of USD 12,821 in materials and supplies and USD 9,158 in current expenses.

Users and operating staff's positive perception:

Opinion polls from the FPA indicate an increase from 50% to 76% of users' satisfaction.

Simplification of processes

CONAGUA has shown a significant 67% reduction in administrative activities by eliminating those that create no value such as report multiplicity, filling forms and sending them by courier or fax.

Management control and transparency

CONAGUA has acquired more control on public work delivery, reception, and execution follow-up, making the processes more transparent by presenting complete information about each work's execution stages. Said transparency caused an increase in the citizens' trust in the government's actions.

Continuous improvement

Through PECTRA BPM Suite, CONAGUA produces complete documents in an automatic way, with the support of operation, guideline and procedure manuals for its use, including the Total Quality Management System, certified under ISO 9001. Additionally, it has been achieved the integral standardization of all the elements that the Treasury Department and Public Credit establishes for the execution follow-up of the federal government's public work and to keep them on-line for public consultation. The results obtained after the implementation show a significant reduction of non-conformities in the bidding procedures.

Modernization and efficiency

The implementation of PECTRA BPM Suite gives the organism the possibility of data and images transmission by means of modern technological platforms, allowing the creation of a link with a data base for the updating of users' register from Districts of more than 110,00 thousand producers. The information generated in the system is the same used for institutional decision-makings and it can be consulted and checked simultaneously by the community and users.

In this way, CONAGUA has changed the task management and organization methods, using a practice that has made it possible to overcome the geographical dispersion barrier, the format diversity and the difficulty of means and time to send the reports. Above all, CONAGUA has succeeded in:

- Optimizing the interactive communication management among local and central offices.
- Improving the interconnection with information systems established by CONAGUA.
- Complying with the rules of both Acts.
- Defining performance indicators.
- Making commitments and links transparent.
- Identifying and linking work instruments.
- Identifying and taking advantage of best practices.

With this practice, the ordinary citizen benefits in two ways:

- The reduction of the contracts' follow-up costs has an impact at the end of the production chain, in that the resulting public work is carried out in a proper and functional way. In this way, the application of public resources is more efficient.

- The reduction of waiting-time for the delivery of restored infrastructure, since it is carried out in a faster way and with better quality.

Productivity

Expected budget functioning and benefits.

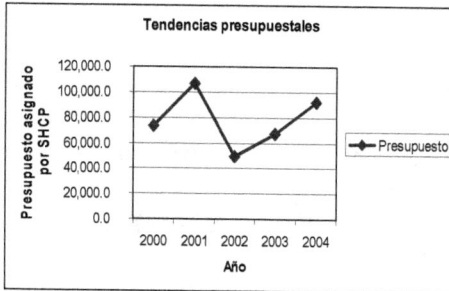

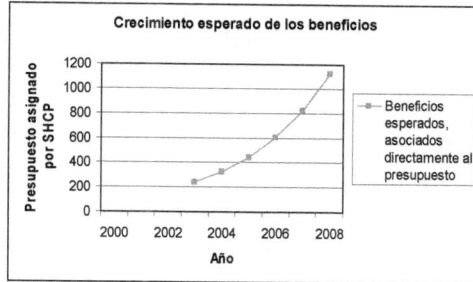

Left table: Budgetary trends/ Budget allocated per SHCP/ Budget/ Year
Right table: Expected benefit growth/ Budget allocated per SHCP/ Expected benefits, directly associated to budget/ Year

Innovation

The innovation development implied by the Hydro-agricultural Management System – CONAGUA identified the technological tool based on PECTRA BPM Suite with this name –, whose core goal is the management and transparency of public work processes, includes the adoption of modern IT and processes management technologies. The practice has achieved the establishment of a system that goes beyond an administrative improvement with short-term aims. It is a change in the way of working, which updates the investment resources management methods to make them transparent for the citizens, granting efficiency and effectiveness to keep performance indicators on-line and in real time. It is a technological development that returns priority to substantive functions in hydro-agricultural subjects, meeting the users' needs and, in general, the needs of the beneficiaries' communities, in every place where it is applied. The technological development starts from the experience and knowledge of the operators of substantive processes from the General Sub-directorate of Hydro-agricultural Infrastructure of CONAGUA, who make possible the fulfillment of the Institutional Mission, around which it makes sense. In this subject, innovating by means of technological development has multiplying effects, offers all the benefits derived from knowledge and experiences -an accumulated intellectual capital that, added to the technological tools applied, produce dramatic improvement and boost. Due to the mentioned facts, in benchmarking terms, the practice stands at a higher level than that of emerging economies. The system with platform – feasible to be replicated in any entity of the FPA – gives options to the federal government for the use of information technology, telecommunications, the overall view provided by the processes approach which, in case of being adopted, creates economies of scale and a greater integration and link between the services provided by the development programs of the TSDs.

Benefit for the community

The system as innovative practice has an approach mainly oriented to the users (internal and external to the Commission) that also includes the possibility of public consultation for a transparent management. The Districts administration and development give as a result the control of water surplus and the exploitation of agricultural lands of the Humid and Sub-humid Tropical areas. The set up infrastructure is not limited to the production activity. Its impacts and effects are systemic; for example, the roads get better with the soil dug up from draining channels and they are used for carrying the agricultural production and any other type of goods, thus increasing the commercial activity in the area near the District, as well as the improvement of the access to schools, health centers and sport facilities.

BEST PRACTICES & COMPETITIVE ADVANTAGES

On April 29th, 2004, the United Nations Convention against Corruption was ratified. Said Convention had been signed on December 9th, 2003 and according to it, the Mexican Government undertook a leadership role by presiding over the writing committee and acting as venue for its signature.

The Mexican Government has the policy of identifying the best practices that promote transparency, control and prevention of corruption.

For that reason, and through the Department of Internal Affairs and the National Institute of Public Administration, the Mexican Government has created a competition, the Annual Transparency Award, in order to acknowledge those entities that present exemplary practices and systems in that subject.

As a result of the implementation of PECTRA BPM Suite, CONAGUA was awarded an Honorable Mention in the Annual Transparency Award 2005 by presenting a system that made the use of public resources 100% transparent in the various works of the Mexican Republic Hydro-agricultural Infrastructure.

The entity was awarded the important mention due to the practice named: 'Hydro-agricultural Management System: Transparency in the use of Public Resources for the Development of the Technified Storm Districts.

Besides, in the year 2005, the System also obtained the Innova Acknowledgement, awarded by the National Presidency, since it was instituted as a process improvement exemplary tool, with management transparency and administration savings and feasible to be used in other stages, both from the government and the private sector.

The General Assistant Manager of Hydro-agricultural Infrastructure, Sergio Soto Priante, highlighted: "the implementation of the Hydro-agricultural Management System with PECTRA BPM Suite gives full assurance to users from TSDs and to the population in general, that the resources for public works are executed with transparency in the various projects under way.

Furthermore, he added, "the implementation of PECTRA BPM Suite has attracted other State and Federal Governmental departments and institutions to create an exchange of experiences, in order to get to know in greater details the results of its functioning in the CONAGUA for a future application of the solution."

PECTRA Technology's IT Department along with its Marketing Department has accomplished this important document. Federico Ignacio Silva, PECTRA Technology's Marketing Manager, has planned the data searching and writing.

Different techniques were used to collect the information. Interviews to the people in charge of the solution's design and implementation were carried out (in an average of two hours each); and also a performance evaluation was carried out in the entire company to respond appropriately to the requirements demanded by the Global Excellence in Workflow Awards for innovation and excellence in workflow implementations.

Geisinger Health System, USA

Gold Award, North America.
Nominated by TIBCO, USA

EXECUTIVE SUMMARY / ABSTRACT

In a move to improve document management and bring greater efficiency to clinical, business and financial processes across its organization, Geisinger Health System undertook a cross-enterprise BPM initiative that has resulted in significant productivity improvements, cost savings and improved customer service. Benefits have included automated document retrieval, faster response on billing and claims inquiries and greatly reduced turn around time on accounts payable processes with resulting cost savings of $1.5 million+ annually.

OVERVIEW

Geisinger Health System is a physician-led health care system in central and northeastern Pennsylvania dedicated to health care, education, research and service spanning 41 counties, 20,000 square miles and serving 2.5 million people. Given the increasing volume and critical nature of the healthcare documents associated with serving a population of more than two million, information managers at Geisinger Health System knew they needed to upgrade their document storage and retrieval system. The goal was to build an enterprise-level system that would enable Geisinger to keep pace with the inflow of documents and make them available within 48 hours of receipt to physicians and other staff at any of the company's approximately 40 outpatient clinics. In addition, Geisinger saw an opportunity to improve workflow in the health insurance component of its HMO customer service unit, as well as the turnaround time in its accounts payable department.

To meet the goals outlined above and bring greater efficiency to clinical, business and financial processes across its organization, Geisinger implemented a Business Process Management (BPM) solution, TIBCO iProcess Suite. This system is enabling Geisinger to execute processes quickly, accurately, and in a manner that can be easily audited and tracked, resulting in performance improvements in three key areas:

1. Clinical document management. Ensuring that health records and relevant clinical documents are up-to-date and readily available to patients and their physicians is critical to both patient safety and to complying with regulatory requirements like HIPAA. BPM is enabling Geisinger to automate and streamline the processing of patient information, greatly reducing administrative time involved and improving real-time access to this information across the organization.

2. Customer service/support for Geisinger Health Plan members. Geisinger's managed care insurance operation wanted to improve turn around time on resolving member contacts (grievances and appeals) related to billing and claims issues. Geisinger leveraged BPM to simplify and automate a complex, multi-tiered process that spanned multiple lines of business, numerous stakeholders (including

external regulatory agencies such as Medicare and DOH), and a diverse customer base.

3. Accounts payable. TIBCO iProcess Suite was deployed to transform a 100 percent manual, paper-based invoice posting process into a 100 percent automated, virtually paper-free operation. The reduction in turn around time on invoice processing has not only slashed administrative hours, it has also helped Geisinger to take advantage of vendor discounts offered in exchange for prompt payment of invoices.

BUSINESS CONTEXT

Five key business imperatives drove the initiation of this project:

1. HIPAA Compliance – ensure process consistency, transparency and availability of records across systems, sites and departments.
2. Patient Safety – automate and streamline the processing of patient information so that the most up-to-date records are available to physicians and patients.
3. Improve Customer Satisfaction – improve turn around time on customer service and support provided to Geisinger's HMO plan members.
4. Reduce Costs – cut administrative costs resulting from manual, paper-based processes and reduce turn around time on accounts payable procedures to capitalize on vendor discounts for on-time/early payment.
5. Improve Efficiency – through streamlined, consistent, automated processes.

THE KEY INNOVATIONS

Business

By automating and innovating cross-enterprise processes, Geisinger has been able to address each business imperative outlined above:

- Greater process transparency and auditing capabilities make it easier for Geisinger to address compliance requirements such as HIPAA.
- Patient safety is enhanced by enabling fast access to critical medical records.
- Customer satisfaction has improved due to the fact that Geisinger is consistently resolving issues experienced by plan members more quickly and efficiently.
- Administrative and liability costs have been slashed due to better records management, faster customer service and reduced turn around times for accounts payable.
- Streamlined processes and a reduced need for manual intervention greatly improve productivity across the board.

Process

1. Clinical document management. By integrating TIBCO iProcess Suite with its electronic content management solution from Vignette, Geisinger was able to establish a foundation for an enterprise-wide document imaging management system (DIMS), and move from a 100 percent manual to 100 percent automated document management process. Incoming records, documents and other data like CT scans,

X-Rays and ultrasounds are captured and indexed by the Vignette software, while iProcess Suite ensures that all patient records are processed, managed and tracked in a consistent way. There is a direct link between the two systems at all times so that patient information can be pinpointed and retrieved instantly, no matter where it is as it flows through the many systems that need to "touch" it. This type of real time access to information is critical to patient safety – if a physician is unable to access a test result or an X-Ray because a physical copy is buried on filing clerk's desk, then patient care is at risk. Prior to implementing electronic content management in conjunction with BPM, Geisinger experienced a 15 million document backlog at the GHS clinics. Providers stated their concerns about not being able to find all relevant data needed to properly manage patient health care needs. Today, all medical documents are scanned and made available within 48 hours. Geisinger has estimated cost avoidance savings (due to reduced liability costs stemming from an improved ability to locate supporting documentation) of approximately $200,000 in year one and $1.2 million in year two and forward (5+ years).

2. Customer service/support for Geisinger Health Plan members. Geisinger has also been able to completely automate previously manual processes involving multiple stakeholders, lines of business, and urgency levels (there are three levels of appeal open to customers, Level 1, Level 2, and Level 3, each of which is associated with a unique, corresponding process.) Case appeals processing time has been reduced by 67 percent, from 24 hours to just eight. This has resulted in administrative savings as well as an increase in customer satisfaction due to the fact that Geisinger is consistently resolving issues experienced by plan members more quickly and efficiently.

3. Accounts payable. Prior to implementing TIBCO iProcess Suite, Geisinger's invoice posting process – which covered the multiple, manual steps involved in receiving and preparing an invoice for payment – required an average of 12-13 days per invoice. Personnel needed to open mail, sort the invoices by hand, and then manually enter the invoice into the appropriate financial system. Today, Geisinger has moved to a completely paperless process, where sorting, data entry, posting and all other related tasks are automated. When invoices arrive, they are now immediately scanned and automatically captured within iProcess Suite. Within several weeks of going live with the solution, Geisinger was able to reduce accounts payable processing time by 86 percent, slashing turn around time to less than two days. This has not only greatly reduced the administrative hours required to process invoices, but has also enabled Geisinger to achieve a perfect record of early payments to suppliers and fully exploit vendor discounts offered as a result. In the first year of operation, Geisinger saved $497,842.00 on early payment discounts from vendors. Geisinger is anticipating savings of approximately $600,000+ over the second year.

ORGANIZATION

In automating processes across specialties, departments, lines of business, systems and locations, Geisinger has empowered employees across the organization to become more efficient as they no longer need to spend as much time on manual data entry and other repetitive tasks.

HURDLES OVERCOME

Management and Business

Geisinger Health System serves 41 counties in northeastern Pennsylvania via 40 clinics and three major hospitals. As a result, patient information, technology systems and personnel are distributed across many physical locations. Yet another challenge Geisinger faces is the need to have optimal visibility and control of organizational processes to meet the requirements of health care industry regulations like HIPAA. However, rather than serving as a barrier, these challenges have been greatly minimized through the implementation of the TIBCO iProcess Suite. TIBCO's independent process layer not only enables Geisinger to better manage and control processes across people, systems and locations, it also provides the transparency and auditing capabilities critical to addressing compliance requirements.

Organization Adoption

The only significant challenge that Geisinger met with in implementing BPM was change management. Personnel accustomed to working in a primarily paper-based environment needed to be comfortable moving to automated processes. This issue was addressed through a comprehensive training effort. Once users learned how to access automated information – and understood that they could access data no matter where documents were the process cycle – their doubts about the "new way of doing things" were eliminated.

BENEFITS

Cost Savings

- Cost avoidance as a result of centralized document management estimated at $213K in year one and $1.2M in year two and forward (i.e. over 5+ years)
- Reduced liability costs due to an improved ability to locate supporting documentation (on average up to $113,000 may be potentially lost per liability case when supporting documentation is unavailable due to poor records management.)
- Estimated costs savings of approx. $400K per year due to early payment discounts from vendors (as a result of reduced accounts payable processing time.)

Time Reductions

- Prior to implementing electronic content management in conjunction with BPM, Geisinger experienced a 15 million document backlog at the GHS clinics. Today, all medical documents are scanned and made available within 48 hours.
- Customer service case appeals processing time has been reduced by 67 percent, from 24 hours to eight.
- Accounts payable processing time has been reduced by 86 percent, invoice turn around time has gone from an average of 12-13 days to less than two.

- Systems are collecting metrics now that can be reported real-time. Prior to implementations, all statistics had to be calculated manually.

Increased Revenues

Geisinger Health System is a non-profit organization. Maximizing revenue is not one of its key motivators. However, impacts have been experienced through cost savings.

Productivity Improvements

- Previously manual processes across document management, customer service and accounts payable are now 100% automated, greatly reducing turn around time.
- Employees across the organization no longer need to spend as much time on manual data entry and other repetitive tasks – leaving time for them to focus on higher value activities.

BEST PRACTICES, LEARNING POINTS AND PITFALLS

Best Practices

✓ Geisinger made sure success was long-term and sustainable with the implementations/projects chosen.

✓ Geisinger ensured it had end-user champions and ownership in all BPM implementations.

✓ Geisinger determined what the key performance indicators were and how they were to be tracked over time to show success to the organization.

Pitfalls

✗ The only pitfall Geisinger experienced could only be described as "with success comes follow on work". Geisinger needed to be better prepared for the interest these successful projects spawned.

COMPETITIVE ADVANTAGES

In a real-time environment such as health care, it is important for organizations to be able to quickly adapt to changing conditions, 24x7x365. More streamlined end-to-end processes serve as a critical foundation for a more agile and productive operation. In Geisinger's case, the improvements realized through BPM have positively impacted a host of competitive goal posts, including customer satisfaction, patient safety, HIPPA compliance and cost effectiveness.

TECHNOLOGY

The business imperatives listed in question 3. are typical concerns for many health care providers. What is also typical, and what Geisinger wanted to avoid, is a tendency for health organizations to address these issues with specialized point solutions or customized, home-grown approaches. Geisinger Health System serves patients via 40 outpatient clinics and three major hospitals. As a result, patient information, technology systems and personnel are highly distributed. Geisinger wanted to implement a single solution that could be used to improve processes across specialties, departments, lines of business, systems and geographic locations – a solution that they found in the TIBCO iProcess Suite. Specifically, three key elements of the solution stood out:

- Enterprise-level solution: Unlike point solutions that may be "hard wired" to address one specific process area (like records management) but not another, TIBCO iProcess Suite is an enterprise-level solution that can be applied across functional areas, systems and organizational departments. Geisinger has been able to take advantage of the solution's powerful process automation capabilities within their clinical, insurance and financial operations and easily sees the value it can bring to a wide variety of scenarios. In fact, the organization plans to apply the solution to 11 more systems in the next 12 months.

- Highly Flexible/Adaptable: In a real-time environment such as health care, it is important for organizations to be able to quickly adapt to changing conditions, 24x7x365. TIBCO iProcess Suite components such as the iProcess Modeler, iProcess Decisions rules engine and iProcess Engine execution engine enable users to easily model, analyze, test and create business rules and execute and modify processes without having to rely on IT help. The solution facilitates fast process design, re-design and reuse and additionally leverages service-oriented architecture (SOA) for quick development and deployment of new applications and processes.

- Independent process layer: Recognizing that a variety of systems may be involved in any one process, TIBCO's iProcess Suite separates the management of processes into an independent process layer that operates across applications, people and organizational departments. By providing an independent environment for creating and continuously improving processes, the solution allows more value to be extracted from existing investments, so that Geisinger can leverage a range of systems and applications – including enterprise content management, financial systems, and document imaging software – to drive cross enterprise process excellence.

Because TIBCO iProcess Suite is built on an open architecture, Geisinger found that it was easy to implement the solution and leverage its existing infrastructure to integrate cross-enterprise processes. TIBCO's iProcess Modeler also gave Geisinger the ability to easily define the flow of complex processes involving multiple applications. The resulting processes were thus 100 percent customized to meet the unique challenges that Geisinger needed to address.

THE TECHNOLOGY & SERVICE PROVIDERS
- TIBCO Software, Inc.: www.tibco.com
- Vignette: www.vignette.com

Louisiana Supreme Court, USA

Silver Award, North America
Nominated by Oracle Corporation, USA

SUMMARY

Over the last two years, the Louisiana Supreme Court (LASC) rolled out a business process management system (BPMS) to help bridge the deluge of paperwork and manual processes that underpinned its organization. The solution unifies legal records pulled from several systems in an online portal, enables online collaboration, document sharing, and paper filing, and structures core processes. This has helped make process faster, more convenient, and more transparent.

The BPMS includes BPM, Portal, Collaboration, Content and Document Management, and Search Capabilities. By implementing the BPMS, the Supreme Court of Louisiana automated collaboration, document sharing, and paper filing for the average over 3000 filings per year, making each user process simple, convenient, and transparent. The BPMS significantly increased employee efficiency with robust collaboration and search tools and allows justices and clerks to access court documents and schedules from any Web client. This highly successful system not only enabled the Court to be more efficient and effective in day to day operations, but also enabled it to service and supports its constituents (the public) during and after Hurricane Katrina.

Currently, the BPMS solution services both the wide public (over 4 million residents of the state of Louisiana) as well as users in the court system (government employees, external attorneys and support staff). We have already streamlined our Certificate of Good Standing process and are currently rolling both e-filing and case management processes. LASC is already recognized as one of the most technologically advanced courts by network world, CIO Digest, and Government

Technology for its ability to recover from Hurricane Katrina and continue to serving its public constituents before, during and after the disaster. Efficiencies and cost savings were only a small part of the ROI, as getting the correct court information at the right place at the right time effects real cases and people an impact that can't be measured by dollars and cents (how do you quantify a wrong result in a court case). As the case management is placed online and integrating with electronic filing, the Court expects to increase productivity by at least 50 percent.

The BPMS was paying strong productivity dividends in the best of times, but paid off in spades after Katrina. Many attorneys lost everything, including records proving their status in the Louisiana Bar. This sudden overflow of requests illuminated the serious shortcomings in the process and screamed for a quick and robust solution, BPMS provided a perfect and quick fit post Katrina and will now allow for immediate access for the states attorneys to this service regardless of the state of the court.

THE KEY MOTIVATIONS BEHIND INSTALLING THIS BPMS SYSTEM

The Louisiana Supreme Court wanted a clearer and simpler way to service its constituents, which includes its internal staff and judges, attorneys and supporting staff, and the general public. Providing a **secure** and **trustworthy** system to uphold the public trust is not easy at the best of times, and was made even more challenging when dealing with emergencies and natural disasters (i.e. Katrina). This motivated The Louisiana Supreme Court to implement a BPMS system that would provide a stable, secure, trustworthy, and fail-safe solution that would allow access to the right information to the right people at the right time. The key areas of motivation were to:

- Provide a clear and simple method of connecting to the courts system
- Provide a simple and stable data sharing, collaboration and common work environment
- Establish a platform for future projects i.e.; e-filing and Virtual Court services and research tools
- Remove the client server environment and keep security concerns at the data center not at each location
- Make use of recognized technology, browsers and browser navigation to reduce the learning curve and gain user acceptance from the largely non-technical user base
- Utilize a tool that provides the court with the ability to change, add to or update without third party intervention
- Implement a complete solution that supports the Justices and staff in their daily tasks and increases the courts ability to provide the highest level of output
- With Hurricane Katrina, the court was forced to move to Baton Rouge, over 75 miles away
- Had to move all operations along with the technical hardware that supports the system
- Realized the absolute need for consolidated tools and single source for work products

The Louisiana Supreme Court did not stop there. It has established a vision of establishing a world-class virtual court solution, the LASC has set out the following goals:

- Business Objectives:
  - *Enhance productivity at district offices*

- *Provide more consistent service to external users*
- IT Objectives:
  - *Centralization for improving efficiency*
  - *Reduction of cycle time for securing good customer service*
  - *Standardization for simplifying processes*
  - *Improved decision-making in risk management*

Additional motivators from business and technical perspectives are as follows:
- Business Aspect:
  - *Reduced virtual court process time*
  - *Unified channel for filing various documents*
  - *Prompt routing based on business rules*
  - *Elimination of complex work environment*
- Technical Aspect:
  - *One-stop access to data stored in various systems*
  - *Interoperability among various existing systems including Active Directory, Security, printing, e-Filing, Case Management and external systems*
- Enhancement of development productivity
- A flexible system that can accommodate continued development of virtual court system

OVERALL BUSINESS INNOVATION, SHOWING IMPACT TO MANAGEMENT RESULTING FROM THE NEW SYSTEM

The Louisiana Supreme Court consists of 7 districts.

Overview of management setup:
- 7 Elected Justices (1 from each judicial district)
- 200 Staff members
- 6 Remote district offices
- 22,000+ external attorneys
- Support staff for all attorneys
- Over 4 million residents of the State of Louisiana with public access
- 2000 to 3000 case filings annually
- Over 5900 CGS annually
- Court of last resort
- IT staff of 6

Implementing and supporting a Virtual Court system (and improving it) that supports such a diverse and wide spread community with only 6 IT staff is a challenge. The BPMS enabled a focused approach to enabling Business (in this case mission focused) innovation.

The core focal points of business innovation on operations were:
- Streamlines a currently paper based and laborious manual system
  - *All filings normally accounted for and done by hand*
  - *Distribution was still paper delivered to staff*
- Allows staff to view reports, memorandums and research documents from anywhere
  - *Great Disaster Recovery risk reduction aspect*
  - *Revolutionize working from home*
- Maintenance and support needs diminished to almost nothing v. almost continued problem support with the previous environment
- Allows courts development staff to customize portal and portlets to suit various staffs v. old static view and tools presentation

- Network managers able to remotely access to resolve issues or make changes during business and off hours, provides the best level of support for the staff
  - *Small staff, allowed us to customize even more for the users*
  - *Provide a web access for staff members to access from remote locations and provide the Justices with data when and where required*
  - *Allows the court to collaborate and provides one stop shopping*
  - *A secure environment that allows the same access to data that exists within the walls of the court, and externally*
  - *Scalable for different groups within the court*
  - *Publishing information is easier and can be done by business owners*

New Capabilities enabled by the new BPMS were:
- Community Discussions with over 6 remote sites with daily access
  - *Employee billboards*
  - *Publishing of Court events (including maintenance by business users)*
    - Evacuation information
    - Staff locator and information (Traffic, maps, etc.)
  - *Calendars (Court functions, Court Room events, etc)*
  - *Documents*
    - E-filing
    - Uploaded files for filings
    - Shared documents
    - News Releases
    - Dockets
- Receives over 3000 filings per year
  - *E-filing, the future, BPM allows for the complete automation of the process*
  - *Will streamline a currently paper based and laborious manual system*
    - All filings accounted for and done by hand
    - Distribution was still paper delivered to staff
- Certificate of Good Standing
  - *Needed by Attorneys to prove status in the Louisiana Bar*
  - *Processing 300 to 500 monthly (over 5,900 annually)*
  - *3 – 5 hours daily to complete*
  - *Formerly, completely manual process*
- With BPM and the application developer
  - *Can be requested by the customer from our Virtual Court system*
  - *Automated entirely*
    - End product is the certificate and the envelope in the printer tray
    - Work savings of 2 to 4 hours daily, equates to 4000.00 in lost productivity to the old manual process
    - Found to be a huge need during a crisis event as Attorney's move around and need to prove who they are to other states

A key area of business innovation that can not be overstated is the new system's capability to ensure trust and security while enabling access to content and documents in a timely manner. As proven by the natural disaster Katrina, a paper based system can cause long-term damage to the operations of any community. This was clearly seen when documents were lost and unrecoverable because they were only in paper format. Many attorneys had their Certificates of Good Standing destroyed or inaccessible because of the disaster. With the on-line BPMS it not only keeps electronic copies of all supporting documents, but also allows requests and renewals on-line with access to supporting documents securely stored. This coupled with the disaster recovery and fail-over plan enables the government to better maintain the public's trust, especially in such an important aspect as law and order.

Example:

Scenario	Business Cost or Benefit
Your attorney's certificate is destroyed and he/she can't represent you.	You stay in jail...
Your attorney can retrieve or get a new certificate allowing a speedy process	Priceless...

OVERALL TECHNOLOGICAL INNOVATION

Using the BPMS, we are able to achieve remarkable technology innovations in the following four areas.

Firstly, we personalized several community environments using the highly end user customizable portal. We can open multiple applications (up to 15 windows to handle one work item) required for the job and build a work environment that enables attachments and opinion exchanges, allowing us a flexible process portal.

Secondly, we improved development productivity and made maintenance easier by simplifying the application development process through the separation of business process from application logic. Also, application logic can be simplified into components and reused.

Thirdly, the powerful Content Management and EDMS comes integrated out-of-the-box with the entire BPMS (Portal, BPM and Collaboration)

Fourthly, we also integrated the BPMS with our security platform, Active Directory, printing, existing applications (i.e. auto printing, and email).

BPMS Solution Development Lifecycle

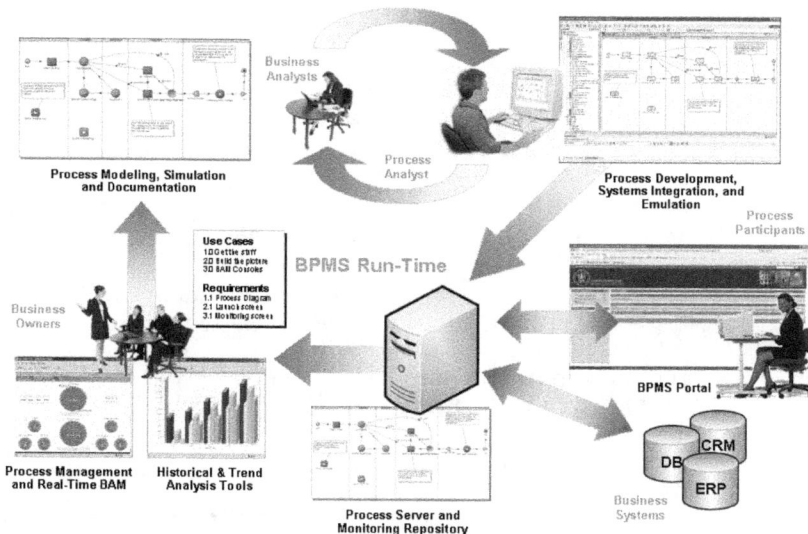

Additional technical achievements may be summarized as follows:

- Various process tracking and history management through process manager and UI manager
- Flexible modification of process data with auditing throughout
- Detailed monitoring of each process in graphical or statistical displays through the process map
- Powerful online monitoring of running processes and completed processes with online keyword search in process manager
- Dynamic process modification — even while the process is in progress — through the "modification" feature

The BPMS system enabled Business and Project leaders at all levels to have better insight and control over the development lifecycle. With only 6 IT Staff to not only implement, but support the system having an integrated tool that matched the solution development lifecycle was essential to our efficiency and effectiveness. The BPMS solution development lifecycle enabled the team to quickly develop, test, and implement enterprise solutions with close collaboration with the business owners. This rapid solution development approach allowed us to not only save time and cut costs, but also avert risks (e.g. stay in touch with the Business) and avoid re-work and allow the business more access to change and administer the BPMS system (e.g. communities, and content).

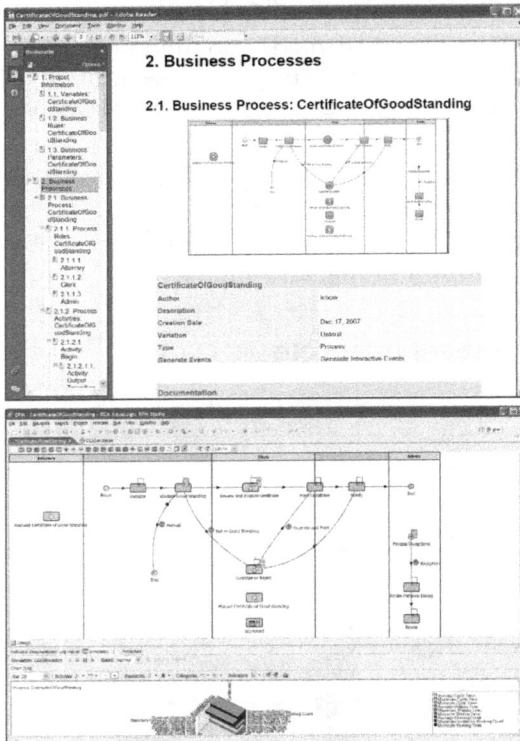

Additionally, for the project team in general the BPMS had powerful time saving capabilities such as auto documentation, simulation and emulation within the Integrated Design Environment (IDE).

Auto documentation in pdf format. Also available as html. Furthermore the BPMS enabled simulation and emulation of the process with the business owners:

The BPMS has built in simulation capabilities to run As-Is and To-Be models with reports and charts and graphs.

Additionally, we are looking at the new round-trip capabilities of the latest release. This new capability would allow data collection of real run-time over periods of time that we would compare with our As-Is and To-Be scenarios.

Simulation of the process with drill down Charts (Bar, 3D, Heat Maps, Line) by units, time, and cost

THE SYSTEM USERS AND WHAT THEIR JOBS NOW ENTAIL COMPARED TO PRE-INSTALLATION

The BPMS includes BPM, Portal, Collaboration, Content and Document Management, and Search Capabilities. By implementing the BPMS, the Supreme Court of

Louisiana automated collaboration, document sharing, and paper filing for the average of 3000 filings per year, making each user process simple, convenient, and transparent. The BPMS significantly increased employee efficiency with robust collaboration and search tools and allows justices and clerks to access court documents and schedules from any Web client. This highly successful system not only enabled the Court to be more efficient and effective in day to day operations, but also enabled it to service and supports its constituents (the public) during and after Hurricane Katrina.

Currently, the BPMS solution services both the wide public (over 4 million residents of the state of Louisiana) as well as users in the court system (government employees, external attorneys and support staff). We have already streamlined our Certificate of Good Standing process and are currently rolling both e-filing and case management processes. Efficiencies and Cost savings were only a small part of the ROI, as getting the correct court information at the right place at the right time effects real cases and people an impact that can't be measured by dollars and cents (how do you quantify a wrong result in a court case). As the case management is placed online and integrating with electronic filing, the Court expects to increase productivity by at least 50 percent.

Previous System:
- No true global data sharing platform
- No collaboration system for projects, groups or departments
- Remote access to the courts data system limited to just a few due to complexity and cost
- Remote offices using dial up, tail circuits and old technology
- Locally installed Fat clients
- Architecture not present to support growth of a web based environment
- Need for a complete upgrade and development of updated tools to support the courts staff and provide a tool for remote use
- Court had to move
- All traditional services halted
- Re-location was difficult at best due to the large influx of other entities, both government and private looking for space
- No central tool for dislocated staff and external customers
- Required managing multiple tools
  - Clients installed on public or family machines
  - Difficult with limitations on support or programming staff
- Overall burden and overhead that comes with "Client" based systems

Improved System with BPMS:
- External customer access that was very apparent during Katrina
- Central system supports collaboration a big part of this dual hat system
- Embedded security and the Active Directory allows for internal and external to work in the same environment without fear of data compromise
- Provides for multiple log on source, i.e.; local source v. Active Directory
- E-filing, BPM allows for the complete automation of the process
- Will streamline a currently paper based and laborious manual system
  - All filings accounted for and done by hand
  - Distribution is still paper delivered to staff
- Allows staff to view reports, memorandums and research documents
  - Great Disaster Recovery risk reduction
  - Revolutionize working from home

- Need for a consolidated tool that allows all to utilize regardless of location
  - Web Based, NO CLIENT
- Easy management, single sign on
  - Allows for cross training with tech staff
  - Allows for integration with many tools that are web based or provide for Portlets managed by business users
  - Web browsers, no need for training
- Gives staff access to needed work tools (one stop shopping)
  - *Very important during a regional event or even a Pandemic where folks will stay home or be ordered to remain home*
    - All the traditional tools inclusive, email, calendars etc. as well as the collaboration tools
- Gives external customers access to tools needed to keep court functioning

Enabled Platform for the future:
- Employment of the BPMS have given the court the ability to move forward with consolidating its tools
- Provides an environment that allows for many application development needs with limited tech staff
- Gives a big leg up on that pesky monster called Business Continuity
- Allows the staff to use a clientless tool (web browser) for work tools, little or no learning curve. Browser is recognized and used technology

The BPMS Virtual Court system for LASC is summarized in the table below.

Item	Details	Remarks
Total Users	4 million+	Information soon available to all Residents of the State Already has general access to Louisiana Supreme Court General Information.
Most likely users	40,000+	Attorneys and supporting staff; court officials and staff
Installation Location	LASC Data Center	Business Continuity Sites
BPMS Collaboration Portal	Supports Most Likely users 40,000+	Users: 40,000+ 10+ Communities 6 remote sites access the system daily
Certificates of Good Standing	5900+ a year	Users: 40,000+ 10+ Communities - 6 remote sites access the system daily
Additional Processes such as Writ Filing	To Be Determined	Users: 40,000+ 10+ Communities 6 remote sites access the system daily Extended to Public

Certificate of Good Standing process workflow (in BPMN)

Attorneys may request a Certificate of Good Standing...

The BPMS has a secure portal that allows several different views based on the users (and what communities and groups they are part of). This enables a very business focused and user friendly access to content and processes while maintaining the integrity of the access privileges.

...which will auto-launch a form for certificate delivery. Form can be auto populated or filled in and has logic for required fields.

As the Official Clerk you have different access privileges and an in-box to process the request for the Certificate of Good Standing

These are some example forms that are given to the end-user in requesting the Certificate of Good Standing.

Once initiated the process with auto-notify the attorney a various stages of the process.

Once completed this with automatically print and the certificate for the mail room to mail-out.

The Clerk can also manually issue a certificate for emergencies. This can be done automatically from the unique Bar-roll Number associated with a valid certificate.

*Note that this automated process reduces all errors as only valid certificates of good standing can be issued

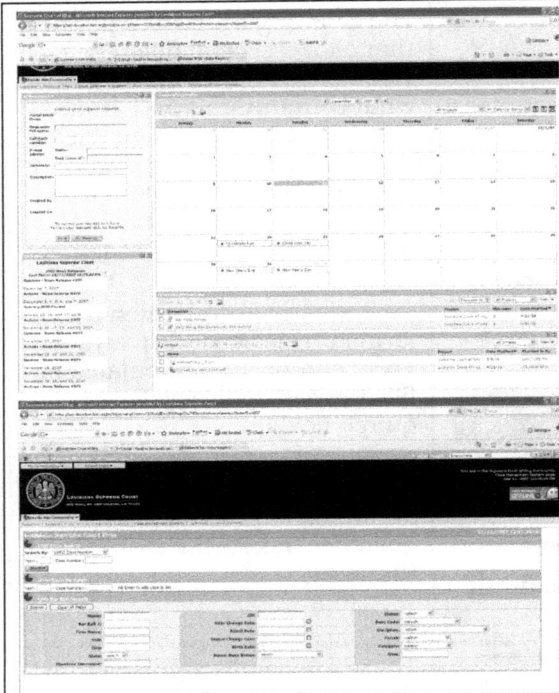

Additionally, clerks, and court staff have access to the Court Calendar, and online support.

Furthermore, permitted users can access the Court Management System and search for Cases and supporting documentation and content.

It is easy to note that enabling a Virtual Court saves a lot of time in searching for and maintaining all the normally paper based content that a Court (especially a Supreme Court) produces and stores over a period of time. This is a truly impactful change to the way a court does its business that can reach to all its constituents including the general public.

THE NEW SYSTEM CONFIGURATION

The entire network and hardware configurations in relation to the BPMS system are as follows:

7 Machines	System configuration
1. Administrative Portal Server 2. Automation, Search, and Services Server 3. Database Server 4. Application Server 5. Collaboration Server 6. BPM Server 7. Web Services	Each machine was configured with: Windows 2003 SP2 2 CPU 2 GB Memory 2.4GHz Processor speed

The diagram below shows the connectivity structure among solutions at the Louisiana Supreme Court.

COST SAVINGS, INCREASED REVENUES, AND PRODUCTIVITY IMPROVEMENTS

As the Louisiana Supreme Court business is to serve the public trust, normal business ROI metrics are not necessarily relevant. However some key metrics meeting the court's mission objectives are detailed below:

- Savings of time
- Adherence to strict budget guidelines
- Visibility and accessibility for the public
  - *Public used to have to make a trip to courthouse or make a phone call but can now access information online quickly and easily*
- Attorneys can access case information, receive Certificates of Good Standing, and very soon, electronically file their case submissions

- Make filings more accessible and minimize or eliminate lost paper, invalid information, shipping costs and hassles
  - *External users used to have to ship or hand carry the large documents to the court – now they can file these documents over the public internet*
- Savings of resources – filing and reviewing electronically saves time and therefore resources, allowing greater attention to detail and frees the staff to better serve the public with other court matters

Example for Case Filings:

2005 Case Filings	2595
2006 Case Filings	3039
This was an increase of	over 17%
2006 Cases Cleared	3325
This means the clearance rate was	109.4%
Paper savings:	
Each case averaged	100 pages
Each case averaged	10 copies
For 2006 estimated pages saved just for case filings	3325000

Example for Certificates of Good Standing:

2005 Certificates of Good Standing	4315
2006 Certificates of Good Standing	5990
This was an increase of	39%
Savings for Attorneys and support staff =	time, paper, mailing (of requests)
Savings for the court several staff =	one clerk
Other ROI: =	Priceless

- Can be requested by the customer from our Virtual Court system
- Certificate of Good Standing is entirely automated
  - *End product is the certificate and the envelope in the printer tray*
  - *Work savings of 2 to 4 hours daily, equates to 4000.00 in lost productivity to the old manual process*
  - *Found to be a huge need during a crisis event as Attorney's move around and need to prove who they are to other states*

Goal Achievement Access:

- Extremely important for remote sites and traveling staff
  - *6 remote sites across the state access the courts system daily, their ability to work is paramount in supporting the Justice for that office*
- Current access was limited to those who had a court laptop with the VPN, remote and security client as well as an internet connection via dial up.
- The Portal provided access to anyone on staff via any internet connection from any PC with a browser
- Security concerns were relieved using Active Directory/SSL and employing at the courts data center.
- Does away with the need for any third party remote or security clients
  - *Moving from the technically complex to the simple while increasing the user base and security aspects*
- Uses recognized browser technology and presents data in a user friendly view
  - *Important, to help reduce or eliminate a learning curve*

- Maintenance and support needs diminished to almost nothing v. almost continued problem support with the previous environment
- BPMS solution allows courts development staff to customize portal and portlets to suit various staff v. old static view and tools presentation
- Network managers able to remotely access to resolve issues or make changes during business and off hours, provides the best level of support for the staff

Goal Achievement Collaboration:

- Enabled collaborative environment where paper walked around before
- Created communities for each Justice chambers (staff)
  - *Allowed immediate sharing of calendars, projects, data and the courts case management system regardless of their login location*
- Allowed court teams to work as one even though geographically separated
- Provided Justice staff members constant access to case data regardless of the author
- Document versioning a huge plus given the number of drafts per Opinion
- Distribution of information through Community pages v. hand carrying

Goal Achievement Ease of Use:

- No true simplistic method of remote access to the courts system
  - *Limited to a few and difficult to use and understand by the average end user*
- Portal provided recognized technology
  - *Eliminated remote clients, security multiple logins and the learning curve*
  - *Reduced by almost 90% the amount of needed support by tech staff*
  - *Use of browser environments was immediately embraced by the staff*
  - *Web surfing is what we all know*
- Learning curve reduced from hours and in some cases days in understanding old tools to minutes
- Flexibility of use
  - *End users can create, edit and control their own views, pages and tools*
  - *Communities are all very similar in look so there is no confusion about what works and how*
- Integration of 3rd party tools quickly completed and rolled out

Goal Achievement Security:

- This was a very important requirement
  - *Court data is sensitive in nature given the spectrum of cases the Justices are called upon to review*
  - *Bigger concern with the remote login and work*
- Accomplished simple and easily managed SSL encryption
  - *Moved control of security to a single point*
  - *Removed the single point of failure with the VPN technologies*
  - *Is not incumbent on the end user*
  - *Allowed for single sign on, simplified the login process for the end user*
  - *Increased level of comfort for the Justices*
  - *Allowed us to secure previously unsecured tools within the Portal*

Goal Achievement Disaster Recovery

- The added benefit of using the BPMS to build a technology lifeboat for the day when everything falls apart

Summary:

- The end result of this tools rollout has been a secure simplified access

- Our return on the investment has been both fiscal and end user
  - *Fiscal, we saw a significant increase in output with less effort*
  - *Provides a consolidated environment for the future which will reduce or eliminate the need for numerous individual tools*
- The biggest benefit has been the ability for the end users to customize their own environments
  - *Web Browser technology reduces or completely eliminates any learning curve*
  - *Rollout of the Portal took about 30 minutes with each employee v. hours of training on splintered older systems*
  - *Clean look*

COMPETITIVE ADVANTAGES GAINED AND HOW WE MOVED THE COMPETITIVE GOAL POSTS

The Louisiana Supreme Court is a front runner in this field of endeavor and this level of technology. Many courts are just now breaking into the tech world and Louisiana Supreme court has far surpassed most. Not only have they implemented a leading technology solution, but they did it in the face of Karina and picked up quickly in the aftermath. The court provides leadership for lower courts and appellate courts to follow and in some cases assimilate – this alone is a huge plus for the state and the constituency that each court serves.

The competitive advantages that we gained from this system include a remarkable improvement in cost savings, cycle time and error ratio through integrating with the legacy system. Our introduction of web-based BPMS technology into the virtual court system is the first in the US and it enables us to provide excellent service to our customers.

The competitive advantages gained from seamless integration between the BPMS and legacy system may be summarized as follows:

1. Enhanced responsiveness to the public and adjustments to changing conditions (e.g. disaster recovery)
2. Improved court image in public relations (industry-leading technology in court system)
3. Reinforced business capability and improved customer loyalty through effective work distribution in communities (central and 6 remote sites)
4. Enhanced customer satisfaction and court reputation resulting from reduced *work errors through automated work processing*

Furthermore, from the holistic point of view, the system:

Firstly, maximizes the efficiency and productivity of the overall processes by facilitating communication with automated work/data flow and enabling the processes to be handled in time.

Secondly, allows flexible adaptation to changes in the workflow or other various elements by separately constructing the process definitions for controlling the workflow and the application necessary for execution of the relevant work, and by implementing the interface between them by defining it in the workflow.

Thirdly, enables continued improvement of processes through monitoring work processes and providing a variety of reports.

As a final word the biggest competitive advantage a court system has is to be true to the public's trust. A court that allows secure, clear access to a non-technical audience that is also reliable and trustworthy even during extreme circumstances, like disasters, will stand the test of time. The BPMS is essential to enable to court to implement a virtual court system to meet these goals.

IMMEDIATE AND LONG-TERM PLANS TO SUSTAIN COMPETITIVE ADVANTAGE

With continued expansion of the BPMS system, we will further strengthen our capability to service our customer (the public) and instill a sense of security and organization essential for the public trust of the state of Louisiana.

Our short-term expansion plans include:
- *Expand* the workflow system to *include* multiple virtual court solutions
- Application of the BPMS to e-Filing and Case Management

Our long-term expansion plans include:
- Expansion of the BPMS to include additional Public to Government and Government to Government access
- Enablement of more Government self-service, Supported Attorney self-service, and Public self-service.

Tasks that have been identified in expanding the ROI and use of the BPMS are:
- Continue identifying and building out more processes to automate
- Continue growth and make use of any technology that allows for information at the court level to flow via the least path of resistance for both the staff and general public.
- Serving the public by supplying the best systems possible and giving the greatest levels of access
- Maximizing our budget by fully optimizing time and resources
- Plan in advance how to survive and sustain natural disaster events

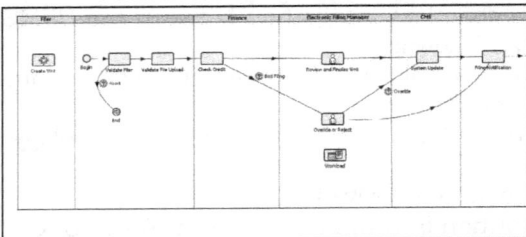

As part of the system infrastructure, the BPMS will be expanded to various processes in Louisiana Supreme Court to strengthen its P2G, G2G and G2B, and internal processing capability. This system is the infrastructure for future IT development.

Writ Filing process is one of the next processes to be implement in 2008

Efficiencies and Cost savings were only a small part of the ROI, as getting the correct court information at the right place at the right time effects real cases and people an impact that can't be measured by dollars and cents (how do you quantify a wrong result in a court case). As the case management is placed online and integrating with electronic filing, the Court expects to increase productivity by at least 50 percent.

Wells Fargo Financial Information Services, USA

Gold Award, North America.
Nominated by Lombardi Software, USA

EXECUTIVE SUMMARY / ABSTRACT

Wells Fargo Financial (WFF) is a division of Wells Fargo & Company (NYSE: WFC) with more than $69 billion in assets. It offers real estate-secured lending, automobile financing and other loan products through their network of stores; offers indirect automobile financing through relationships with more than 18,000 franchised automobile dealers in the U.S., Canada and Puerto Rico; offers consumer and private-label credit cards and commercial services to consumers and businesses. WFF also provides credit cards and lease and other commercial financing. Headquartered in Des Moines, Iowa, it serves 8.8 million customers in the US and internationally.

Wells Fargo Financial was challenged with increasingly complex processes that are paper-intensive and have a large number of manual steps and handoffs resulting in errors (for example, in typing, misplaced files, etc.) and inefficiencies. WFF elected to incorporate Business Process Management (BPM) into their architecture to reduce the time and cost between process re-design and re-deployment into production: from >12 months to <4 weeks.

OVERVIEW

In 2006, Wells Fargo Financial embarked on an initiative to improve processes and overall reduce costs. It created a SWAT team to oversee this process improvement effort. One of the key areas that the company focused its efforts on was the setup process for "dealers" that offer WFF's financial instruments (e.g., mortgage and retail lending, and credit card accounts).

WFF began implementation of their first process improvement effort under the new SWAT program using BPM software from Lombardi® (Teamworks®) in February 2007, and placed it into production in April 2007. The total time-to-market was 7 weeks. A critical factor to WFF was the ease and speed of deployment, better process visibility and tight integration to Microsoft Outlook as compared to their corporate Enterprise Content Management (ECM) system.

By automating numerous mission-critical processes in their complex retail credit organization with Lombardi as a single BPM platform, WFF has identified several key areas of benefits:
- Increased process visibility
- Increased process automation
- Increased data quality and integrity
- Leads to faster "time-to-market"
- Reduced administration processing cost
- Reduced length of process life cycle
- Provided value-added customer services
- Centralized all processes onto one standardized platform

Those benefits have generated firm metrics including reduced staffing costs; a reduction in cycle-times for internal and external stakeholders; as well as a substantial increase in employee productivity. In sum, BPM has significantly improved operational efficiencies and more deeply integrated the Wells Fargo Financial processes into its customers and business partners.

BUSINESS CONTEXT

Beginning in the second half of 2006, Wells Fargo Financial launched an initiative to improve processes and overall reduce costs. One of the key areas was in the management of "dealer setup", a labor intensive process that requires hundreds of changes each week. Many others were identified as candidates as well, including processes related to the company's "non-real estate Centralized Disposition Team."

The initial 'as-was' Dealer Setup process at WFF was paper based and manually handled. When a request to set up a dealer (or change) came in, the application was submitted to the WFF Home Office, and a decision was made to approve or decline the request. The requests process involved the use of 2 systems, 3 MS-Access databases and more than 20 spreadsheets, as well as 38 FTE's.

At the time, WFF was receiving enough requests that the company was considering the addition of 4-6 more FTE's. Additionally this practice had a cost associated with it. Sales representatives spent unnecessary time manually tracking the process by sending emails, and/or answering phone calls. Similarly, management spent 30 minutes or more each day developing report data to track the performance of the process. As such, the process was an ideal candidate for automation and optimization through BPM and workflow technology.

THE KEY INNOVATIONS

Business Innovation and Impact

As an organization, Wells Fargo Financial is relentlessly focused on continuous process improvement. Its goal is to deliver process ownership into the hands of the business whenever possible. One way that the SWAT team works to accomplish this goal is by incorporating the concepts and practices of LEAN within the organization. As such, each project that it undertakes with BPM also has a LEAN aspect. The Dealer Setup process was no exception.

To date, the implementation of BPM to automate the WFF Dealer Setup and other processes has yielded very good results. By automatically pre-qualifying the vast majority (80+ %) of dealers without manual intervention, the team is now able to work on higher value activities, better handle exceptions to the "happy path," and reduce rework.

The new process automates the entire process, eliminating all manual tracking efforts, thus making it much less labor intensive. Management now has access to real-time visibility reports, allowing them to accurately measure the results of the process at any point in the day. In turn, users of the process have become much more productive. With the new automated system in place, WFF now processes hundreds of Dealer Setup requests each week, without any increase in FTEs. As previously stated, WFF was considering the addition of 4-6 FTE's to handle the load. The cost avoidance of ~6 FTE's, correlates to ~ $438,400 annually, which is a significant cost savings.

The radical change in development productivity and ability to iterate quickly has also improved their corporate agility significantly.

As a by-product of implementing WFF processes using BPM software (in Teamworks), the company is able to quickly show compliance with the Equal Credit Opportunity Act (ECOA), Federal Reserve Regulation B, and Office of the Comptroller of the Currency (OCC) charters.

Additionally, the business has much more input into the design process and the skill set that is required to help build the applications is less stringent. As a result, business acceptance of the application and overall satisfaction are both deemed higher as well. Through BPM, the company also has a single tool that gives managers visibility into their process performance, as well as track, measure and report on the productivity of specific employees at any time.

Such visibility increases WFF's ability to manage business and supplier relationships, expedite important orders, identify and quantify exceptions, and improve the process over the long term.

Process

Wells Fargo Financial evaluated several software packages including extending the FileNet enterprise content management (ECM) system that it already utilized, but determined that the core problem was in the workflow of their business process itself. The goal was to automate the previously manual activities, as well as pre-qualify dealers so that team members could better handle business growth and enhancements. By eliminating hand-offs from the mix, WFF could increase productivity and reduce cycle times, especially as it relates to communication with the company's Sales Representatives.

The 'as-was' state of the process included nearly 40 full-time-equivalents (FTE's) to handle the process volume. The team was quickly growing beyond its manual processes for handling applications. Setting up new clients and Dealers required multiple hand-offs and handling of paper apps (often delivered incomplete or in the wrong order), and frequently required data to be entered multiple times. Additionally, the process was being handled (slightly) differently in Canada from that of the US. With over 100 applications and more than 300 changes requested every week, the process was too slow to support the projected sales growth.

Today, WFF has automated the process electronically using BPM software. Coupled with the LEAN concepts, the SWAT team modeled, developed, tested, and deployed a new process solution (on Lombardi Teamworks). The resultant process automates much of the previously manual activities, and ensures data consistency and quality. Streamlined hand-offs allows team to support more business without more staff. Real-time visibility warns management of bottlenecks before they become problems, and coupled with automated reporting, reduced efforts by over 50 hours per week.

At any time, the business user can see the status of the process on a single screen instead of mulling through numerous systems and/or paper documents. WFF now has considerable atomic visibility into the status of client and Dealer request that they receive. The entire effort of automating the human workflow for the Dealer Setup process was completed and delivered in under 4 months (total elapsed time). The actual programmer time in terms of the number of days of effort was between 1 to 1½ months for each project.

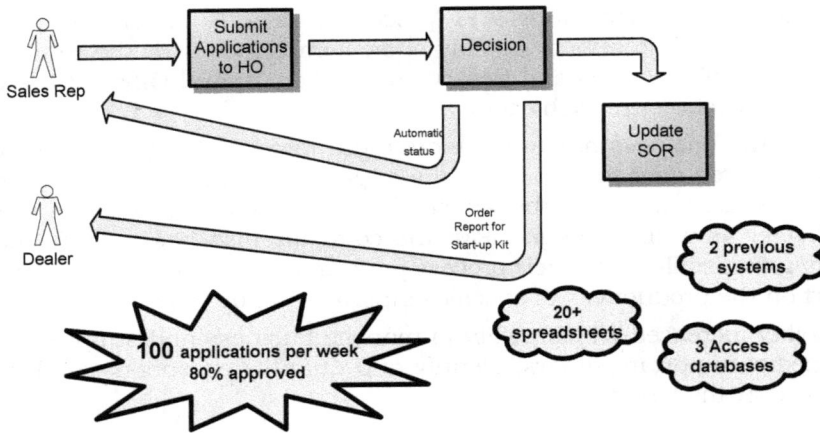

© *2007 Wells Fargo Financial - Simplified schematic of the process*

Most importantly, the new process provided WFF with a solution that applies Lean and continuous improvement concepts, and delivered process ownership into the hands of the business – a primary corporate objective.

With a flexible BPM infrastructure in place with Teamworks, WFF realized that it could iterate on the process quickly (and easily) and therefore determined that the next area of improvement for the process was to increase the straight-through processing (STP) of the workflow in both this and other processes.

One of the key lessons learned during the implementation was the importance of adopting a platform that can be continuously improved in short development cycles with minimal impact to existing processes and the option of them inheriting the improvements.

ORGANIZATION

The new process has had a positive impact on the employees involved. Prior to the BPM implementation, employees interacting with the process were frequently frustrated by handling paper applications and change orders, and they were required to spend a lot of their time communicating via e-mails and/or phone calls. Now, the streamlined hand-offs in the new process allows the existing team to support more business without more staff. The increased communication and automated hand-offs reduce the number of emails and phone calls that they must undertake. Real-time visibility warns management of bottlenecks before they become problems, and coupled with automated reporting, reduced efforts by over 50 hours per week.

The SWAT team within Wells Fargo Financial can be considered comparable to that of a Competency Center (or Center of Excellence). Since each member was trained in LEAN concepts, the primary challenge it faced was with learning the nuances of the BPM tool and how best to approach process development.

User comments related to the success of the project include:

- ✓ *"Easy to use, made my job a lot easier"*
- ✓ *"Reduced the steps to get to the same spot"*
- ✓ *"Reporting is easier to access"*

✓ *"I know how I am performing without having to wait until MPP (i.e., performance review) time"*

HURDLES OVERCOME

Management

Being such a large organization, Wells Fargo Financial did experience some initial hurdles during the project.

The company is dedicated to institutionalizing continuous process improvement. As such, there were few management-related hurdles to overcome, since the support for the improvement program was top-down led. Steven Smith, CTO at WFF, has been a key executive sponsor and champion for the BPM improvement efforts.

Business

There was initially a lack of consensus about what the right approach to process improvement for the company was. Initial conversations centered around whether WFF should search for an external BPM vendor to augment the existing ECM system, or if they should build the capabilities themselves in the ECM tool. Ultimately, they elected to augment the existing system using BPM.

Also, there were several competitive BPM and SOA solutions that potentially could have suited WFF's needs, but they did not deliver all of the capabilities that the company was looking for. The company had many constituents that needed to be satisfied that the tool they selected was the right one. WFF performed extensive due diligence on the companies and selected a BPM suite with standards-based capabilities that met the company's requirements both for today and into the future.

ORGANIZATION ADOPTION

Once the initial process was in place and the initial results were clearly positive, team members were eager to participate, as the improvements that were put in place allowed them to do their jobs more effectively. Similarly, the real-time visibility and reporting now offered to management eliminated large inefficiency in their daily jobs, thus adding to the success and adoption.

Due to this, the SWAT team has received numerous requests from other parts of the organization to be included in the process improvement schedule.

BENEFITS

There have been many benefits received by the Lombardi BPM implementation including reduced cycle times, lower error rates, fewer lost orders, lower paper costs, and it is expected that over time WFF will be able to measure increased customer and partner satisfaction as well.

According to a WFF Operations Manager:

"Fantastic! This is great! This is what we need to help us move forward in an efficient manner and easily embrace an increased workload. And, this tool allowed us to prove what we had always thought – we don't need 3 steps or 3 people in the initial process."

BEST PRACTICES, LEARNING POINTS AND PITFALLS

Best Practices

✓ *Don't boil the ocean. Start with the current process, and deliver small efficiencies - the learning curve is condensed and less "painful" to users who resist change*

✓ *Iterate often (run numerous playbacks) with users to get feedback and buy-in through out the development process*

✓ *Business Sponsorship is crucial – the business owns the process, IT enables the solution*

✓ *Encourage evolution – agility can be your greatest differentiator*

✓ *Metrics (goals) around the processes needs to be defined in the beginning*

✓ *Have an extensive (and documented) change control mechanism in place*

Pitfalls

✗ *Ensure that role of the business and IT are clearly defined*

✗ *Know how your process is performing (Before... during... after) or you can not quantify improvements*

✗ *Learn the nuances of the tool and how best to approach development of the solutions before beginning a "visible" project*

✗ *Look for a business problem – not a BPM problem*

✗ *Be prepared to deal with software bugs, and infrastructure setup*

COMPETITIVE ADVANTAGES

The financial services industry is highly competitive. Inn order to better serve customers, faster and at a lower cost, WFF determined that it needed to quickly grow beyond its manual processes for handling loan applications and other financial instruments. With multiple hand-offs and handling of paper apps (often delivered incomplete or in the wrong order), the process was just too slow to support the projected sales growth in the company.

These new processes raise the bar for our competition, which we hope will be easily measured with both increased sales and improved customer satisfaction.

The Teamworks advantage has spread virally above and beyond the processes described above, enabling it to become a strategic platform for designing, executing, and improving processes within the Wells Fargo Financial organization.

By adopting a platform that lets them build processes in 90 – 120 days or less and iterate them just as easily, WFF can respond to changing market conditions and take advantage of new opportunities faster while empowering the business users to be much better aligned with IT. Through continuous process improvement, WFF depends on Teamworks for a long term sustainable advantage.

Due to the highly sensitive nature of the financial services industry, we are unable to disclose future areas within the organization targeted for process improvement.

TECHNOLOGY

Technology Innovation

By implementing Lombardi Teamworks as an agile BPM development platform, Wells Fargo Financial is now able to much more quickly build and iterate its processes. With Teamworks, WFF can manage all process flows are defined graphically even at the screen-by-screen level of detail. The graphical development approach not only vastly reduces the amount of code WFF needed to develop (and ultimately maintain), but also provides a better framework to ensure business users and IT are on the same page as to the application definition and implementation. Increasing the role of the business analyst in the development process was a crucial aspect of WFF's success. The development time for new major process iterations has averaged between 60-90 days as opposed to being measured in months or years.

Wells Fargo Financial also has a more standards-based infrastructure. Teamworks is a 100% J2EE application that fits completely within the WFF technology stack. Teamworks runs on WebSphere and DB2 and all the interfaces are web based. Since the process model is BPMN-compliant, and the product relies heavily on XML, SQL and JavaScript, there are no proprietary languages that WFF had to learn.

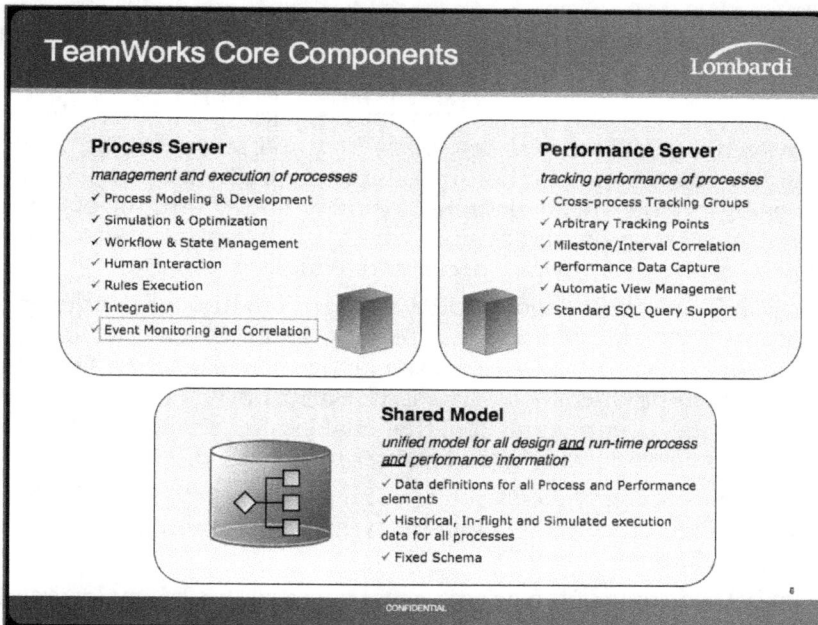

151

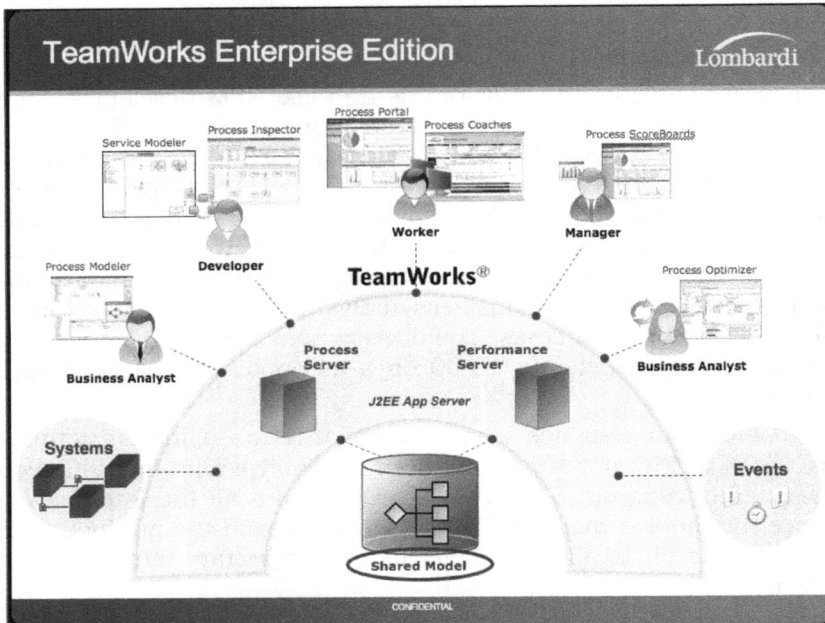

THE TECHNOLOGY & SERVICE PROVIDERS

Lombardi® is a leader in business process management (BPM) software for companies, systems integrators and government agencies of all sizes. The company offers award-winning BPM technology, know-how and services to help its customers become Process-Driven. Lombardi products are built on open standards, and provide ongoing prioritization, planning, visibility and control of business processes, increasing the speed and flexibility with which organizations can manage their business process activity and decision-making.

Teamworks® is Lombardi's flagship BPM software product for designing, executing, and improving business processes. Teamworks for Office™ makes it easy for anyone to participate in business process management using the familiar Microsoft® Office System products. And Lombardi Blueprint™ is the only on-demand, collaborative process documenting tool that enables companies to map processes, identify problems and prioritize improvement opportunities.

Lombardi's unique, shared model architecture, is designed to be easier to use and faster to deploy than other BPM solutions, reducing the overall total cost of ownership of the resulting processes.

Lombardi is behind some of the largest, most successful BPM implementations in the world. Its customers include Allianz Life, Aflac, Banco Espirito Santo, Capital One, Dell, El Paso Corp., ING Direct, Maritz Travel, National Bank of Canada, National Institute of Health, Rabobank, Safety-Kleen, Sprint, T-Mobile, Universal Music Group, Wells Fargo Financial, Xbridge, and numerous governmental agencies. For more information, visit www.lombardi.com.

Section 4

Pacific Rim

Daewoo Shipbuilding & Marine Engineering (DSME), Korea

Finalist, Pacific Rim
Nominated by DNV Software, Norway

EXECUTIVE SUMMARY / ABSTRACT

In the business world's race for companies to perform faster, better and cheaper, Business Process Management (BPM) and Workflow have been launched as the "Holy Grail" to success. Many of the BPM vendors are developing templates and frameworks (best practices) covering traditional industry verticals such as finance, manufacturing, telecom, and also government sectors. The marine and offshore industry is faced with the same fierce competition as the rest of the business world and must also continually improve performance. But, best practices from other industry verticals are not readily adapted to this industry segment. The workforce of the marine and offshore industry consists of highly qualified knowledge workers undertaking complex design work spanning a long time frame. Their business processes are typically concurrent, multi-discipline, iterative and highly complex. Such organizations pose severe challenges to process management and workflow implementation supporting their best practices.

Korea is the world's largest shipbuilding nations, and the three largest yards in the world are located here. The second largest yard in Korea, Daewoo Shipbuilding and Marine Engineering Ltd. (DSME) has over the past years carried out various attempts to improve performance in design activities. Because of competition from "new" shipbuilding nations like China, it has become a vital issue to increase the efficiency in also the management and execution of the design and engineering processes.

To achieve this goal, an engineering process management system has been developed, named 'DSME Engineering Wizard System' which aims to accelerate process performance by managing execution, promoting collaboration and maximizing engineering data reusability based on workflow concepts.

OVERVIEW

DSME launched a project in 2005 with the objective of developing a workflow production system to support their engineers in their daily work. The initial scope of the project was to cover three different work processes:

- Marketing Design (MD)
- Hull Basic Design (HBD)
- Vibration Analysis & Noise Free Design

The **Marketing Design** process is the most complex business process of the above. The Marketing Design process at DSME involves about 150 engineers and more than 10 different engineering disciplines. The process covers the pre-contract engineering work at the yard. The pre-contract projects are characterized by a short duration involving substantial collaboration and communication not only between the project participants, but also with the client (owner) and different makers. DSME typically carry out in excess of 200-300 pre-contract projects every year. In order to conduct all of these projects in a timely manner and with quality, it is of crucial importance to utilize the DSME ship experience base. The

DSME ship database consists of all ships delivered by the yard and holds vital information to quickly determine weight and cost estimates for the ship used as a basis for the final building cost. This working environment posed the following challenges to the solution: not only must the process framework handle the process flow, but also allow for the participants to contribute and exchange information along the way in a flexible manner. All decisions should be logged for later reference and experience feedback (learning). A seamless integration with the DSME legacy systems for document management, project management and ship database was also required.

The *Hull Basic Design* process is involves 20-30 engineers working with the *ship hull* structural design. It is part of the contract work at the yard and the objective of this work process is to produce the information (drawings and calculations) required to obtain class approval by a *classification society*[1].

The process framework must provide management and sharing of documents and drawings that are produced during basic structural design. The system also provides management and integration with applications that are used by the engineers during the process. One of the main challenges is to support a seamless integration with the DSME legacy drafting system, providing easy access to all drawings as part of the process framework.

The *Vibration Analysis & Noise Free Design* process is also part of the contract work at the yard involving 10-15 specialists. This work process is characterized by spanning a long time frame, and the work is usually conducted by one or two engineers. The vibration analysis work starts during the ship design phase, continues throughout the building period and also covers the 1 year warranty period of the ship starting from the delivery date. The total time span for a vibration project can be as long as 2-3 years. During the project period, all relevant documents and information must be maintained. In the course of the project, it is likely that the project resource(s) have to be exchanged. The process framework must support the re-assignment of the work and the knowledge transfer to the new engineer. The new engineer assigned to take over the project, must be able to easily see the progress and status of the project, find all relevant documents, and be able to track all previous decisions.

Figure 1 shows the project phases from initial proof of concept (pilot) to deployment and production.

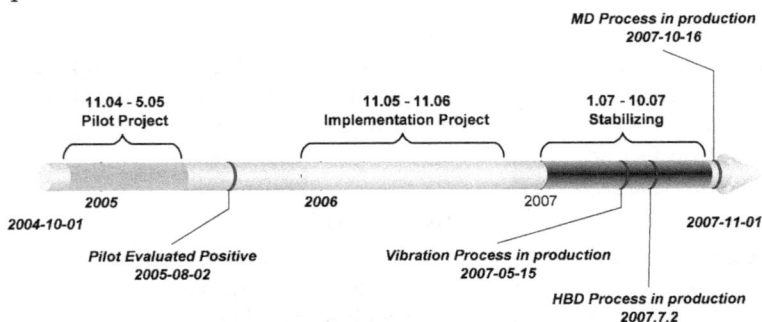

Figure 1: Project history

---

[1] Classification societies are organizations that establish and apply technical standards in relation to the design, construction and survey of marine related facilities including ships and offshore structures. These standards are issued by the classification society as published rules.

The development was undertaken from Norway (at DNV Software head office and development centre), while testing and deployment were carried out on site at DSME's shipyard at Geoje, South Korea. The distance to the customer (both geographically and in time) posed great challenges to the project team. These were partially resolved by supporting DSME from DNVS regional office in South Korea with a single point of contact (SPOC). The SPOC was responsible for the daily contact with the customer, and capable of collecting requirements and communicating these to the development team in Norway. In addition, several work session was carried out at the yard involving the development team from Norway.

The developed system supports the following features:
- Ability to see if a document has changed without actually opening it
- Capability to receive scheduled notification of changes by email leading directly to the change
- Document management and control solutions
- Ability to establish levels of user security and access rights
- Open instant messaging
- Track history for all changes
- Easy exchange of key data and notification if data has changed

BUSINESS CONTEXT

The main sources to engineering inefficiency in existing work procedures at DSME were identified as:
- First, there exist different work practices among engineers even when they are involved in the same kind of work because a standardized process is not defined.
- Second, despite the fact that most of the deliverables produced from engineering work are data in a document format, there is not a management system in place for supporting engineering work itself (how to work).

Putting these together, the business environment can be described as tasks, people, data and tools managed separately through individual practices and resulting in different experiences and works which eventually pose a barrier against business productivity. Figure 2 illustrates the business environment before the process changes were implemented.

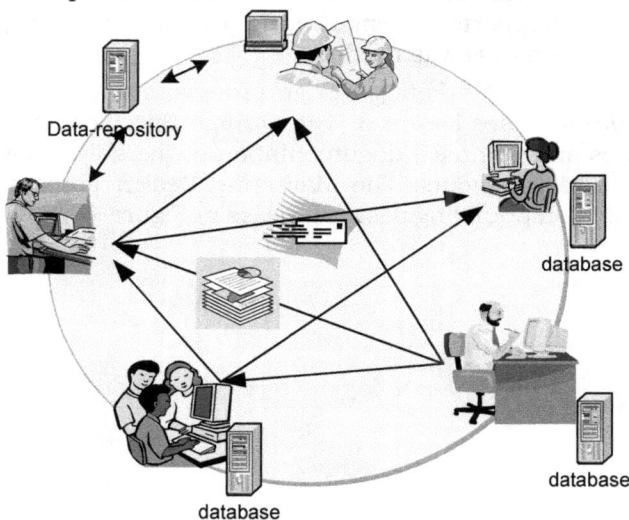

Figure 2: Business Environment before implementation

THE KEY INNOVATIONS
4.2 Business

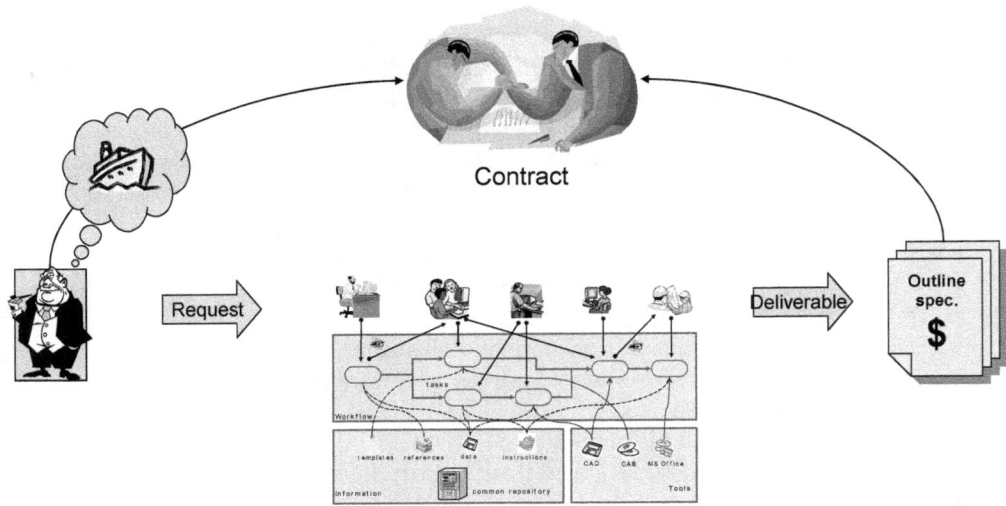

Marketing Design Process

Figure 3: The Marketing Design Process as part of the overall business objective

4.3 Process

When carrying out a project involving process improvements of any kind, the process owner's commitment and participation is vital in order to succeed. And even more true when person-to-person and person-to-system processes are involved. Realizing this fact, DSME established a *Committee of Practice* (CoP) with members consisting of process owners, stakeholders and end-users. The CoP works closely with the project team assuring acceptance of the solution during all phases of the implementation project (design, development/configuration and deployment 2-3 iterations was usually required to reach final consensus.

During the initial work with the CoP to establish the requirements, it was realized that a system which supports the engineering process and manage all the information as part of the process was needed.

The business goal for the Marketing Design process is to produce what is called an *Outline Specification, see* Figure 3. The Outline Specification includes weight and cost estimates and technical documentation of the ship answering the shipowners functional requirements. The Marketing Design process is depicted as part of the overall in shipbuilding design process in Figure 4.

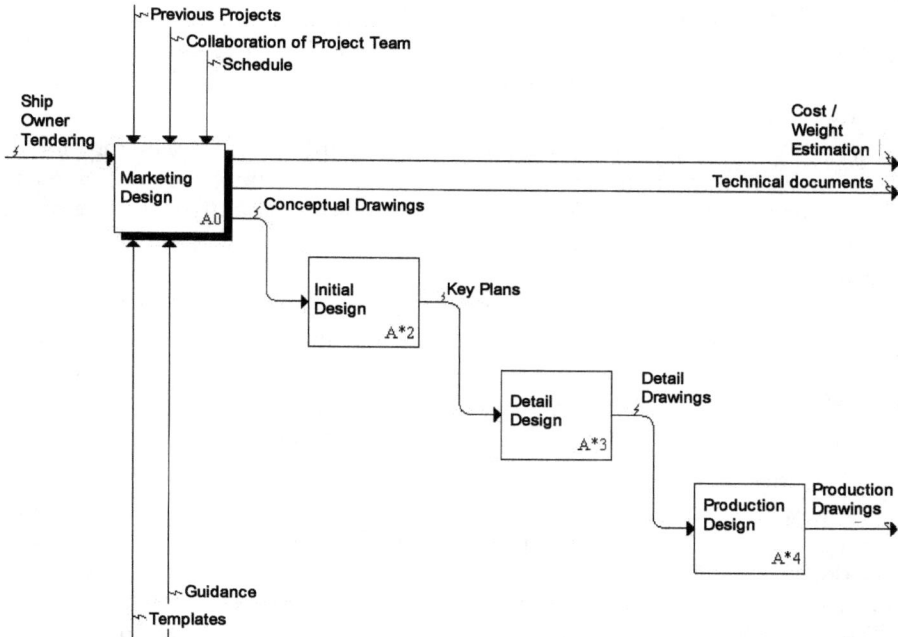

Figure 4: Marketing Design as part of the Shipbuilding Design Process

The Marketing Design process starts with the project setup and ends with the publishing of the final deliverables. Use Case diagrams were applied to analyze the activities and roles in more detail, as illustrated in Figure 5.

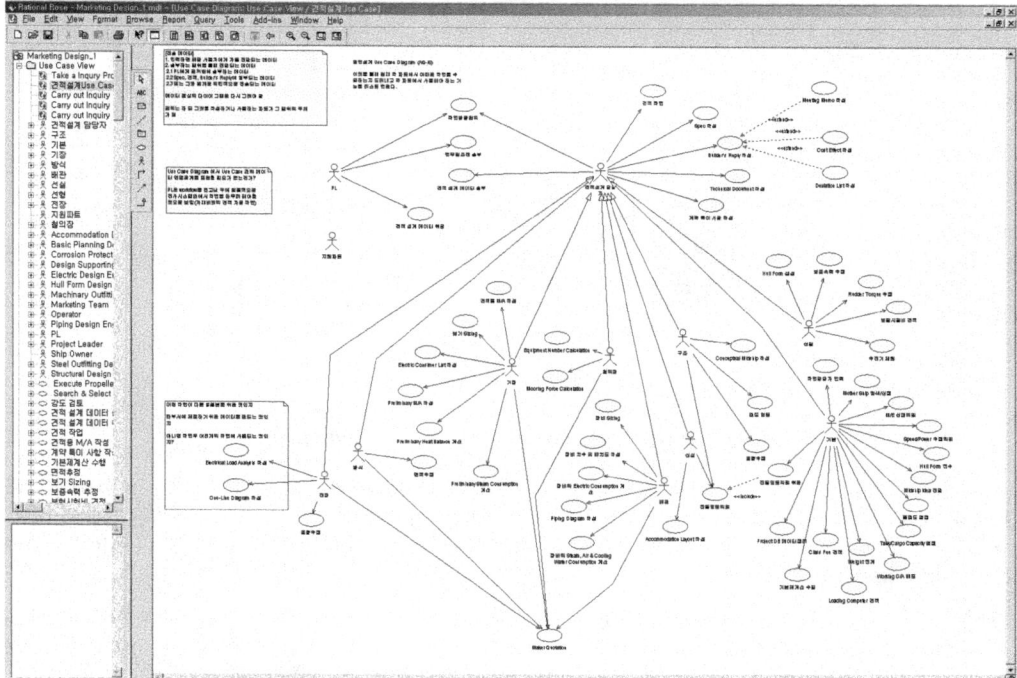

Figure 5: Use Cases Diagram for Marketing Design

Workflow Templates

Using the Process Editor of the workflow module in Brix Foundation, the Marketing Design process was organized into one common workflow template process definition.

The Marketing Design process was analyzed mainly by interviewing end users over a period of time. The process was disassembled into part activities which were necessary in order to achieve the overall business goal (the Outline specification). For each activity, relationships (sequence, dependency, pre- and post conditions) were identified.

Necessary tools providing functionality for the different activities like collaboration, data management, reviewing, notification, messaging, etc. were also identified.

Process Execution

The framework used for this system provides a Workflow Explorer which allows users to view and execute the processes.

While the flow from one activity to the other is automated by the workflow engine, the project leader is orchestrating the real process through the system. The process flow does not only depend on the mechanism defined by the template but also on the project leader's intervention. The other participants carry out their tasks according to his intervention which is notified to them by the system.

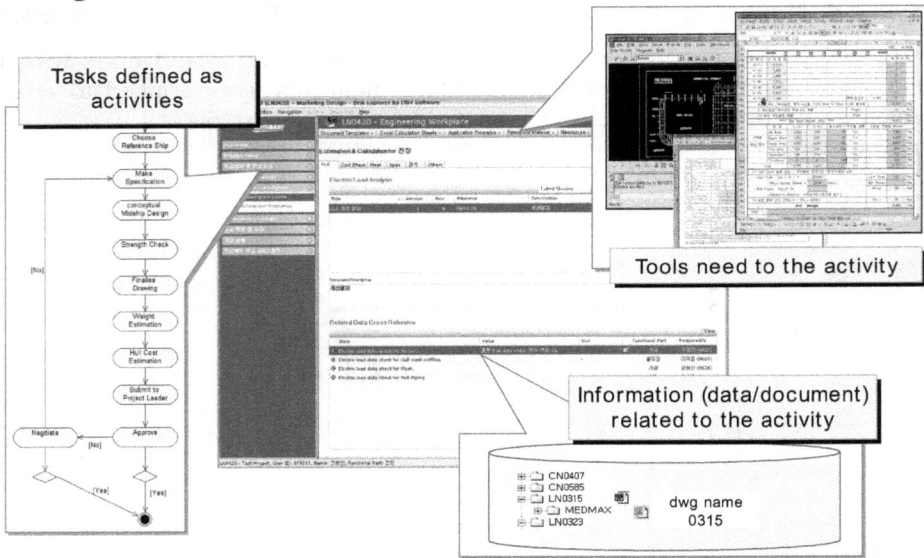

Figure 6: Integrated Work Environment

One instance of the workflow template is initiated when a new inquiry project is registered. All participants can see the specific project through the explorer and contribute to progress participating in the defined activities using the related tools as exemplified in Figure 6.

Basically all communication and data/document management for the Marketing Process are designed to be supported by the system. By providing one solitary engineering workplace environment including all participants working together, project progress is easily monitored as well.

"Ad hoc" workflow is introduced as part of the solution in order to increase end user flexibility. As an example, the engineer which works on the Hull Basic Design process always has to carry out the *Rule Scantling* activity. For this purpose, he/she has a set of calculation tools (applications) provided by the classification societies at hand. For the main stream of projects (designs), these applications are sufficient. But from time to time, a design needs to be developed or studied in more detail. For this purpose, the engineer has to carry out a more detailed analysis using an application based on Finite Element Method (FEM). During the process analysis phase we realized that this behavior is an exception to the normal flow. Rather than modeling this activity into the standard flow of the Basic Structural Design process, we allow the user to dynamically add a sub-process to the activity of the running process when a more detailed analysis is required. The user can chose from a set of pre-defined templates covering the majority of expected exceptions. By this way, we keep the standard flow as clean as possible, and leaving the decision to the knowledge worker of when a detailed analysis is required. It is important to realize that the ad hoc changes only apply to the instantiated process template (running process). The changes are saved together with the process for later evaluation and experience feedback. If one encounters many similar changes to the same process, the process owner may chose to incorporate these as part of the *template* process.

4.4 Organization

Many independent management systems and databases are used for each individual engineering task in the Marketing Design process. This makes it difficult to introduce a workflow system for daily work because the users will have a barrier against an additional system which does not contribute directly to their productivity.

Hence, the new system was designed to yield one common workplace to carry out the Marketing Design process from the beginning to the end. The process is supported as activities defined by process templates and data are provided for each activity. With this approach, the users can carry out the Marketing Design process in a single environment.

As illustrated in Figure 7, one single environment serves information and tools related to tasks controlled by a workflow system.

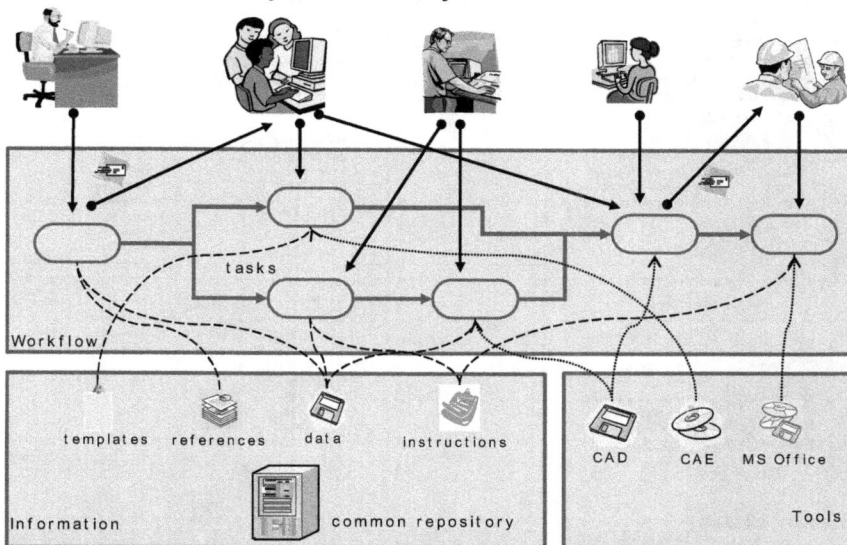

Figure 7: Marketing Design process showing the business environment after implementation

The interview of the CoP further revealed that users tend to choose different ways to collaborate like email, yellow stickers, hard copies and telephone. The communication history could not be maintained nor traced. Consequently, exchange of information tends to be duplicated or omitted.

During this phase, we soon realized that it would be very difficult to represent the process with all exceptions in a workflow context. It was simply too many exceptions and roles involved. Rather than trying to fit all participants into one common template process, we adapted another approach. The Marketing Design process is characterized by being collaboration intensive. By introducing a collaboration mechanism as part of the framework, we were able to define a much simpler process template. The deviations to the template flow are left to be resolved through the built collaboration mechanism in stead of explicitly modeling it into the flow. The mechanism is simple but effective: by introducing a messaging scheme which is part of the framework, the engineer can request information at any time from any workflow participant. Hence, all communication became part of the system so that every participant could easily refer to the latest data and trace the change history. Ownership of key data were defined as part of the process, and the role responsible for creating data or documents uses the system to distribute these to the workflow participants and the system keeps track of the history. The conversations are logged and kept as part of the process history for later analysis and learning.

As an example of data sharing, Figure 8 shows a screen where participants input each data whenever they created or modified. Each change is notified using the messaging mechanism. When a workflow participant is in need for data for a particular task, and the data items are still not inputted yet, he can request the information through the request function. The role with the ownership to the information/data receives the request and can act accordingly.

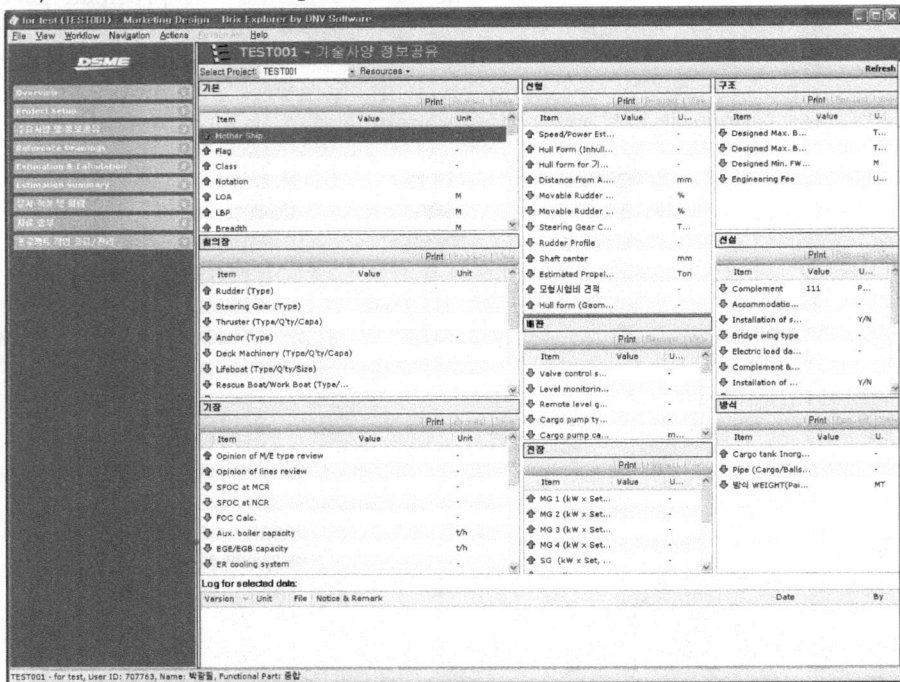

Figure 8: Engineering Data Sharing and Reuse

HURDLES OVERCOME

5.1 Management

The project was initiated and supported by the top management in DSME. This secured the necessary project resources and attention. The CoP represented the process knowledge needed to identify existing procedures and to develop the best practice.

5. 2 Business

The CoP was actively involved during the implementation of the system. Before the final acceptance testing, the CoP members and other key users were trained in operating the system to make the transition as smooth as possible. The training was also used to motivate the users to translate from the old way of working to the new work environment.

5.3 Organization Adoption

No organizational changes were address during the implementation project.

BENEFITS

6.1 Cost Savings and Time Reductions

DSME has estimated the total man hour savings to around 5,000 M/H per year for the Marketing Design process. This is a very conservative estimate, and the savings are expected to increase as more knowledge (projects) is available through the system as reference information. The quality is expected to improve as the process becomes much more transparent and each participant can easily share information and knowledge.

6.3 Increased Revenues

The throughput of projects will increase, leading to a higher possibility for securing more contracts with the ship owner.

6.4 Productivity Improvements

BEST PRACTICES, LEARNING POINTS AND PITFALLS

7.1 Best Practices and Learning Points

- Management support for projects involving process changes is absolutely essential.
- Make sure to have necessary process knowledge readily available to the project. In the current implementation this was solved through a Committee of Practice (CoP) covering the engineering disciplines involved in the work process.
- Take a process centric approach to implement changes when working with knowledge intensive organizations.
- Do not forget to support person-to-person processes.
- Realize that knowledge is sticky and humans have barriers to sharing knowledge. The solution should cater for this.
- Compensate for geographical distance by utilizing Webex (desktop sharing on the web) and Instant messaging (ICQ)
- Deploy frequently to get end user feedback early up
- Plan and carry out regular on-site workshops
- A good chance to attract any process centric attention to the very early stage in shipbuilding business
- The first try to describe this business as a process template - during the development, user group kept modifying the template to find a better way

to do and still there is a good basis this business template can be improved.

- Document management is integrated with the process.
- System design with active user group - all functional design parts participated in designing and refining the process and system. It is important to establish end user buy in.
- Brought a mind shift from individual ownership of data and knowledge to a common information asset and sharing of knowledge.

7.2 Pitfalls

- There are cultural differences between Europe and Asia in what is perceived as good user experience and graphical expression.
- People have a tendency to perceive a workflow system as monitoring of their work which reduces each individual's empowerment. This need to be addressed from the start of the project through end-user involvement.
- Be careful to include exception handling as part of the system, especially for knowledge intensive processes like the Marketing Design process. The process will be far to complex to carry out if all possible exceptions should be modelled explicitly into the process.
- There are many commercial workflow packages and systems available in the market. The main reason for selecting Brix Foundation was the strong process centric support. The system is weaker on more traditional workflow support (document handling and routing) which had to be developed more from scratch. It could be an alternative to adopt an out-of-the-box workflow system and customize this to the business domain for part of the functionality.

TECHNOLOGY

DNV's experience from implementing digital business process support internally and for external clients has lead to the development of a process centric framework - Brix™ Foundation. The overall aim of the framework is to provide solutions that enable an organization to capture and spread its knowledge effectively, see Figure 9.

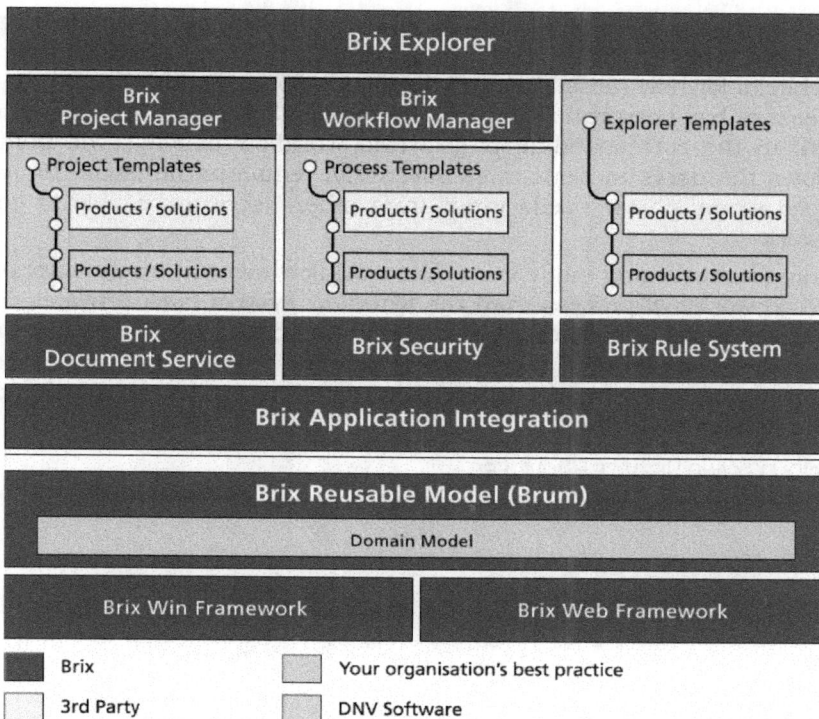

Figure 9: Brix Foundation

Brix Explorer is the application that hosts the organizations engineering portal; providing access to business processes, project management tools, business rules, and engineering tools. It can provide personalized views for different users or user groups.

Brix Workflow Manager is a full-scale workflow system allowing an organization to define business processes as templates. The templates contain information regarding activities or tasks, information flow, application integration, user roles, and security aspects. Process templates are used to create detailed activity schedules.

Each time the user wants to run a business process, a workflow is created based on its template. The system monitors and manages the running processes and updates project plans.

Brix Rule System is a full-scale rule system enabling knowledge such as business rules and design standards to be easily understood by engineers and designers.

Messaging Service

The messaging module allows the users of the system to send simple notifications (messages) to other users. The recipients of a message are workflow roles (not specified users). The message history is thus kept even if a workflow role is reassigned. For example, if the project leader role for some reason needs to be reassigned to another user in the middle of a project, the new project leader will have access to all messages sent to the project leader for the total duration of the project. A message is also linked to a workflow activity, allowing the recipients of a message to go directly to the relevant workflow activity when receiving a message.

To fully make use of the potential in the messaging module, a notification agent was developed which runs on each client computer. The notification agent periodically checks for new messages, and displays a popup notification to the user if a new message has been received. From the notification agent, the user is given a direct link to the corresponding project and workflow activity. The notification agent allows the users to work more effectively, reducing the delay that may be experienced when a user needs input from other users to be able to continue his/her work.

By including a messaging module into the workflow system, we get support for a more ad-hoc workflow process than the workflow system itself provides. The users may assign parts of the work to be done in an activity to other users, on a per project basis. In addition, the messaging module's notification agent provides support for a more efficient ad-hoc workflow, enabling instant notification of work that needs to be done.

THE TECHNOLOGY AND SERVICE PROVIDERS
- DNV Software. http://www.dnv.com/software/

Ministry of Labor, Republic of Korea

Finalist, Pacific Rim
Nominated by HandySoft Global Corporation, USA

1. EXECUTIVE SUMMARY / ABSTRACT

In the spring of 2005, following three years of government-mandated innovation in knowledge-based administration techniques, the Korean Ministry of Labor faced the daunting task of redefining their knowledge management methodology while substantiating and improving business processes. Exploratory efforts to determine strategic goals, core values, core guidelines, and a methodology for on-the-job knowledge integration revealed an ardent need within the Ministry for implementation of an automated process management solution. Upon review of available solutions, the Ministry of Labor chose HandySoft's *Handy BPM* (known as BizFlow in the U.S.) and *Handy PAL* (Process Asset Library), which were utilized in successfully structuring a **Process-based Knowledge Management System** (PKMS) for the Ministry between 2005 and 2007.

The fully operational Korean Ministry of Labor PKMS now enforces transparency and responsibilities for administrative action, improves the way in which employees work and share knowledge, enhances on-the-job safety, integrates processes across the Ministry, annually saves millions of dollars in operating costs, and — as the world's first PKMS model introduced for administrative work — has even facilitated government-wide innovation.

2. OVERVIEW

In June 1996, the Korean government initiated a *Master Plan for Information Promotion*. One of the plan's primary objectives was to create a small yet efficient electronic government. Since then, the Korean government has continued to introduce and promote knowledge-based administration techniques with the aim of implementing an electronic government and bolstering national competitiveness.

Accordingly, the Korean Ministry of Labor was tasked in 2002 with laying the foundation of a world-class knowledge-based work system for managing, sharing and using key knowledge relating to labor administration affairs. The resulting home-grown systems were designated the **Knowledge Management Center** (KMC) and the **Government Knowledge Management Center** (GKMC), both of which were designed to link up and share knowledge with various administrative agencies.

However, the Ministry's KMC project wholly failed to provide the core information necessary to facilitate day-to-day work. Also, the standardization and optimization of business processes was not properly implemented, which led to reduced work efficiency. Analysis of the first three years of operation indicated that knowledge-based management across the Ministry was still not functional, and that there was a dire need to link business processes with knowledge management systems.

In light of these findings, the Ministry determined that automated business processes were needed to identify and remove inefficient work, to improve the speed of process-oriented work, to ensure consistency in work, and to optimize processes overall. After considering a number of relevant solutions, the Ministry selected **Business Process Management** (BPM) solutions from HandySoft: *Handy BPM* (known as BizFlow in the U.S.) as the BPM-based process management solution and *Handy PAL* (Process Asset Library), designed to standardize and continually improve company-wide processes.

From the introduction of these BPM solutions in 2005, the Ministry created a pilot **Process-based Knowledge Management System** (PKMS) as well as a second-phase PKMS within the same year. With this new system, the Ministry defined 34 different business processes in the fields of industrial safety & health and labor supervision standards. They also registered and enabled the use of 12,000 pieces of job knowledge in 2005 alone, including job-related application cases, learning materials, and work manuals.

The Ministry's PKMS, brought completely online in February 2006, is designed to establish business processes, to create knowledge boxes by task in each processing stage, and to link together processed knowledge. Additionally, the PKMS is designed to help search and use necessary knowledge during process run-time and automatically stores knowledge created in the course of work execution. The PKMS is also designed to link knowledge to associated processes, enabling the sharing of relevant user-experience and job knowledge in a one-stop, just-in-time, context-specific environment. Monitoring of the PKMS improves run-time efficiencies and provides a method by which the Ministry can conduct fair evaluation to reward staff efforts based on measurable performance.

In monetary terms alone, PKMS is saving the Ministry of Labor over $16 million annually in operations and salary costs.

The goal of the Ministry's PKMS is to structure the real-time enterprise (RTE) system to allow all members of the organization to share information and knowledge in a concerted effort to attain proactive service administration. The Ministry structured its PKMS to link work and knowledge to provide an integration service for the entire process of planning, executing, and improving all work both within the Ministry of Labor and across the Korean government.

3. BUSINESS CONTEXT

Before the Korean government's *Master Plan for Information Promotion* and the advent of the PKMS, employees of the Ministry of Labor acquired job knowledge through a variety of circulars, job manuals, and laws and ordinances, preventing speedy and concise knowledge capture. A lack of a systematic management and classification methodology for internal and external knowledge resulted in ineffective sharing and use of individual organizational knowledge and experience.

With the absence of standardized business processes, work was dependent upon individual employee experience and knowledge, limiting improvements to a process of trial and error. The need to create a common language/methodology shared by employees to improve this process was clearly evident. They also needed to implement an accountable administration system to facilitate the collaboration between headquarters and local agencies by establishing standard policy processes — from policy formulation to policy implementation — in order to improve poor accountability that resulted from the separation of the establishment and execution of policies (which explained the need for policy quality management manuals).

In addition, the information for projects was separately managed, creating difficulty in re-tasking the data. Accumulation of information by focusing on inputting action results caused difficulties in extracting the statistical data necessary for supporting policy establishment.

Overcoming these issues required the creation of a one-stop, integrated working environment to use next-generation development platforms that facilitated easy maintenance and repair, as well as simplified management of changes in redeveloping business specialization systems. Introducing a knowledge management system to ensure real-time availability of knowledge and processes, and to link knowledge and processes, was essential for improving productivity across the Ministry of Labor.

In brief, a system was urgently needed to integrate business processes (not simply workflows), knowledge and learning functions, diverse knowledge, expertise, practical techniques, and the knowledge necessary for performing jobs — as well as to manage all major business-related processes of the Ministry. The answer lay in business process automation.

4. THE KEY INNOVATIONS

Through its business-style redesign using process automation, the Ministry of Labor reshuffled its organization and assigned roles to achieve a higher degree of efficiency, eliminated unnecessary work, standardized business processes, linked together work and knowledge, and laid the foundation for *mobile* administration using tablet PCs.

4.1 Business

Applying PKMS to maximize productivity and efficiency in their processes for business innovation, the Ministry reinforced the link between its mission strategy and knowledge management systems. Not only are they able to effectively link work and knowledge, but employees are now able to identify relationships between workflows and knowledge from a customer viewpoint.

Ministry labor supervisors can now provide real-time required knowledge specific to the tasks at hand and are able to determine bottlenecks at local agencies and analyze their workloads. In this way, the Ministry has achieved transparency into work-handling and process bottlenecks and has enhanced the quality of labor administration affairs service. By efficiently providing professional knowledge suitable to relevant purposes in a timely manner, and by shortening the work handling period, the Ministry improved administrative service quality and thereby increased customer satisfaction.

One of the most significant innovations for the Ministry was the ability to confirm industrial accident cases — and even prevent industrial accidents — through the use of tablet PCs. Providing such knowledge instantly to the field is an enormous benefit to supervisors and customers alike, and allows users to immediately document incidents and quickly pull up similar incidents that occurred in the past to facilitate immediate and appropriate resolution.

In the past, for example, business owners were not made properly aware of dangerous fall hazards during roofing work on construction sites, although they were given verbal explanation. Through the use of PKMS-linked tablet PCs, supervisors can now show cases of accidents to business owners using their tablet PCs, increasing awareness of these hazards. Supervisors can also take administrative action (corrective orders, suspension of use, suspension of work, etc.) through the PCs.

4.2 Process

By applying the PKMS, the Ministry established an environment that provided an integrated service for all processes for planning, execution, and improvement of labor administration affairs.

The hierarchy of all business processes was established in accordance with the standard business classification system, assuring consistency with established processes. Processes within the Ministry were classified down to the lowest level, establishing a Ministry-wide process classification system.

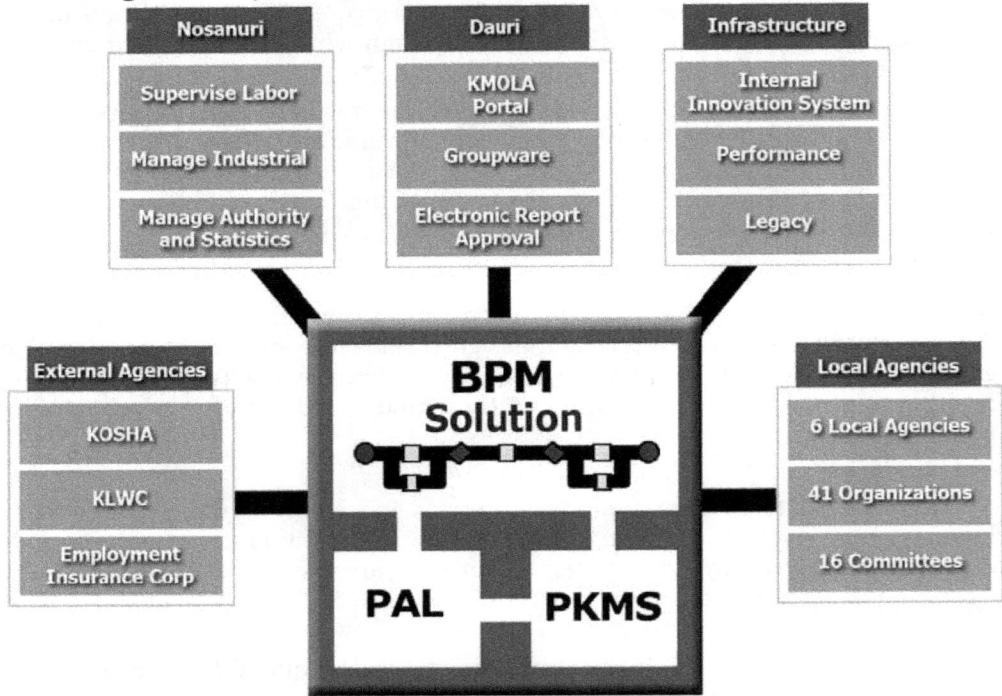

Schematic: Korean Ministry of Labor's automated PKMS solution

In order to provide necessary knowledge in a timely fashion, it is necessary to link together individual knowledge units and individual tasks to fit standardized processes. To perform such work, it is necessary to conduct prior review sessions to redesign and link together the knowledge classification system to fit processes.

Also, with regard to inefficiently managed processes within complex groupings (as revealed in PI or BPR consulting), the system manages company-wide processes according to standard procedures such as process change proposals, change approval, modeling and disclosure, and continues to improve business processes.

Other process capabilities are outlined as follows:

- Links processes between Ministry headquarters and remote agencies through work screens
- Analyzes rate of knowledge use provided by PKMS
- Measures task bottlenecks by process by local agencies and analyzes workload
- Traces diverse processes and history management through BPM progress management tool and manager's user interface

- Uses process management tool to search processes by keywords, and identify progress and history, enabling online audit
- Uses BPM change function to enable dynamic process changes on-the-fly

4.4 Organization

The old, unsystematic practice of transferring know-how and job knowledge from one employee to another was markedly improved by standardizing business processes, capturing knowledge required for performing jobs, and developing job learning units using job profiling methodologies. This permits newly hired or transferred employees to acclimate to their new job and conduct work more easily.

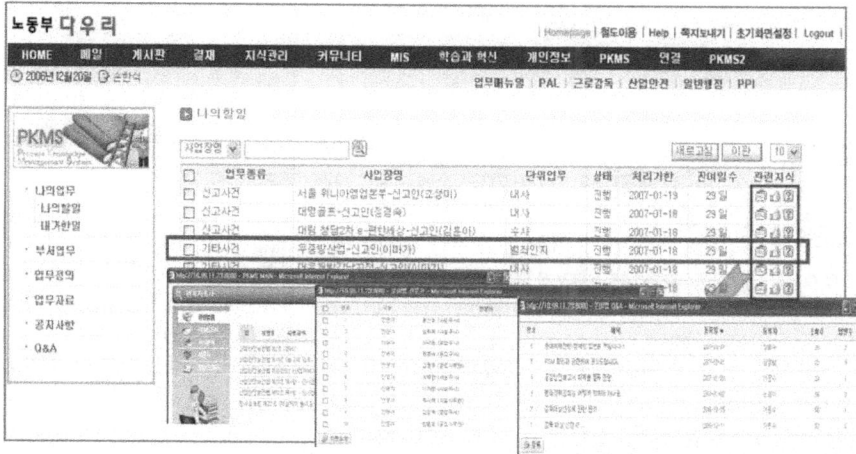

PKMS Menu "My Work To Do"

Under the previous system environment, users found it necessary to move to individual systems to conduct work. Under the BPM system, users can search and conduct work simultaneously, maximizing work efficiency.

Users under the previous system, after logging in, had to click on their own work menu through several steps or to return to the main screen in order to refer to other work, repeating the same process from the beginning. Under the current system, users can log on to the Dauri system (the Ministry of Labor's integrated work portal system) linked to the PKMS system, which shows a list of today's work as well as actions to be taken in advance of each process stage.

Compared with the existing offline work processing methods of accessing individual systems, the current PKMS system enables streamlined processing. While the previous system required users to access it, the current system automatically and proactively shows information, boosting the convenience and simplification of use. Above all, the current system allows users to see processes interconnected between departments at a glance, preventing work delay and enabling quick action.

Employees at the Ministry now access the intranet system, Dauri, using their IDs and passwords to conduct work. Through the To-Do list of the portal screen, they search the status of their jobs which are tasked to them or in which they are participating, as well as monitor the progress of their jobs.

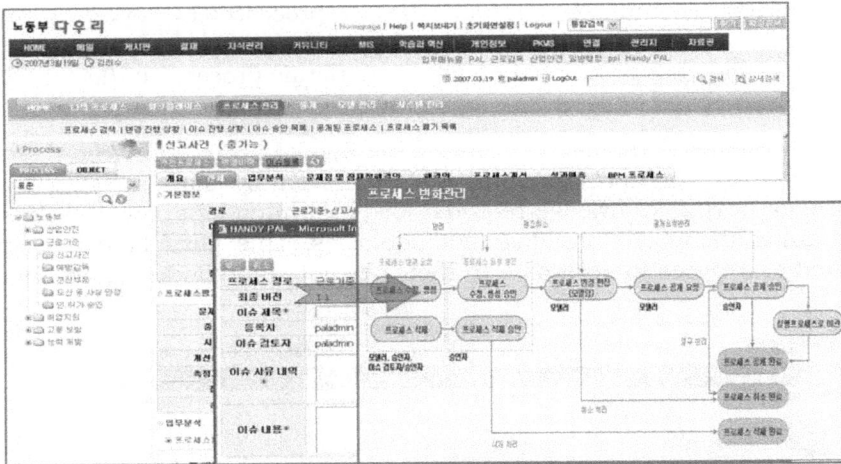

Managing Company-wide Process Change

5. HURDLES OVERCOME

From the outset of the Ministry's PKMS project in 2005, management was acutely aware of a number of obstacles to rapid and efficient implementation — the most daunting of which were exclusively human obstacles. This drove management in their efforts to educate and encourage Ministry employees in PKMS participation.

5.2 Management

Early on, it became apparent that the PKMS project was lacking in vision and goals, and that launching it would require a new mindset on the part of both Ministry employees and management. In an effort to reshape the prevailing mindset, top managers took the initiative to begin educating employees and to publicizing the vision and goals for the project.

Ministry employees were more than apprehensive about the new system; they were afraid of change and weren't confident about the effects of BPM on a public agency. Managers responded by monitoring employee concerns, reinforcing project publicity, and stepping up employee education. The Vice Minister himself led the publicity campaign, making BPM a regular topic of discussion in meetings with high-ranking Korean officials.

A particularly confounding hurdle was the lack of BPM experts within the Ministry of Labor. Education by BPM developers was offered to boost employees' understanding and confidence, a PKMS support group was organized, and one-on-one communications were conducted between specialists from BPM development companies and Ministry employees.

Even as employees were coming to accept the prospect of the PKMS, the change in work procedures and knowledge caused some confusion and difficulty in following amended laws. Selecting likely targets for BPM enhancement within the Ministry also proved difficult for managers.

In response to these additional hurdles, the Ministry managed changes to information and interpretation of the Ministry-enacted and amended laws.

Another important solution was linking the Ministry's law information system and the PKMS, enabling the search of details of laws to meet individual task requirements.

Finally, Ministry management developed a methodology suitable for a public agency to select BPM targets.

5.3 Business

Aside from the human obstacles to PKMS implementation, the Ministry considered a number of challenges to improve PKMS in the areas of labor supervision, industrial safety and health (as structured in phases one and two of the project), as well as to improve other processes to which the system could be applied in creating a process-based work environment. However, surmounting such business process-related hurdles was precisely the task for which the Ministry's BPM solution was selected.

The tasks for coping with these challenges included:

- Linking to other systems (such as digital budget and accounting systems)
- Standardizing diverse laws and their relations
- Providing the history of enactment and amendment of laws for referral in process work
- Structuring a system to optimize the management of change.

Still other business hurdles called for:

- Structuring an organization-wide PKMS
- Establishing an efficient system to cooperate with PKMS operation groups, relevant departments, committees, branch agencies, etc
- Standardizing knowledge types and classification system by work
- Providing knowledge optimized to the standardized classification system.

Establishing standards for the Ministry's work-knowledge linkage system and complying with the established linkage standards to maintain consistency of relevant information represented yet another hurdle for the PKMS implementation project. Minimizing work processes, reinforcing search functions, and achieving integrated monitoring of work were also hurdles.

5.4 Organization Adoption

Lastly, the Ministry faced some obstacles in the adoption of the PKMS by the organization itself on a more technical than human level. Such hurdles were not unexpected and were/are addressed in the following manner:

- Standardized core process and support process to redesign knowledge
- Performed work in a single-view linking processes of the headquarters and local agencies
- Creating measures to activate the use of tablet PCs provided for field work
- Determined bottlenecks of tasks by local agency and process, and analyzed workload
- Analyzed the rate at which PKMS-provided knowledge is used
- Designed an optimized To-Be model process to approve process changes
- Changed meta information according to change in PKMS work knowledge
- Applied process changes to actual processes
- Tightened interface with existing systems
- Provided user-friendly interface to encourage the use of the system
- Monitored work progress between headquarters and local agencies
- Monitored process progress history to continue to improve processes
- Increased user ability to manage processes
- Fostered Process Innovation (PI) team within the Ministry
- Continued to learn the process change management system
- Continued to advance connection to future systems

6. BENEFITS

While many of the long-term benefits of the Ministry's PKMS implementation from 2005 through 2007 are yet to be realized both within the Ministry itself and across the Korean government, significant benefits were apparent from the early days of deployment. By the end of 2006, for example, the Ministry had listed 28,000 pieces of knowledge while operating in 500 communities, as well as reporting 10,000 cases through their hotline, thereby laying a solid foundation for sharing knowledge.

During the same time frame, the Ministry established a strategy for furthering development of the PKMS with plans to utilize the system as a government-wide model of innovation. This project earned the Ministry of Labor the *Prime Minister Prize for Superior Knowledge-based Operations*, organized by the Korean Ministry of Government Administration and Home Affairs.

6.1 Cost Savings

In the areas of industrial safety & health and labor supervision, the Ministry recently confirmed cost savings attributable to business process innovations between 2005 and 2007:

- Total personnel costs were cut by 5.7 billion *won* (6.75 million USD) annually
- Guidance and supervision was improved, yielding cost reductions of approximately 3.5 billion *won* (3.7 million USD) annually
- A reduction of supervisory work due to increased efficiency provided salary savings of 3.5 billion *won* (3.7 million USD) annually
- And the area of labor standards saw annual cost cuts of 2.2 billion *won* (2.34 million USD)

6.2 Time Reductions

The areas of industrial safety, health, and labor supervision confirmed the following:

- Processing time of an average safety and health case was reduced from 29.8 days to 20.8 days, a reduction of 9 days
- Processing time of an average safety and health case decreased from 30 days (2005) to 26 days (2006)
- Between 2006 and 2007, the Ministry's processing time of average inspection and supervision case decreased by 20.8% from 49.7 days to 41.4 days
- Required time for educating newly-hired or transferred employees was reduced from 1 year to 6 months

6.3 Productivity Improvements

Due to more efficient automated processes, the Ministry's total supervisory manpower was reduced by 33% in 2007, while the average number of safety and health cases handled per worker increased by 1.4% and the average number of inspection and supervision cases handled per worker increased by 5.9%.

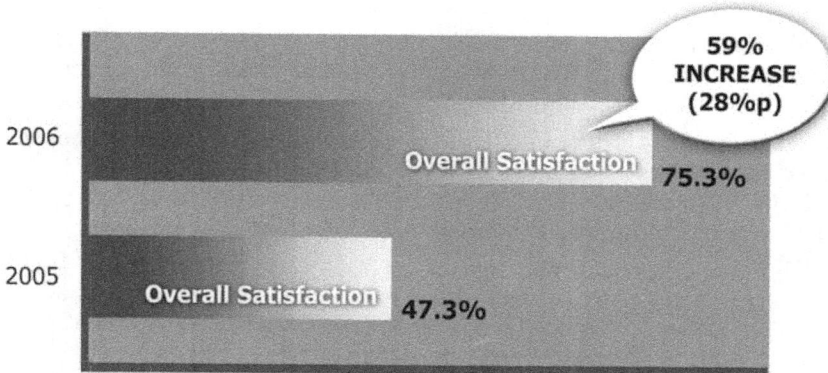

With these productivity improvements, customer satisfaction following the introduction of PKMS-linked tablet PCs and field work improvement increased to 59% from 47.3% in 2005 and to 75.3% in 2006. Internal customers' satisfaction also improved, discouraging talented employees from quitting their jobs, leading to an enhanced profile of the Ministry (these effects are difficult to quantify).

Qualitative effects achieved by the introduction of PKMS:
- Shared specialized expertise, and increased newly hired employees' understanding of their jobs
- Accumulated knowledge assets minimize job vacancy during the transfer of employees involved
- Increased the efficiency of administrative work through innovative business processes for headquarters and local agencies
- Standardized work handling procedures and processes, systemizing the handling of work
- Achieved the transparency of work execution through monitoring
- Provided an integrated service of knowledge assets, and converted knowledge into assets, improving the organization's competitiveness
- Through the integrated law information system, and a customized knowledge management by process, provided value-added administrative knowledge service
- Enhanced the quality of labor administration affairs service
- Efficiently provided professional knowledge suitable to relevant purposes and shortened the work handling period, enhancing administrative service quality
- Accumulated labor administration affairs-related knowledge, linked it to work, provided high quality administrative service, and fostered field administration experts

7. BEST PRACTICES, LEARNING POINTS AND PITFALLS

7.1 Best Practices and Learning Points

In order to overcome employee resistance to the innovative PKMS program early on, the knowledge-based administration called for strong commitment and leadership from the top management. Sessions reported the progress of the PKMS project to the Vice Minister of Labor. CKO sessions were held twice in 2005, 5 times in 2006, and 3 more times until August of 2007, with the attendance of directors general, headquarters head, team leaders, and higher-level officials.

This provided a strong driving force to the Ministry's innovation through knowledge-based administration. Meanwhile, frontline employees participated in the reclassification of knowledge fitting into business processes and structuring of the system which substantiated innovation.

In 2005, when problems through BPR were determined, 20 frontline employees participated in 4 workshops devoted to the establishment of the PKMS model. In 2006 and 2007, 2 exclusive working groups made up of 4 and 7 people, respectively, were formed to analyze businesses, conduct process modeling, and redesign knowledge.

Ministry of Labor employees participating in PKMS workshops

A PKMS support group made up of 20 to 40 people also joined in the project. Compared with the usual system structuring projects led by the administration publicity team or the innovation team, the PKMS project attempted to reflect frontline requirements more accurately in order to structure user-friendly systems and reflect such demands inherent in the policy.

Diverse measures were reviewed and led to the standardization of business processes and the development of job learning units by means of a work profiling methodology designed to determine job knowledge and analyze job requirements. With the help of HR-related outside experts, workshops were held to develop the Ministry's learning units; and, job-duty-tasks were determined with job learning units designed by classifying them into basic knowledge, laws and regulations, practical skills, and analysis of cases required for tasks.

Thus, field employees could confirm what knowledge is required for individual tasks, capture knowledge required of them, and automatically or additionally register knowledge produced in the course of performing jobs. Employees could acquire knowledge required for performing work through education by linking to the education system, thus enhancing work performance.

Employees' diverse external activity achievements were recognized as their learning hours, linking to their evaluation knowledge produced in the course of education through the Learning System which was systematically accumulated and linked together, making it practical.

PKMS operation group members were concerned whether they could effectively transfer their accumulated job expertise to customers in the labor administration and their subordinates while striving to establish PKMS firmly in 2005 and 2006. Members continued their efforts to quickly apply the PKMS to work, to clear system hurdles through corporation between relevant employees and the system development team, to establish logics, to research and coordinate work between co-working departments and support departments, and to develop technology.

These efforts reshaped the driving force to implement the system in a way that it would link work, knowledge and learning. They can now conduct real-time knowledge change management following the enactment and amendment of relevant law. Also, participants in the project endeavored to practice the new work process instead of the existing method, to change employees' mindset on knowledge based administration, and to play a creative role in pursuing the project.

7.2 Pitfalls

In February 2006, the phase-one pilot PKMS was applied to the industrial safety category with full force. Collecting and providing knowledge alone initially was thought to improve the efficiency of work; however, the system failed to provide expected effects. In an effort to drastically improve the way in which veteran expertise and work capabilities were transferred in the form of tacit knowledge, experienced worker input into the system had been unsystematic.

For frontline labor supervisors who were familiar with the existing Ministry system, the PKMS change itself was regarded as added workload, and they voiced complaints at the beginning of the project. Although they, in principle, agreed on innovation, they resisted the introduction of a new system.

8. COMPETITIVE ADVANTAGES

The competitive advantages gained by the Ministry through the PKMS system included, among many other things, the fact that the world's first PKMS model was introduced to administrative work. This improved the way employees work and the way support for service is provided, facilitated government innovation and enhanced its perception among the public. The innovated labor administration reinforced transparency of and responsibilities for administrative action.

The Ministry perfectly linked together its high-tech PKMS, Dauri (the Ministry of Labor's integrated work portal system), Nosanuri (a system to handle industrial safety and health, and labor standards-related work), Work-net, HRD, and employment insurance system, thereby producing the following competitive advantages:

- Reinforced the transparency of and responsibilities for labor administration
- Won *Premier Prize in the Knowledge-based Superior Agency Evaluation* conducted by the Ministry of Government Administration and Home Affairs (MOGAHA) in November 2006
- Won the *Home Minister Prize* in the category of administration productivity in the 3rd *Government Innovation Superior Practice Competition* organized by the MOGAHA in October 2007, leading the PKMS to be developed as the government-wide innovation model
- Embodied a leading model of knowledge systems which are internal and external customer-oriented in knowledge-based administration
- Structured a positive circulation management system between business processes and entities of managing knowledge, structuring a con-

stant-based system to monitor and manage a change in core knowledge (monitoring of the process of the enactment and amendment of laws)

- Substantiated the integration of labor knowledge-based administration activity in terms of the organization, work, and knowledge, structuring infrastructures to maximize work performance as a positive work innovation circulation system and to support policy decision making.

The Ministry is committed to furthering the application of the PKMS system with a view toward reinforcing the sustainable innovation of labor administration, and internal and external competitiveness.

Immediate plans are as follows:
- In 2008, apply PKMS to labor insurance, occupational capabilities, and equal employment
- Structure work management systems in such areas as policy quality management, task management, document management, and instruction management
- Consulting for converting processes into assets (PAL methodology)
- Create databases of standard work manuals in line with work classification, and structure a system to manage a change in processes
- Link with BPM to structure a process execution model
- Link PAL process indicators with the measurement of processes, and structure BPM-based performance measurement indicators
- Continue to further the structuring of business processes disconnected between key systems through BPM
- Continue to monitor processes to improve processes and reflect the results
- Form and operate groups of experts in core fields, activating a culture of sharing and cooperative work
- Promote the culture of managing and sharing processes through performance evaluation
- Positively conduct activities to establish organizational culture through education and consensus meetings
- Define processes as a core asset of the organization and refine them to be collected, managed, and shared, and form operating specialist teams to that end.

Long-term plans are as follows:
- Link up strategic goals and Critical Success Factor (CSF)-based key performance indicators with processes to continue to analyze process performances
- Analyze process performances and accumulate and use customer-oriented indicators of customer service, quality, cycle time, and costs, laying the groundwork for conducting a fair evaluation of each department and employees
- Define necessary knowledge by process, identify knowledge location, provide information right where it is needed just in time, and accumulate process performance results and turn them into useful knowledge
- Redevelop common administration work systems and link them to work specialization systems
- Manage work relating to policy affairs between the headquarters and local agencies
- Structure electronic conference system

- Secure process agility for laying grounds for RTE (Real Time Enterprise).

The Ministry will apply the PKMS system to all its business processes, substantiating processes and converting them into assets, and will eventually link up processes and performance management indicators. This will speed up a structural change into a process-oriented organization with goals and visions, and create a framework to efficiently measure process performances fairly.

9. TECHNOLOGY

Through the use of *BPM*, technological innovation was achieved by integrating and linking together dispersed knowledge resources centering on processes, and through *HandySoft's PAL*, standardizing the organization-wide processes and continuing to secure infrastructure for improving processes.

By applying the PKMS, the Ministry established an environment that provided an integrated service for all processes for planning, execution, and improvement of labor administration affairs.

Diverse work support systems, which were introduced and used for individual purposes, were perfectly integrated centering on BPM; thus, an environment was established to facilitate a more flexible system infrastructure and to provide integrated knowledge immediately at the point of job execution.

In addition, diverse systems devoted to individual purposes such as Nosanuri, Dauri, and Web services were reconfigured centering on BPM.

A key aspect of the system is that it has the capability to provide an integrated work environment for users who in the past accessed individual systems independently to process work. Also, the structure was established to quickly apply relevant applications to permanently change processes, ensuring maximum flexibility in system changes.

Business process and application logic was separated to simplify the development of necessary applications, enhancing development productivity and facilitating ease of maintenance and repair. Application logic was simplified and its components were made available.

A portal site that provides a single path to knowledge and information created internally and externally allows team members to work together online. An environment was provided to freely create custom interfaces allows the Ministry to tailor the working environment to individual users. Also, multiple applications necessary for processing work were provided consistently in a single view with an integrated work environment, including the ability to attach files and exchange comments. This, in effect, enables user-customized work portal sites.

Based on the results of a Process Innovation (PI) or Business Process Re-engineering (BPR) review session, HandySoft's PAL was used as a verification tool, and business processes were standardized and converted into organizational assets. Process change management systems were established and work knowledge was shared, creating an environment for continuing business process innovation.

On the strength of the established modeling guidelines for process logic flows and characteristics, support was thus provided for modeling. Additionally, roles and responsibilities centering on processes were defined, and performance indicators, relevant documents, and information were mapped, enabling the identification, use, and analysis of processes from each user's viewpoint.

10. THE TECHNOLOGY AND SERVICE PROVIDERS

HandySoft is the leading global provider of Dynamic Process Management solutions, and the first company in the BPM industry to seamlessly integrate and automate both ad hoc tasks and structured processes to drive visibility, control and productivity across *all* work within an organization.

For more information, visit www.HandySoft.com

Mallesons Stephen Jaques, Australia

Silver Award, Pacific Rim
Nominated by Metastorm, USA

EXECUTIVE SUMMARY / ABSTRACT

Mallesons Stephen Jaques made a strategic business decision to embed BPM into its core technology infrastructure upon which it could develop 'circuit breaker' applications that reduced or removed non-productive and non-billable process overhead from the business.

Mallesons' BPM initiative, known internally as Pulse, is an agent of change. Successfully modifying work culture and practice is rated more highly, and considered of more enduring value to the business, than the efficacy of the BPM tools used to enable this change.

Since 2004 Pulse has delivered demonstrable financial benefits, savings in time, fostered transparency, removed regional differences, improved service quality and delivery, eliminated re-work and duplication, provided consistency, accuracy, and repeatability of processes, assisted enforcement of firm policies and improved managerial oversight and decision making.

OVERVIEW

An exhaustive review over several months culminated in the submission of a detailed BPM business plan to Executive Management. The plan was adopted to become a cornerstone of Mallesons' change management program. The objectives of the business plan were clear:

- To rationalize and automate non-productive and non-billable processes that add no value to the business and its clients.
- Capture for productive and billable purposes time freed by the application of BPM.
- Remove overhead from functions of the business.
- Improve the quality of service of internal business units.
- Impact positively on the firm's profit margin.
- Support the strategic goals of the business, for example, by removing center and regional differences from processes.

As per the plan, the initial focus was to re-engineer high value 'back-end' administrative functions of which over 200 had been documented and ranked in value according to a number of business criteria. This tactical direction for development was designed to achieve a number of 'quick wins', to ramp-up internal development expertise and to steadily build a solid base of support for BPM based change.

Once the confidence of the business was earned the focus increasingly shifted towards the more demanding and sensitive processes that involve legal practice and client interaction.

BUSINESS CONTEXT

Mallesons is Australia's most successful commercial law firm focused on advising major corporations and financial institutions in Australia and Asia. Mallesons is resourced by approximately 2,100 employees, including over 1,200 legal staff.

To be successful in a highly competitive market, Mallesons needs to be constantly improving, changing and innovating and to always be mindful of the financial drivers that influence profitability.

To this end, Mallesons invests significantly and continuously in technology to extract strategic, financial, competitive and productivity dividends for the business and its clients.

Mallesons was the first major law firm in Australia to institutionalize BPM into its core infrastructure. This provided a launch pad for a rolling change management program focused on taking cost out of the business and redirecting time to more productive or billable pursuits that directly impacted margin, one of the four key profit drivers in a law firm.

THE KEY INNOVATIONS

Innovation is a natural byproduct of solving the technical and business challenges that an 'out-of-the-box' BPM solution is unable to address directly.

For Mallesons, customized development delivered richer more directed outcomes for the user community and the business, provided a range of complementary tools and allowed the exploitation of value-add integration options enabled in the BPM platform.

The sum effect of aggressively pursuing a program of innovative customization that leveraged the underlying BPM platform was increased user satisfaction, a much smaller training footprint and less demand for support.

4.2 Business

Each evening, for example, a Pulse digest email is sent out. This email aggregates outstanding To Do list items and highlights any unacknowledged alerts and notifications. The items are grouped in order of importance, with client related activities highlighted as a top priority. For many items that appear in the digest there is a 'one-click' approve or acknowledge button **(Appendix B)**.

The digest was designed to support a commonly held work practice of many staff which was to review and action 'administrative' tasks within a 'block' of time usually at or near the end of a working day.

Separate email alerts or a taskbar alert were regarded as intrusive and irritating. The digest was instrumental in accelerating the uptake of and engagement with BPM enabled processes.

For staff, particularly process administrators, who prefer or need to monitor and action tasks throughout the day there is ubiquitous access via the intranet to constantly updated To Do and Watch lists **(Appendix A)**.

4.3 Process

Pulse is a long-term program to entrench BPM into the foundation of Mallesons. The two person development team has an aggressive target of one new or upgraded process in production each month. Over 40 processes have been deployed **(Appendix E)**.

The high level of customization has the developers spending up to 50% of their time doing web development and application and database integration work. Key

BPM tools used are the forms designer, business rule mapper, APIs and the underlying 'engine' and database functions which bind the workflow solutions together.

Performance indicators and evaluation criteria are in place to measure system reliability and user participation. This was done by tracking user support and issue management systems, and by monitoring system logs, for example capturing data on the length of time items remained in a person's To Do list.

4.4 Organization

Eighteen months into the Pulse project a program was put in place to gather feedback and measure the results being experienced by users. This exercise included 13 focus groups involving over 70 partners and staff in different centers.

Pleasingly the feedback was generally positive with average ratings of 7-8 out of 10. The principle user and organizational benefits recorded were:

- A greater appreciation and insight of a process from end-to-end.
- Roles and functions were more clearly defined.
- Firm-wide processes helped to break down center and regional differences.
- Less time being spent on mundane and tedious administration and consequently additional time to spend on more productive work.
- Time was saved and data quality improved by increased "self-service".
- Integration of processes with core applications and data repositories greatly improved the quality of data and reporting.

HURDLES OVERCOME

Pulse introduced fresh, but exciting, technical and design challenges for Mallesons' developers and infrastructure specialists and it raised new business, procedural and people issues as the implementation of BPM applications set about changing work practices.

Any possible threats arising from these challenges were met and contained by adopting a project management methodology that is highly transparent and communicative, promotes consultation and participation, focuses on business outcomes and involves personal responsibility and accountability.

5.1 Management

A senior executive or partner was appointed 'sponsor' to each BPM project to provide the necessary gravitas, authority and credibility to the project. Most importantly, the sponsor championed a project throughout the business.

5.2 Business

A business case was drafted for each proposed BPM application to provide a commercial reality check on key business deliverables.

A business case also subordinated technology to business objectives, ensured high level engagement, tightly integrated communications and training into projects and demanded intensive analysis, benchmarking and modeling of quantifiable benefits.

5.3 Organization Adoption

A 'process owner' was appointed from a business unit or practice team as the knowledgeable 'go-to-person'. The process owner worked closely with the BPM developers and other specialists, such as Trainers, in pre and post deployment phases.

Managing the expectations of participants and accentuating the positives from change were also key factors in winning the business to BPM driven change. Removing laborious, repetitive and tedious paper-based or quasi-automated systems that suffered from high error and rework rates was ultimately viewed as liberating by many staff as their roles changed to be filled by more interesting and rewarding work.

BENEFITS

An effective way to measure financial benefits and to 'sell' process change to the business was to calculate and attach a dollar savings to a transaction. Reducing the financial benefit to the lowest denominator for individual processes conveyed a simple but powerful message to staff, for example, "$6 is saved each time you submit an automated leave request form" (**Appendix F**).

Major benefits identified from formal feedback mechanisms included:

- Greater transparency and improved process cycle times.
- Better governance and quality of decision making.
- Improved levels of service and quality of data and reporting.
- Removal of cost, time and waste from processes.
- Standardization of processes for 2,000 plus staff across nine offices.

6.1 Cost Savings

Costs savings have been identified in a variety of business activities as a consequence of BPM, for example:

- An analysis of the cost and time savings from automating the leave process alone showed a AUD$615k positive 5 year Net Present Value (NPV).
- It took just 1 year to recoup the 3 year amortized cost of the BPM solution.
- Ongoing consumerable savings, for example, AUD$20,000 p.a. is being saved by removing paper from the leave process alone.
- Data collected on meeting room usage has helped to better plan and reduce the cost of an expensive refit of conference room facilities in the Sydney office.

6.2 Time Reductions

Illustrative examples include:

- Reducing from 5 days to less than 1 day the time taken to publish articles to Mallesons' website or to distribute articles by email to clients.
- Reducing lapsed time in the leave process from 7 to 2 days.

6.3 Increased Revenues

To date an annualized financial benefit of over AUD$350k has been calculated.

6.4 Productivity Improvements

Illustrative examples include:

- Managers of secretarial staff spend, on average, 5 hours less per week managing staff leave and during peak leave periods, such as Easter and Christmas, this figure rises to 10 hours per week.
- 0.25 of full time equivalent (FTE) saved in removing need to file leave records.
- Equivalent of 1 FTE saved in staff managing secretarial staff due to reduction in leave administration burden.

- Equivalent of 2 FTE saved in the area of managing staff moves and office/floor 'restacks'.
- One working day per week saved for 2 staff responsible for managing the largest paralegal pools.

BEST PRACTICES, LEARNING POINTS AND PITFALLS

7.1 Best Practices and Learning Points

✓ *Time taken to research, consult, analyze before starting.*

✓ *Buy-in from the business at the most senior levels.*

✓ *Business case for each process.*

✓ *Motivated sponsors and process owners.*

✓ *Application of a structured project management methodology.*

✓ *Right mix of skills in development and project teams.*

✓ *Managing business and user expectations particularly through lucid inclusive communications.*

7.2 Pitfalls

✗ *Better identification and qualification of possible process targets to avoid time being spent on a business case only to find the outcome or value was not compelling enough to proceed.*

✗ *Due to pace of development there was the occasional failure to focus on post-production tasks such as adequately measuring benefits and ensuring savings in time were directed to more productive / billable work.*

✗ *Time spent overcoming unexpected pockets of resistance within the user community which impacted the speed at which some processes were implemented.*

✗ *Occasional poor choice of project sponsors and process owners whose failure of ownership and engagement hindered both development and deployment.*

✗ *Made an incorrect assumption that the 'out-of-the-box' user interface would be adopted by the user community. To remove a perceived barrier to participation scarce development resources were redirected towards producing a customized interface tuned to the requirements of the general user community.*

✗ *There was the occasional failure to adequately communicate with and support members of the user community.*

COMPETITIVE ADVANTAGES

To maintain competitive advantage and leadership in professional services, Mallesons continues to invest early and persistently in innovative, and award winning technology enabled business solutions. To realize a return on this investment Mallesons seeks out and attracts the best talent available to provide the requisite intellectual capital and know how.

Pulse has delivered a number of competitive advantages:

- Irrespective of office location an increasingly homogenous and seamless Mallesons approach to many processes is making it easier to service clients.
- Minimizing and removal of center and regional differences has harmonized and unified work practices across business and practice teams freeing time to be more productively spent on client activities.
- Processes integrated with Mallesons client management, messaging and web systems mean that Mallesons is frequently ahead of its competitors in getting communications, invitations and publications delivered to clients and potential clients.
- A capacity planning process assists in the timely and appropriate allocation of legal staff resources to better manage the deliver of legal services to clients.
- A fee estimates process integrated into the Mallesons' financial system tracks and alerts partners and clients when matter estimates reach or exceed an agreed threshold. This pro-active process brings visibility and discipline to fees management an often contentious area of practice and client relations.

TECHNOLOGY

Pulse development, with Metastorm BPM® at its core, is modeled on the classic 3 tiered development infrastructure which is replicated to a disaster recovery 'secondary' data center site **(Appendix G)**.

The highly customized BPM applications being developed add complexity. Experience has shown however that this is more than off-set by a positive impact on the user community and in providing more value add to the business which is not necessarily possible with 'out-of-the-box' BPM solutions.

Illustrative examples of process customizations include:
- Forms were given a Windows 'look-and-feel' incorporating Windows type functionality for navigation and actions, even the color palate is standard Windows **(Appendix C).**
- Integration of the Metastorm BPM platform with core technology infrastructure including: MS Exchange (messaging); HP Service Desk (user help system); Keystone (financial system); PeopleSoft (HR); Web environments (intra and internet); InterAction (client relationship management); DeskSite (document management); Blackberry handheld devices and the Cisco phone system **(Appendix D)**.
- Staff can, for example, book a meeting room directly from a Cisco handset.
- Training, leave and secondment processes feed data directly into people presence information shown on the intranet corporate directory **(Appendix H).**

THE TECHNOLOGY AND SERVICE PROVIDERS

Following several months of consultation, research, analytical and comparative work a business case was submitted to Executive Management for approval with Metastorm chosen as the preferred vendor. The business case was approved, and work on Pulse using the Metastorm BPM platform began.

APPENDIX A

The Pulse "homepage" on the intranet which is accessible from several points of entry across Mallesons' systems.

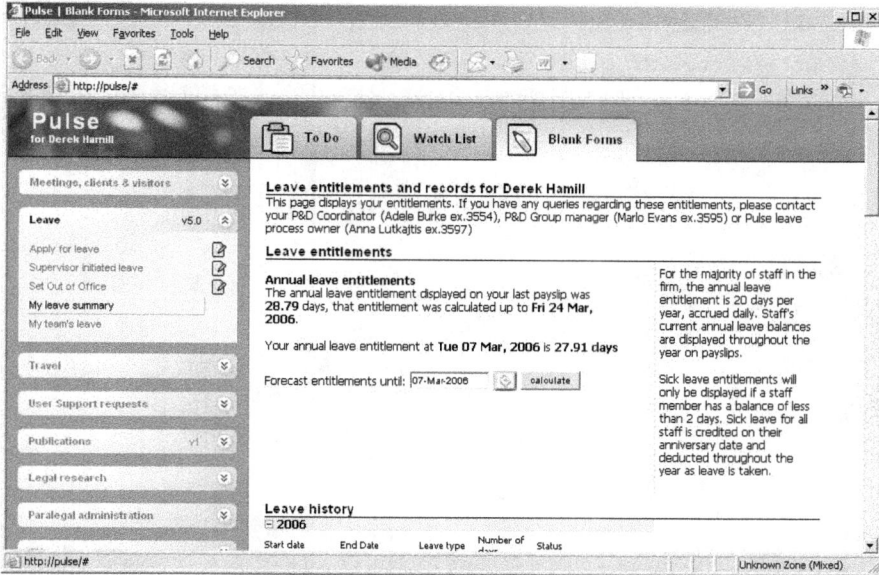

APPENDIX B

The Pulse digest email is sent out each evening. The digest aggregates all To Do list items and alerts for a user. Many items can be approved or acknowledged with 'one click'.

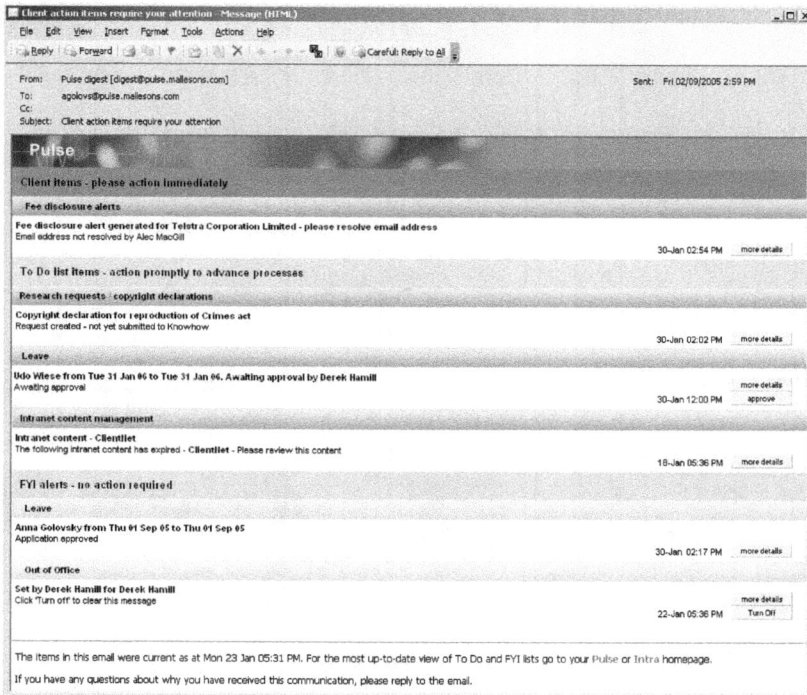

APPENDIX C

An example of the customized user interface developed to present a Windows 'look-and-feel' that incorporates Windows type functionality for navigation and actions eg use of tabs, data input fields, buttons, pop-ups and narration.

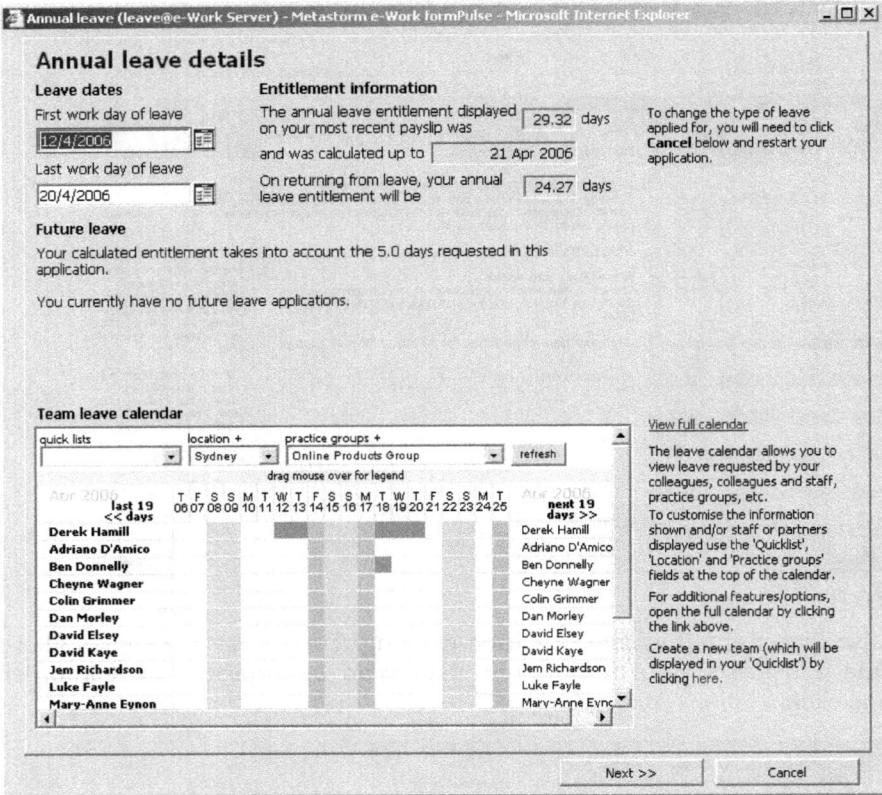

APPENDIX D

Pulse integrates with most of Mallesons' core applications and databases.

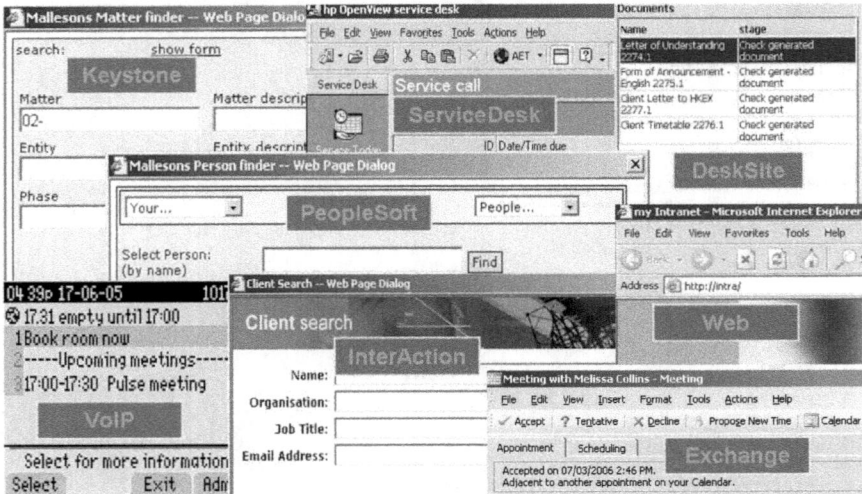

APPENDIX E

Since 2004 over forty processes have been developed and put into production.

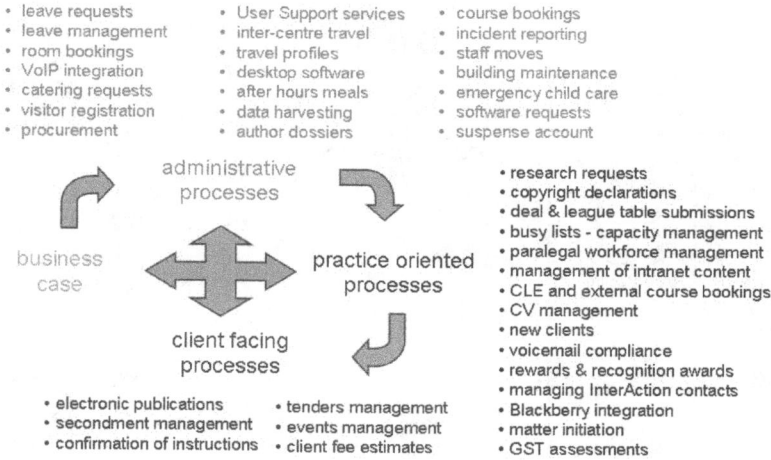

- leave requests
- leave management
- room bookings
- VoIP integration
- catering requests
- visitor registration
- procurement

- User Support services
- inter-centre travel
- travel profiles
- desktop software
- after hours meals
- data harvesting
- author dossiers

- course bookings
- incident reporting
- staff moves
- building maintenance
- emergency child care
- software requests
- suspense account

administrative processes

business case

practice oriented processes

client facing processes

- research requests
- copyright declarations
- deal & league table submissions
- busy lists - capacity management
- paralegal workforce management
- management of intranet content
- CLE and external course bookings
- CV management
- new clients
- voicemail compliance
- rewards & recognition awards
- managing InterAction contacts
- Blackberry integration
- matter initiation
- GST assessments

- electronic publications
- secondment management
- confirmation of instructions

- tenders management
- events management
- client fee estimates

APPENDIX F

Financial benefits have been realized and volume of activity increases steadily.

Annualised financial benefit of over AUD$350k

1 year to recoup the 3 year amortised cost of BPM solution

Approximately 2.8 million actions performed (by user or systematically) p.a.

Process	Volume of transactions p.a.	$ benefit per transaction
Paralegals	1,000	$72 per work request
Room bookings	79,000	$4 per booking
Leave	19,000	$6 per request
Course enrolments	24,000	$4 per enrolment
Staff moves	4,500	$22 per staff move
User Support	3,000	$6 per request
Equipment loans	3,500	$5 per request
Busy list updates	16,000	n/a
Catering requests	13,000	n/a
Intranet page reviews	2,000	n/a
Fee disclosures	3,000	n/a

APPENDIX G

Pulse infrastructure which is replicated in a secondary disaster recovery center.

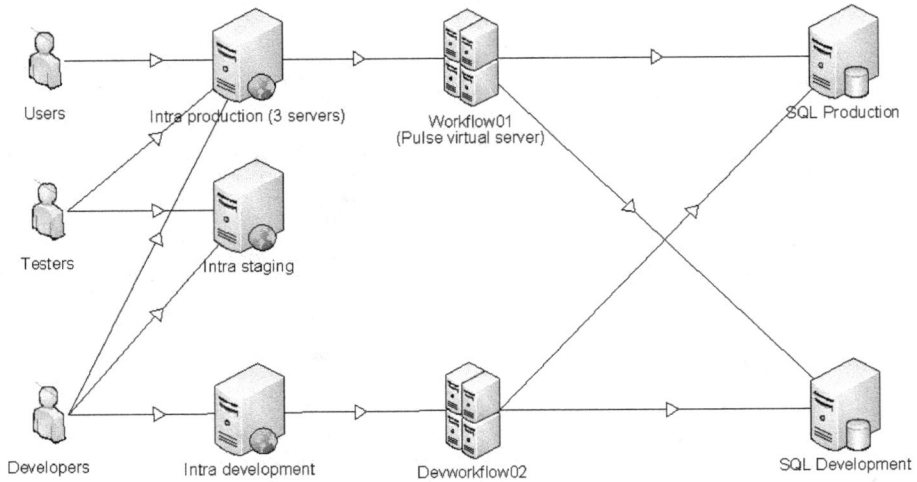

APPENDIX H

Training, leave and secondment processes feed data directly into people presence information shown on the intranet corporate directory.

Leave		Denisha Anbu
Training		Julie Anderson
Secondments		Sonia Bastida Corral
Leave of absence		Alexandra Crammond

Satyam Computer Services Limited, India

Finalist, Pacific Rim
Nominated by Satyam Computer Services Limited, India

1. EXECUTIVE SUMMARY / ABSTRACT

Satyam has operations spreading across 60 countries, and revenues growing at more than 30% annually. The growth has been possible and can be sustained only if transformational changes are made to the way business processes are managed. We conceived and implemented such a transformational initiative by way of creating an Integrated Service Virtualization platform. We have designed this as a workflow based shared services platform to automate and virtualize business processes. Thereby, we have provided "Agility" to the organization to respond to its business demands. Apart from this, from an organisational strategy viewpoint, we needed to selectively link our external stakeholders to our business processes to gain competitive advantage. In other words, we needed to incorporate these stakeholders into our workflows. Our platform which is innovative, home grown and which leverages the best practices in business process and workflow management achieved these objectives.

A Center of Excellence was created to implement the platform which has developed a proprietary framework for Integrated Service Virtualization. Using this framework, 150 business processes are being managed delivering 9 million service requests annually that range from self service to simple transactional services to complex knowledge services.

The benefit of this BPM innovation over the past few years has been manifold. On the operational front, there has been a significant impact on productivity and utilisation rates of employees. On the strategic front, as an organisation we have expanded our footprint outside organisational boundaries, through strategic outsourcing of business processes to low-cost-high-efficiency remote locations within India. We have been reaping direct benefits of several million dollars every year on a sustainable basis. We expect the benefits to grow at further in the forthcoming years. The platform has also a unique impact of helping the organization achieve its stated social responsibility objectives.

2. OVERVIEW

This project is about creating a process for Integrated Service Virtualization pertaining to various business processes of the organisation on a platform characterised by automated workflows and business rules to achieve multiple stakeholder delight. The platform tightly combines processes, technology, infrastructure, and service delivery to virtualize business processes and transact them as shared services. The key stakeholders are employees, investors, customers and the society. The services are aimed at meeting the business process requirements of these stakeholders. Since we take a "services" approach when we analyse any business process, we would use the words "services" and "processes" interchangeably through the remainder of the case study.

The stakeholders are given role-based accesses to the components of this platform and would be able to execute their business functions from anywhere in the world by accessing the platform through the Internet. Moreover, the platform has multiple layers of access assigned to stakeholders. These are called "workbenches" in our parlance and are an output of the service-oriented architecture principle of "policy-driven service availability". For example an employee, based on one's role in the organisation has access to different kinds of workbenches like employee workbench, manager workbench, administrator workbench, projects workbench, sales workbench, etc. Similarly, external vendors and service providers have access to what we call the "vendor workbench". This, in a way signifies the depth of the platform. We have built this platform in-house at the company's internal IT department "eSupport".

There is a vast array of business processes, transactional and high-end that has been covered under this platform and the main advantage we have with this is a seamless integration of business processes and services. The portability and replicable-nature of the platform has given our organisation ways to integrate external stakeholders into our business processes. We have been able to improve employee productivity and reduce cycle times. We have also integrated various activities related to our social responsibility objectives onto the virtual platform. The key breakthrough for us is the way we are able to establish the footprint of our platform across the organisational boundaries.

The main challenges in implementing this virtual platform as we would explain in later sections pertain to change management (organisational and extra-organisational adoption), dynamically changing business scenarios, and rapidly evolving technologies. Our platform has evolved since its inception, overcoming these challenges. Unique workflow engineering and an excellence in BPM practices have been the key enablers in the successful implementation of this Integrated Service Virtualisation platform. .

Through this platform, currently we have 9 million requests being served annually relating to 150 business processes.

3. BUSINESS CONTEXT

Background

The company started off with employee strength of 70 and about $ 360,000 in revenues at inception. The company has a strong vision to emerge as one of the world's most valued integrated IT services companies. As a part of this vision the company grew 25,000 times in revenues since inception. This saw a phenomenal increase in the employee base of the company to about 45,000 in the current year.

Need for Integrated Service Virtualisation platform

In this journey, as the company expanded operations to more than 60 countries, we realised a need to create an extremely agile and scalable platform that can integrate various business processes by taking due care of geographic and cultural consideration. Without such a platform, managing stakeholder priorities across various geographies, time zones and cultures would be extremely difficult and resource-intensive.

Stakeholder-oriented services have to be launched with alacrity if we are to maintain our competitive edge. These services can range from simple ones like employee travel arrangements to more complex knowledge-oriented services like market intelligence. These services should be so designed that they can be delivered virtually from anywhere in the world.

This prompted the organisation to develop a state-of-the-art BPM methodology (proprietary) and invest in workflow management to create an Integrated Service Virtualisation platform that can host a variety of services to the stakeholders.

4. THE KEY INNOVATIONS

Our key innovation is the creation of an ***Integrated Service Virtualization platform*** to cater to the needs of various stakeholders. Using stringent BPM methodologies and innovative workflows, we could define a platform that is service-oriented.

4.1 Business

The key business impact has been the way we are able to engage our service providers using our workflow based platform. The identified service providers deliver support work to our organisation from various locations across the globe. Some of the services are transactional in nature like employee travel arrangements, vendor bills processing, recruitment support, etc. Yet other services are high-end in nature like medical counselling to employees by contracted doctors, meta-tagging of documents to create Corporate-wide taxonomy etc. We used the adaptability of the virtual platform to create pertinent roles for our service providers through an institutionalised policy implementation. We reengineered our workflows innovatively to give selective access of business process transactions to our service providers. This required us to follow our stringent BPM methodology, as we had to plug-in additional components into business processes to suit such an exercise.

4.2 Process

The Integrated Service Virtualization platform supports several business processes (performance management, procurement, travel, recruitment, accounts payable etc). Each of these processes has its own virtualization requirements but what we have implemented is a common framework for all these processes.

Process of Virtualization

Before the project, a lot of business processes were carried out either manually or through decentralised applications that had very little integration with each other. Collaboration between various strategic business units was very difficult. Most of the communication with external stakeholders used to happen either through e-mail or over phone. This usually resulted in inefficiency of business processes as prioritisation of tasks was quite difficult. After the implementation of the virtual platform, interaction within business units has become more seamless and moreover, external stakeholders have also been integrated into the system through our unique workflow engineering.

The overall process architecture after virtualisation

	Business Process 1	Business Process 2	Business Process 3	Business Process 'N'
Web-based Service				
Access & Security	Availability/Authorisation/Authentication			
UI Standards	Workbenches/UI Standards/Notifications			
Workflows	'n' Stage Processing/Business Rule Engine/BAM			
Data Management	Data Access/Master Database/Data Integration			

The process architecture was originally defined to be intranet based catering to employees of the company. With the rapid growth of the organisation we expanded the scope of the architecture to include external stakeholders (vendors, service providers, etc) as well on the Integrated Service Virtualisation platform. Basically the architecture has a web-based service layer onto which component services (applications) are embedded. The workflow layer is the most critical of all and it is through a careful engineering of this layer that we were able to give role-based accesses to external stakeholders. The platform's influence now extends beyond the organisational boundaries.

Service Oriented Architecture

SOA is an inherent trait of the workflow based Integrated Service Virtualisation platform. Service being the end deliverable, we invariably have a service component built into every process that is brought onto the virtual platform. For example, the user helpdesks which are a part of the service layer have simultaneous access to multiple applications (services). Any new service launched on the platform will immediately be reflected on the helpdesk menu as a service item. Apart from this, the key SOA principles that we stress on are:

- *Reusability;* we have built and tested services like Authentication, Meta Data Management etc. that are reusable across various processes that are brought onto the platform without any major code changes
- *Clear policy definitions* that make services available as per eligibility and entitlement
- *Platform neutral* so that the Integrated Service Virtualization platform could connect two ways from other systems within the company. No special installations or additional coding is needed at the end-usage point

4.3 Organization
Impact on employees

Employees, who are key stakeholders in the organisation, experienced a significant improvement in productivity levels with the implementation of the virtual platform. Improvement in productivity in turn has led to employees spending more than 85% of their time on core and productive work (from internal statistics from a baseline of 70%). Further a small but significant cross section of about 100 associates have been redeployed to better suited roles by strategically outsourcing their non-value adding work to low-cost areas. This outsourcing was made possible because we could accommodate external service providers on the platform, as the platform is completely workflow driven.

Centre of Excellence

The Virtualisation Centre of Excellence within the ambit of eSupport was formed in 2006-07 when there was a strategic shift to get more than 70% of business processes virtualised. The Centre of Excellence has developed a robust BPM methodology for internal support processes. It has been instrumental in persuading leaders of various support units to bring their business processes onto the virtual platform. As on today, the CoE has the mandate of transforming this platform into a virtual enterprise information hub – a movement up the value chain. We have shown our BPM methodology in the following figure. It shows the integrated services approach in virtualisation covering the process, infrastructure, technology, and service delivery.

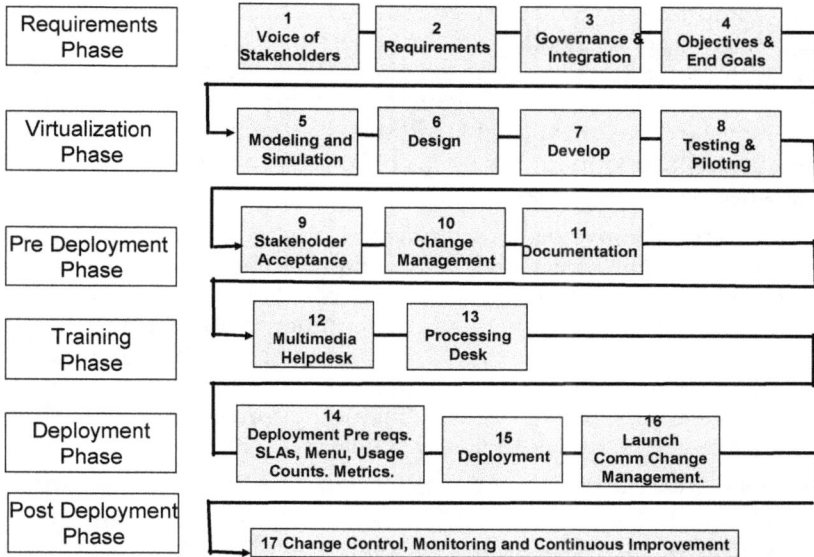

Requirements Phase	1 Voice of Stakeholders	2 Requirements	3 Governance & Integration	4 Objectives & End Goals
Virtualization Phase	5 Modeling and Simulation	6 Design	7 Develop	8 Testing & Piloting
Pre Deployment Phase	9 Stakeholder Acceptance	10 Change Management	11 Documentation	
Training Phase	12 Multimedia Helpdesk	13 Processing Desk		
Deployment Phase	14 Deployment Pre reqs. SLAs, Menu, Usage Counts. Metrics.	15 Deployment	16 Launch Comm Change Management.	
Post Deployment Phase	17 Change Control, Monitoring and Continuous Improvement			

The main challenge in sustaining the change initiative was in getting commitments from business leaders of the organisation. On the other hand, identifying a suitable architecture for the platform was a daunting challenge. The success of the initiative would depend on the adaptability of the platform with respect to the humungous growth of the organisation's size and also rapidly evolving technologies. With a robust combination of people, processes and technologies, the CoE has been able to establish an agile platform that has the capability to adopt to dynamic scenarios.

5. HURDLES OVERCOME

Management

An initiative of this scale has been possible because of unstinted commitment from the management. Nevertheless, to establish the viability of such an initiative was a major challenge in the inception stages. An approach of showcasing successful case studies helped in garnering management commitment.

Business

Lack of precedents was a major problem at the time of conceptualizing and implementing the Integrated Service Virtualization platform. We did not have access to best practices or generally accepted methodologies. No other company has attempted to virtualize and integrate all their business processes on a single platform.

Understanding of the platform by our business partners was minimal, leading to certain discontinuities in the way we conduct businesses. A few of our business partners were averse to using the platform as they could not easily do away with their traditional methods. For example, in spite of using the platform, some of the partners still stuck to maintaining records in spreadsheets, leading to delays in deliverables in a few instances. We could overcome this difficulty by inviting such users for proper orientation on the platform and its features.

Organization Adoption

One of the key characteristics of this initiative is the inevitable need for automating workflows and many business rules. This often leads to resistance from many top managers and also intended users, as generally is the case with any deviation from status quo. Sometimes, but not too often, there is a general sense of insecurity and skepticism among top managers, as they perceive a threat of losing control of their long-held organizational territories. In the initial days of the initiative, driving organizational adoption was a big challenge which was overcome through:

Innovative change management

But over the years, we have evolved innovative change management practices to deal with issues related to organizational adoption. One of them is a sustained organization-wide campaign stressing on the benefits of the virtual platform to employees and also to their businesses. Yet another is a contribution-linked recognition system, carefully aligned with the accepted HR methodology, wherein business leaders (of strategic business units) and their teams are rewarded based on the percentage of business processes (including transactions) they bring on to the virtual platform. This has been a very successful strategy.

At the business level, the implementation of our workflow based solution to integrate business processes created some discontinuities. For example, some users felt that their productivity was getting affected because of this platform. This was mainly due to unfamiliarity with the concept of virtual platform at various levels in the organization and also a slight apprehension in parting with time-tested and traditional methods of conducting their businesses. The team came up with the idea of creating help lines on an ad hoc basis to assist business leaders, employees and external stakeholders for any queries related to the usage of this platform. These help lines over a period of time evolved into full-fledged helpdesks and are now a part of the "service" component of the Integrated Service Virtualization platform and can act on behalf of the users. We still have a challenge in persuading a large number of vendors and customers to use our virtual platform to connect to us.

Governance model

To overcome such challenges, as a part of our BPM philosophy, we have developed a governance model that inherently integrates various stakeholders at the outset. We have also perfected the build-operate-own-transfer methodology, where in most of the case the intended user departments ultimately are given the entire ownership of the component of the platform relevant to them.

Top-down, bottom-up strategy

Of course the most important thread in all these change management strategies is a subtle balance between top-down and bottom-up approaches. Where we find it extremely difficult to persuade business leaders, we definitely take a top-down approach and ensure that the adoption becomes almost mandatory. But the virtual platform now being a proven model, we are in a position to reduce the top-down component of the strategy.

6. BENEFITS

6.1 Cost Savings

A primary objective of the platform was to optimize the costs of the support structure surrounding the core business units. Prior to the platform's inception, the Selling, General & Administrative expenses in addition to the support unit personnel costs were a cause of concern at 28% of revenues. This led to shrinking EBITDA margins at 36.51% (compared to peers at 50%).

The platform has over the years achieved its objectives of containing the costs through automation, effort reduction and innovative sourcing. We have taken publicly available information (annual reports of the company) about the company and to establish the impact of the implementation of our workflow based Integrated Service Virtualization platform.

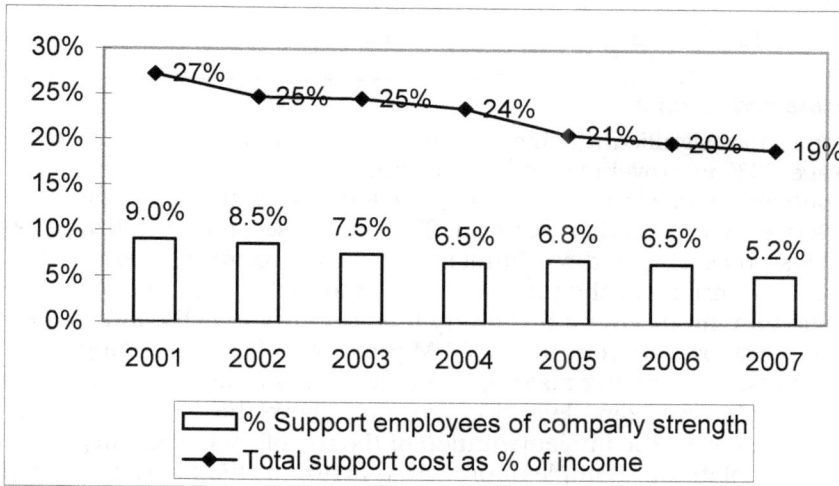

Since its implementation in 2001-02, the platform enabled us to control the increase in support unit costs in relation to the incomes. There has been a consistent decrease in the support unit cost as a percentage of revenues. During 2004-05, with the second wave of services coming on to the platform, we could realize a reduction in this figure in spite of a marginal increase in the proportion of support unit strength. We <u>do not</u> attribute the trend entirely to the virtual platform, but we do believe that the innovative use of workflows has had an impact to a significant extent. The support unit cost mentioned in the above graph is a combination of support personnel cost and the SG&A expenses.

6.2 Time Reductions
Reduction in time per transaction

Due to automation of workflows and creation of the Integrated Service Virtualization platform, the average time-to-process a business transaction has come down from about 12 minutes to about 5 minutes over the lifecycle of the transaction. This figure has been arrived at by taking into consideration the weighted average time of about 9 million transactions classified across 3 categories – indenting, approvals, service type requests - that are recorded annually by the virtual platform.

The baseline of 12 minutes per transaction was extracted from an earlier industrial engineering study conducted prior to the creation of the workflow based Integrated Service Virtualization platform. Wherever baselines are not available, we have taken statistically significant samples of business-process transaction times to arrive at estimates.

An example of how the transaction times of the activities of a typical process were reduced is given below:

Activity	Time taken prior to Integrated Service Virtualization (minutes)	Time taken after Integrated Service Virtualization (minutes)
Receipt & Acknowledgement	1	0.5
Pre Verification for Completeness	2	0.5
Running Business Rules	5	3
Delivery and Feedback	2	0.5
Accounting and Reporting	3	1
TOTAL	12	5.5

Cycle time reductions

One of the most significant achievements in the recent past is that, we could get an average 50% improvement in delivery time for processes that we could strategically outsource to scalable service providers using the workflow based Integrated Service Virtualization platform. Though these processes (travel bookings, vendor bills processing and recruitment support) account for about only 172,000 transactions annually of the total 9 million recorded by the platform, we can attribute such an improvement in delivery time completely to the innovation that we did in our workflows and our strong BPM principles. This is a strong case of intelligent workflow engineering making its impact across the organizational boundaries. This is just one example and is over and above the basic cycle time reductions that came with the implementation of the workflow based Integrated Service Virtualization platform. Sample approach to arrive at this figure along with baselines for these is as follows:

Process	Average. cycle time before (days)	Average cycle time after (days)	Number of transactions over the time bucket	% improvement for the process
Bill processing	15	7	300 bills	53%
Travel arrangements	1	0.25	200 bookings	75%
Joining formalities follow up	3	1	300 follow up calls	67%
Recruitment support	0.5	0.4	250 attendance confirmations	20%
Weighted average improvement (number of transactions is the weight)				53%

6.3 Increased Revenues

We do not have an estimate of the impact of our innovation on revenues, since we do not have a mechanism to track the same. For example, some of the services rendered through this platform like cold calling, market research, etc do have a direct impact on revenues in terms of new customers. But it is difficult to entirely attribute the growth in revenues to the Integrated Service Virtualization platform.

6.4 Productivity Improvements

We have mentioned productivity improvements in section 6.2

7. BEST PRACTICES, LEARNING POINTS AND PITFALLS

7.1 Best Practices and Learning Points

Best practices

- ✓ Institutionalization of BPM methodology
- ✓ Creation of a framework supported by technology and policy
- ✓ Establishing a dedicated R&D sub-unit under the Centre of Excellence to keep abreast of rapidly changing technologies and business scenarios
- ✓ Creation of teams with techno-functional capabilities to handle organizational requirements end-to-end

Learning points

- ✓ Change management is an integral and critical part of new initiatives that have organization-wide impact
- ✓ Technological capabilities have to be properly complemented with policies. Policy-making is a very important part of any organizational initiative
- ✓ It is a good idea to design systems futuristically so that have all the flexibility to accommodate changing business scenarios
- ✓ Stakeholders love to be recognized for their contribution to an organizational initiative. They should be acknowledged and rewarded appropriately through a credit-sharing mechanism
- ✓ Management commitment is of utmost importance for a project to be successful
- ✓ Innovative workflows can bring about a transformation that transcends organizational boundaries, as we saw in the case of two villages becoming a part of the mainstream economy

7.2 Pitfalls

- ✗ Unclear objectives of BPM / Workflow in terms of scope, quality of service or cost should be avoided
- ✗ Technology and business should not be viewed in isolation
- ✗ There should not be too many stop-gaps or workarounds; so that things do not become unmanageable when it comes to integration
- ✗ Things outside the accepted methodology, be it BPM or project management should not be entertained or should be addressed and resolved before embarking on a new project

8. COMPETITIVE ADVANTAGES

Innovative sourcing

In the industry (IT) we operate, human resource being the most critical differentiator of competition, it gets difficult to attract and retain the best talent. With the workflow based Integrated Virtual Services platform, we have been able to open up new avenues to source human resources.

We are now uniquely positioned to reach out virtually to vast pools of untapped skilled resources to conduct our business processes at their base locations, rather than moving the resources to the location of work. Our study shows that employee attrition in such locations is a mere 4% per annum compared to the industry average of 25%. With the innovative use of our workflow based virtual platform, we experimented with sourcing some of our business process related transactional work from such areas. These experiments have been quite successful and we believe that as this sourcing model matures, it would help us reduce employee attrition, thereby supplementing the innovative efforts of our HR managers.

Short term plans for sustaining competitive advantage

In the short term, we propose to maintain this competitive advantage by bringing more and more business processes onto the Integrated Virtual Services platform.

Long term plans

In the long term, the Virtualisation Centre of Excellence has proposed that high-end tacit work related to business processes also be brought under the ambit of the virtual platform. This has a potential to bring in about huge savings annually by empowering the associates and providing them the right inputs in terms of learning, research, analytics etc. Pilots have already begun and have started yielding results. In the long term, savings would result from productivity improvements at the higher levels of organisational hierarchy and also as an extension of the benefits of strategic outsourcing using our innovative workflow based virtual platform. We have a five year vision for this to happen.

Sustaining Competitive Advantage

To sustain the competitive advantage, we have a clear vision to work towards excellence on the following 4 parameters:
- Business model maturity
- Service innovation
- Delivery model maturity
- Technology innovation

9. TECHNOLOGY

The architecture

The entire platform has been developed by us in-house on a multi technology environment. The Integrated Service Virtualization platform has the following architecture:

User Helpdesks

Business users
Employees | Process Owners

External Consumer Access
Vendors | Service providers

Internet & Intranet

Load Balancer

Firewall

HTTP Server | HTTP Server | HTTP Server

Web Infrastructure

Enterprise Trusted Network

Web Services (Private) | Business Services | Reports | Application Services | Content Management | Learning Services

Application Services

Metrics | Data Management | Security Services | Common Services | User Administration | Workflow Management

Platform

Domain Services | Enterprise Security | Legacy Systems | Network Systems | Transaction Services

Enterprise Infrastructure

Enterprise Systems

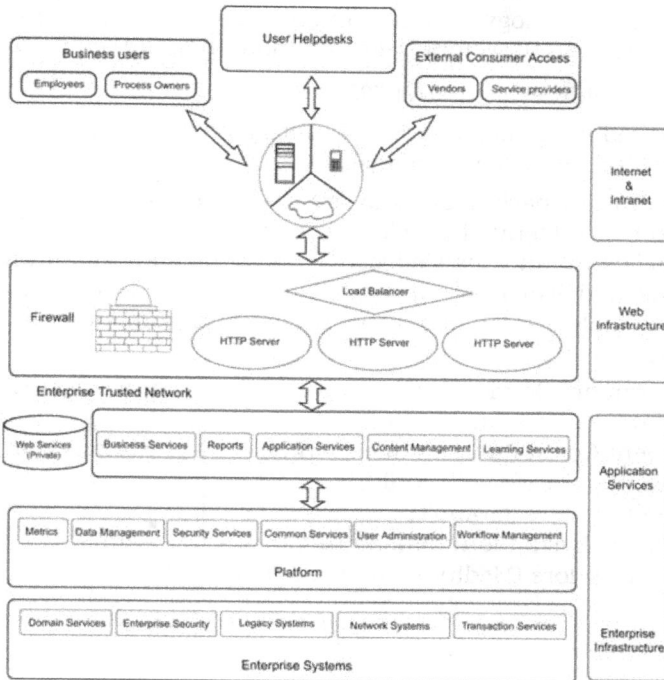

We have used Microsoft technologies extensively to meet the complex customer requirements with state of art hardware platform and with database clustering supported by high end load-balancing web-server technologies.

Benefits of the technology architecture

- This architecture has helped in giving agility to the virtual platform. We have the advantage of being able to replicate the platform very easily and build various applications on it as and when need arises. For example, we have perfected certain processes like employee leave management and re-imbursements as components of the platform.
- The platform is so agile that it can expand laterally to accommodate a large number of such processes and there are around 150 services running on it. At the same time it can support a concurrent load of about 1500 users accessing it at a time.
- Strategic outsourcing mentioned in previous sections was also a logical outcome of this agility.
- Another benefit of this architecture is the integration of various applications with third party business intelligence (BI) tools that were embedded onto the platform as a part of the vision to make it a virtual enterprise information hub.

Yet another significant benefit of this architecture is the "service component" that becomes inherent to the platform. The architecture hosts services that individual processes / applications can reuse.

The implementation

Technology was implemented using our rigorous in-house Integrated Service Virtualization BPM methodology. It is an organization-wide implementation catering to the needs to about 40,000 employees and more than 200 external users.

10. THE TECHNOLOGY AND SERVICE PROVIDERS

The workflow based Integrated Service Virtualization platform for our organization has been developed completely in-house.

There are certain third party tools that are embedded on the platform after converting them to our Integrated Service Virtualization framework. These relate to services like collaboration (knowledge management and communication), business intelligence and learning management systems. However, the redesign of these third party tools was done internally with minimum assistance of the technology providers.

Using this platform are Service Providers both internal and external to the organization. Some of the external service providers are:

- Recruitment Consultants (Names withheld for reasons of confidentiality)
- Travel Agents (Carlson-Wagonlit)
- Rural BPO Centers (GramIT;
  http://www.byrrajufoundation.org/html/gram-it.htm)
- Health Counselors (MedIndia; www.medindia.in)

Shanghai Commercial and Savings Bank, Taiwan

Gold Award, Pacific Rim and International Global Award
Nominated by Flowring Co. Ltd., Taiwan

EXECUTIVE SUMMARY

In the case study, we present how Shanghai Commercial and Savings Bank (SCSB) operates as the workflow application services provider (workflow ASP) via SCSB's e-Bank portal. Using workflow applications not only in the back-office, SCSB pushes the workflow technology to the customer-side by providing VIP enterprise customers with financial transaction approval workflow services through the e-Bank portal, in which it allows enterprises to define and manage their own workflows and business rules for e-Bank transactions. By initiating the project implementation, SCSB aims to establish better environment and mechanism to enhance both security and services of e-Bank by integrating workflow approval processes with the financial transactions to prevent un-authorized e-Bank transaction that violates the business rules of customer's enterprise.

SCSB benefits from the workflow-integrated e-Bank services to satisfy more VIP enterprise customers by making them happy with their e-Bank transactions more auditable and compliant to enterprise rules.

OVERVIEW

Company profile - About Shanghai bank

First established in Shanghai in 1915, Shanghai Commercial & Savings Bank, Ltd. (SCSB) is today one of the largest privately held banks in Taiwan. It is a premier choice for small and medium sized enterprises and recognized for its efficient trade finance and foreign exchange services. Together with its subsidiary Shanghai Commercial Bank Ltd. (SCB) in Hong Kong, SCSB manages total consolidated assets of US$ 22.4 billion and capital of US$ 452 million, and has a shareholder's equity of US$ 1.45 billion as of year-end 2004. As of 2004, it also manages over US$3 billion of private wealth and achieved FX transactions volume of USD70 billion.

SCSB (and its subsidiary) operates 106 branches worldwide, including 59 branches in Taiwan, 42 branches in Hong Kong, 5 branches overseas (London, New York, San Francisco, Los Angeles, and Shenzhen) and 1 representative office in Shanghai. SCSB is the only Taiwanese bank with a full Greater China network, and is the first bank in Taiwan to receive approval in 2002 from the government to conduct direct remittances with financial institutions in China. The Bank operates the largest volume of remittances from Taiwan to China and is reputed to offer the "fastest possible remittance between Taiwan and China."

Project information

BPM technology has been widely used in the bank's back offices for routine processes such as processing credit card applications or loan applications. However, it is new to extend the BPM technology to integrate both enterprise-side financial transaction approval workflows and the bank's back offices processes together on the same bank-operated IT platform.

The project **Multi-authentication financial transaction system** *(now changed to more user-oriented name: Global Pass-Through Financial Web)* is initiated according to SCSB's security policy decision to adopt process technology to enhance e-bank security by enhancing the financial transaction with enterprise-side approval process, in which a financial transaction should only be executed at the bank-side after a pre-defined sequence of approval activities are conducted at the enterprise-side that run through the authorized managers and supervisors.

Before the deployment of the project, SCSB had already industry-standard e-bank services, the only plain, one-step transaction services are provided in the e-Bank portal. In the e-Bank portal, the enterprise customers' account and transactions are protected by well-known PKI and SSL technologies. For stronger protection on important transactions, the enterprise customers may be asked to perform two-factor authentication.

To enhance the financial transaction security by enforcing the users at the enterprise-side to co-work through a workflow that enforces the pre-defined business rules, SCSB must manage to provide an environment for enterprise users to define their own enterprise financial transaction workflows and business rules. The project team setup the requirement baseline for implementing the environment:

- The underlying workflow management system (WFMS) must be flexible and capable to process large volume of financial approval workflows
- The workflow and business rule definition tools must be simplified enough so that financial-domain users can easily create and maintain the workflows and business rules through the Web browser
- The WFMS must host thousands of enterprises in the same platform with shared hardware and software resources. Virtually every enterprise's system is isolated and independent with others. Each enterprise customer can define their own financial-related roles/users as a small organization chart; define their own business workflow and rules according to their own enterprise policies. Although sharing the same hardware and software platform resources, each enterprise in the system should not be able to access other enterprise's workflow information. From technical view point, SCSB hosts a platform to operate as the workflow application service provider that serves thousands of enterprises WFMS core services
- The WFMS should be able to integrate the enterprise-side workflow together with bank-side's back-office workflow or financial gateways. The enterprise-side workflow and bank-side workflow are separated for security issues, however the enterprise-side workflow is related to corresponding bank-side workflows
- The process-oriented security mechanism implemented in the project should work with the network-level security infrastructure PKI and SSL to form more secure e-Bank portal services

In the first-phase implementation, the e-Bank workflows provide the enterprise users with basic transaction services such as transfer among accounts, loan applications. As system growth, more e-Bank workflows can be added into the system

BUSINESS CONTEXT

The driving motivation for initiating the project begins with solving the e-Bank security problems, but it finally produces surprising financial transaction solution services after detail business analysis by the SCSB team.

PKI, SSL, and even two-factor authentication have been applied to protect e-Bank transactions for a long time. It seems the protection is enough for individual e-Bank users, however in the enterprise context, e-Bank services are still vulnerable to un-authorized use of transactions. The employees at the enterprise-side who legally hold the security tokens issued by the bank may take moral risk to make un-authorized transaction in the e-Bank but the bank-side still regards it as authenticated and allows the transaction executed. It is not rare to read news about un-authorized and un-audited on-line financial transactions inside the enterprise.

The people aspects of risk cannot be solved solely through PKI technology. SCSB notices that enterprise customers who resist to adopt e-Bank services because of fearing the people aspect of risk. Especially, the small and medium business (SMB) that can not establish good security practice and IT systems tend to avoid performing financial transactions on-line, and stay with old-style and time-consuming face-to-face bank services.

In the business context, SCSB team identified the consequence of the project implementation lead to more business values for SCSB and provide better service to the enterprise customers. These can be addressed in following two categories:

1. Security enhancement:

- PKI/SSL infrastructure in the e-Bank portal can work as the underlying user authentication and transaction data privacy and integrity protection. It implements the hard security requirement from the technical view point.
- Enforce financial transactions in the e-Bank portal to pass through a pre-defined approval sequence at the enterprise-side (however the system is hosted at the SCSB's information center.) It reduces the security risk from the people aspect. In addition, it implements good security management practice. It is also more persuasive for SMB decision makers to adopt e-Bank services so that SCSB can reduce face-to-face operation cost.
- Allow enterprise-side administrator to create local accounts for enterprise users to login the system so that they need not share single account to access e-Bank services. In addition, all local accounts of enterprise-side also receive PKI security tokens issued by SCSB to authenticate themselves to the e-Bank portal.

2. Better financial services to increase customer satisfaction

- The financial transaction approval workflow application provided to the enterprise users reflect more real business scenario than plain web applications in traditional e-Bank.
- It helps the customer enterprise to establish controlled and auditable financial transaction processes on the reliable IT system
- The customer enterprise can save the software development cost to build financial transaction approval application system
- Process-enabled e-Bank services bring more opportunities for SCSB to develop value-added and sophisticated financial services, in which multiple iterations of negotiation steps between bank and two or more enterprises can

be realized. Traditional e-Bank portal provides only one-step transaction services rather than multiple-step application processes.

- Support enterprise with OBU (over-sea business unit) accounts to perform global financial transaction processes worldwide.

THE KEY INNOVATIONS

The key impact from the project can be summarized as the following:

1. The enterprise customers obtain better e-Bank services in terms of higher-level security protection. It also reduces the security concerns from the people aspect.

2. The enterprise customers obtain free and flexible workflow-automated financial transaction management processes from SCSB. Therefore the customers prefer to do financial transaction on SCSB's platform. For SCSB, the platform costs only reasonable IT investment but provides significant incentive for the customers to do financial transactions on SCSB's platform. The reason is that the enterprise customers can save the cost to construct similar and duplicated applications by themselves.

3. The automated processes at the enterprise-side can be further linked with the bank-side back-office approval processes to reduce the total cycle-time of financial services applications.

4. On the e-Bank platform, SCSB can provide more advanced and value-added financial cash-flow management processes, such as *factoring*, by integrating independent enterprise e-Bank processes.

5. Both SCSB and enterprise customers can have more transparent financial transaction processes and defined business rules for approving different amount ranges. In addition, the financial transaction process can be clearly tracked and become more auditable.

4.1 Business

Applying workflow technology to e-Bank customers brings several innovations. The first innovation is *multi-authentication processes* that provide more trusted transaction process management. Multi-authentication is a mechanism to make sure a financial transaction is actually executed by the bank-side only when a series of authorized stakeholders all agree with the transaction content. No single person can execute a financial transaction without going through the multi-authentication process.

From SCSB's view, multi-authentication can be applied to reduce the security risk factor from the people aspect. To pursue more customers to do financial transactions on the e-Bank platform, only PKI and SSL protection between network-link of bank and enterprise seems not enough. Therefore, SCSB decides to provide e-Bank services that implement best-practice for customers to follow when they are doing e-Bank transactions. The result is to implement and deploy a suite of workflow applications that control the intra-enterprise financial transaction processes for the enterprise customers to use.

The second innovation is to *operate financial workflow applications in the form of ASP-model* to reduce the duplicated software development and maintenance cost of enterprise customers. For small-to-medium enterprise owners to allocate budget to establish and maintain best-practices for managing intra-enterprise financial transaction processes is still a heavy economic burden. Therefore, SCSB decides to host the multi-authentication financial transaction services inside the e-Bank platform so that their enterprise customers can save the cost to develop and maintain the software applications. It means the enterprise customers need not to invest on software or hardware to operate the applications. Each enterprise need only apply for a virtual workflow domain from SCSB, they can obtain a logically exclusive workflow system for their own enterprises. In each virtual workflow domain, the enterprise can define their own organization structure that describes the stakeholders in the intra-enterprise financial transaction processes. For the financial transaction processes, the enterprise can flexibly customize the approval processes based on the process templates provided by SCSB according to the enterprise-dependent business rules.

The third innovation is *optimized cross-enterprise cash-flow management*. Knowing the information inside the workflow processes of each enterprise on the same platform, SCSB can provide customers with more advanced cash-flow management services – "reserved-payment loan". The detail of the service process is described in detail in the next subsection.

4.2 Process

Before the project deployment, the financial transaction processes, such as money transfer, at the enterprise-side are very straightforward. For small enterprise, the case usually begins with the financial specialist filling paper form to obtain the approval of managers or supervisors. After the approval, he then uses the enterprise's username, password, and PKI security token issued by the bank to enter the bank portal to do the money transfer. The transaction is conducted by normal web applications. Although the transaction is protected by SSL and PKI to make sure the integrity and safety of the transaction content. The bank can make sure the transaction is requested from the enterprise users. However it cannot prevent un-authorized use of the bank portal. The risk exists in the enterprise that the money transfer is made through the portal without the enterprise's legal approval process.

With the new system, SCSB guide the enterprise customers to define their approval policy based on enterprise's business rule. All stakeholders in the financial transaction process have separate accounts to login the bank portal. Thus both the bank and enterprise can keep detail transaction history and approval detail about each financial transaction in the portal. It helps the enterprise financial transaction processes transparent for future audit requests.

In addition, the new system solves the problem of SCSB's major enterprise customers to perform the financial transaction approval processes across several country offices. For example, the financial specialist is located in Taiwan, the manager is travelling in China to monitor regional business, and the supervisor is in US or Europe to expand business opportunities. The Web-based approval processes hosted by SCSB can easily support the business scenario.

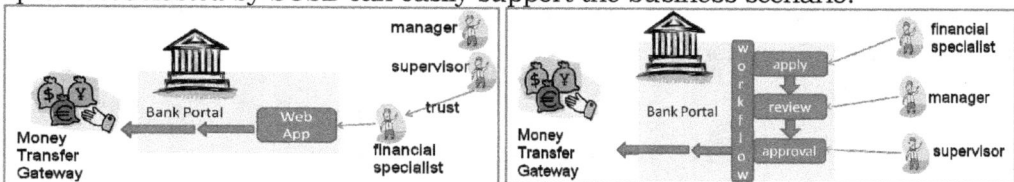

Figure 1. The money transfer scenario before and after the project deployment.

In the project, it allows enterprise to define enterprise-dependent business rules to guide the approval process of each financial transaction. The innovation can be observed by how SCSB supporting enterprises to customize their own processes through the process template instead of directly manipulating the process design diagram. In Figure 2, it describes how SCSB project team plan the supporting architecture according to the business requirement.

In the environment, there are the following process roles:
- Bank-side portal administrator (also called global administrator)
- Enterprise-side site administrator (also called local administrator)
- Bank-side back-office staffs, including reviewer and decision maker
- Enterprise-side employees, including applicant, reviewer, and decision maker.

For security consideration, the two BPMS systems for enterprise customers and bank back-office are installed on two separated machines and communication are filtered by the firewall. The workflow between back-office and customers are linked through inter-workflow engine API, by which workflow processes can be initiated and process status can be accessed.

The global administrator creates a virtual workflow domain for enterprise 1, 2, 3,..,n in the enterprise customer's portal on the enterprise's request. For each virtual workflow domain, a local administrator is assigned to act as the technical contact and administrator to define the customer's organization structure, business rules, and approval processes in the virtual workflow domain. SCSB predefines process templates in the site configuration functions to simplify the process definition procedures. The enterprise-side administrator only assigns the organization structure, adds members, binds roles and members, plans the amount-ranges that some roles can be authorized to approve. The steps of approval processes can be inserted or deleted during the customization based on enterprise's business rules.

After the enterprise-side administrator complete the configuration for his enterprise (e.g. Ent1), the users of Ent1 can login to SCSB portal to perform daily financial workflow processes as if it is operated only for Ent1. When a money transfer process at is instantiated, the enterprise-independent template process is instantiated first, it then reads and interprets the site-configuration for the process variation defined by Ent1 administrator at run-time. Figure 3 illustrates the relationships of template process, enterprise-side process adjustment, and the final process instance variation for different enterprises. By introducing the concept of template process, SCSB can keep the main structure of typical financial approval processes while allow enterprises to make necessary configuration variation to meet their own business requirement. The template process designers are responsible for making the template process more generalized to act according to the configuration variation as well as providing enterprise-side configuration GUI to assign the configuration variation.

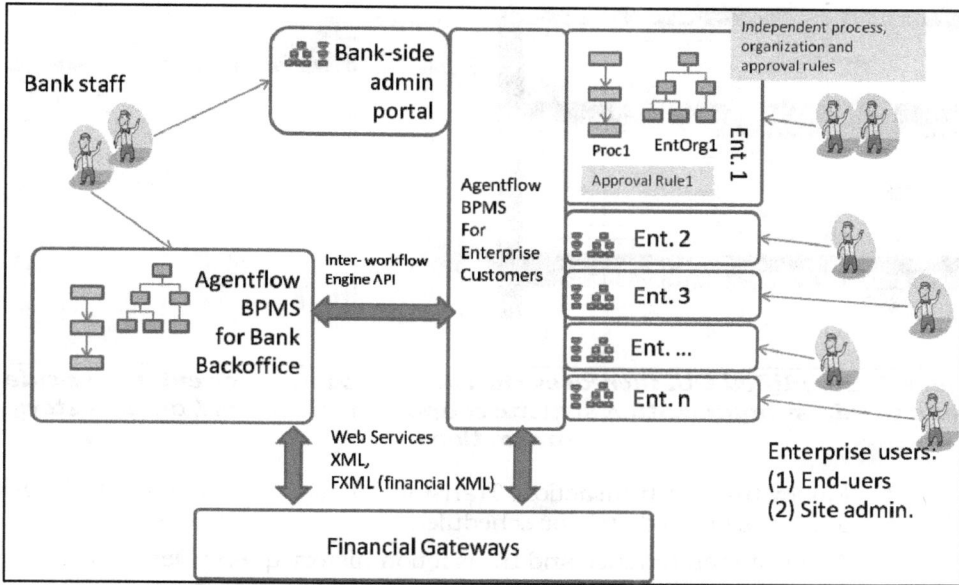

Figure 2. The SCSB e-Bank process architecture to support enterprise with independent processes and organization structure.

In addition to the financial transaction services such as money transfer or loan applications mentioned before, the e-Bank portal provide full-set of process-enabled services as shown in Figure 5. It includes:

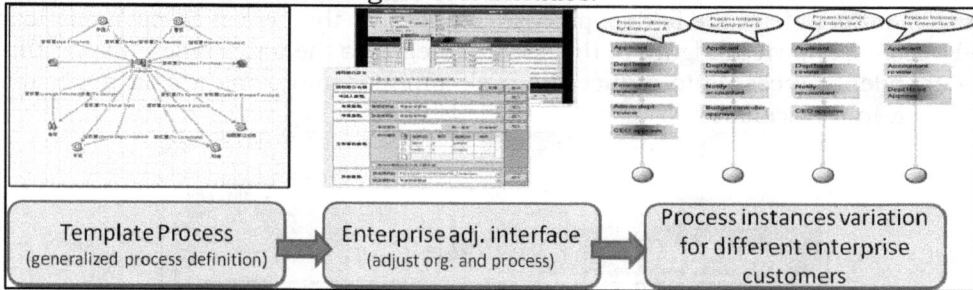

Figure 3. A well-designed template process allows process variation at run-time through GUI adjustment in organization and process structures

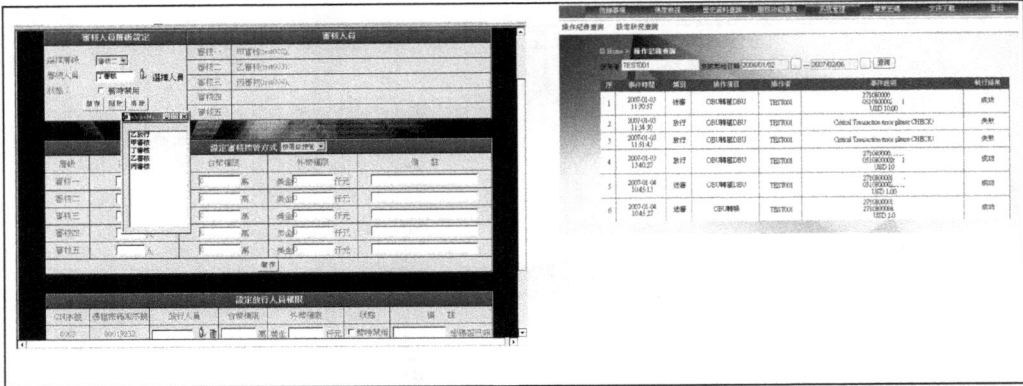

Figure 4. Simplified GUI increases the system usability for enterprise-side users to adjust organization structure, approval rules, and audit history transactions.

1. Money transfer transaction: Transmitting money between OBU/ODU accounts (immediately or scheduled)

2. Account maintenance and transaction history query: Demand account, saving account, checking account, time deposit

3. Mutual funds

4. Trade import/export services: L/C advising, L/C transfer, L/C negotiation, outward bills collection, trade finance (D/A, D/P loan)

5. Loan services: normal loan services, reserved-payment loan services

6. Site administration

One mentionable value-added process services is the "reserved-payment loan" services. As shown in Figure 6, the service integrates the information among three independent processes to reduce the cycle-time for approving a loan application request. In the scenario,

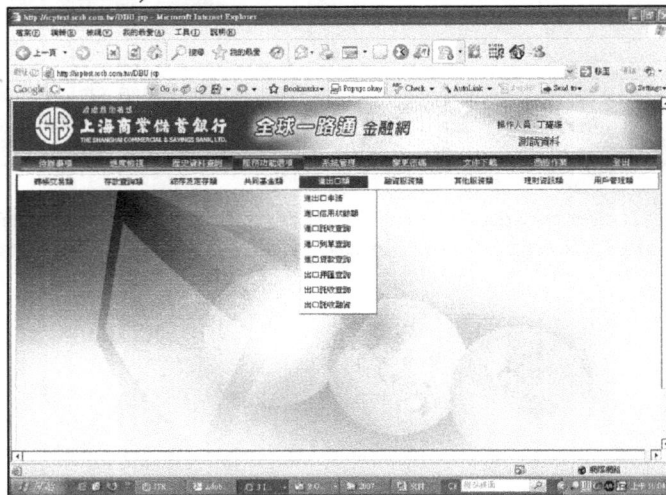

Figure 5. Enterprise customers access workflow-enabled financial services such as money transfer, mutual funds, import/export trade, loan applications.

1. EnterpriseA sells goods to EnterpriseB, the invoice amounts $150,000.
2. EnterpriseA initiated a $100,000 loan request process to SCSB.
3. SCSB receives the loan request and continues the internal (back-office) process.
4. EnterpriseB has already confirmed a payment $150,000 to enterpriseA in the advanced (scheduled) payment process.
5. Knowing the payment plan between Enterprise A and B, SCSB can decide to approve the loan request by reserving the payment.
6. EnterpriseA obtains the notification from SCSB about the loan approval and the date that EnterpriseA can use the approved loan quota.

By integrating the information from processes running on the same platform, the bank obtains more judgement information when approving a loan application, and the customers enjoy more efficient capital utilization for their business.

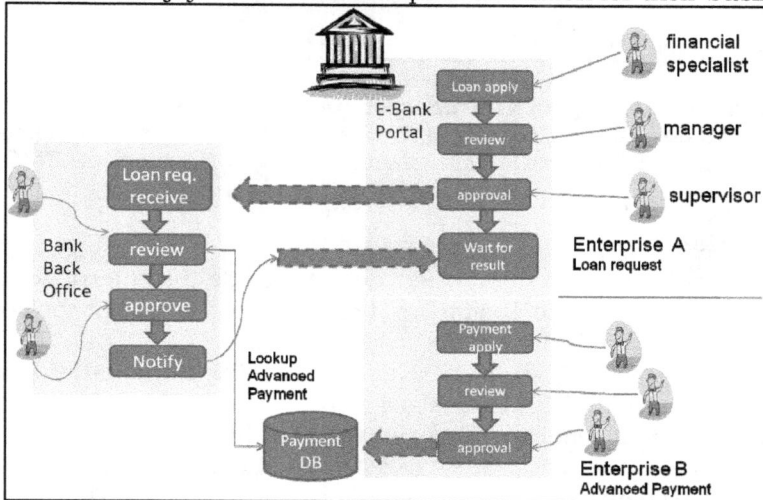

Figure 6. The bank can shorten the loan approve cycle time for enterprise A by knowing enterprise B has already confirmed a scheduled advanced payment to enterprise A

In the back-office processes and approved financial transaction execution, it is often for the processes to interact with bank mainframe systems or external financial gateways. The workflow applications work well inside the bank's SOA infrastructure. In SCSB, it deploys BlueStar middleware to enable mainframe host transaction as Web Services. The middleware also help to integrate with applications that developed under BPEL engine, BizTalk, TIBCO BusinessWorks.

Based on SCSB's ready-to-integrate SOA environment, the project implementation pays less effort to communicate with legacy mainframe systems and different financial gateways. To commit a money transfer in the workflow process, it only need to write code to invoke Web-services or sending XML messages in the process script to the middleware stacks. Other financial transaction services to backend such as money transfer to domestic/foreign banks, factoring database, SWIFT & L/C (letter of credit), can be done in the same manner.

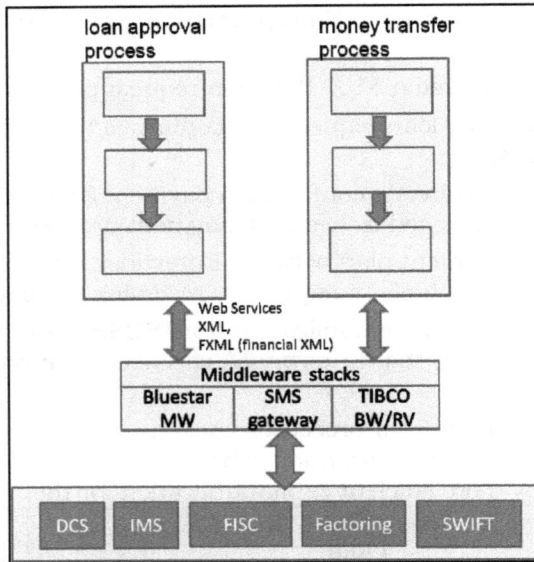

Figure 7. Back-office approval processes and customer financial transaction requests can access backend financial services gateway through (Bluestar + Tibco BW) middleware stacks via Web Services or XML messages

4.3 Organization

The organizations involved in the project context include the enterprise customer, and SCSB. For the enterprise customers, their work environment for performing financial transaction is improved in the following way:

- Enterprise users need not to share the security token and e-Bank account to perform financial transactions as before.
- With independent security token and account, the role and responsibility in the financial transaction process can be clearly defined and tracked.
- It is easier to track the process progress in the e-Bank portal.
- In comparison with traditional e-Bank services, the workflow they perform reflects their real business needs.

For the bank employees, although the basic financial transaction services such as money transfer is mostly done by the automated computer system, newer services types have been developed in the portal. They still can interact with the enterprise customers in the same workflow process like a virtual team. In consequence, they can pay more attention to provide high value-added enterprise finance service to the customers.

HURDLES OVERCOME

The stakeholders in the system need to think through several aspects to present a good service to the end users. At the SCSB side, it needs both the service requirement department and the platform operation department to work together. For the implementation team (vendor of SCSB), they needs to integrate both team members from financial and workflow domains. Several hurdles are overcome during the project lifetime and described as the following:

Management hurdles

In the beginning the project at the SCSB-side are lead together by two department managers. One is responsible for technical and site operation issues the other is responsible for service content. Issues that require trade-off between technical and service content sometimes need long time to confirm.

Solution:

For these issues, the project team help prepare documents for these issues and alternative solutions. They then arrange a decision making meeting based on the prepared document. Their higher-level manager is also invited to join the meeting to help negotiation and decision making. This hurdle reflects the importance of process owner assignment in BPM deployment.

Business hurdles

When deciding whether to make the approval process execution at the bank-side or enterprise-side, it raises a trust problem. Do the enterprise customers agree to store their internal financial transaction information (including approval rules, workflow execution detail) at the bank-side? Some enterprise customers doubt about the privacy problem. It needs clarification when promote the e-Bank to enterprise customers.

Solution:

The enterprise customers can understand the privacy issues and the impact by explaining that the workflow-powered financial transaction services are hosted in SCSB's information center. The software and hardware environment of the system are protected carefully in the same security level with other financial services system they are currently use. Except for authorized SCSB staffs, no one can read their transaction information. The degree of financial information exposure in the e-Bank portal is the same as in traditional e-Bank services. The additional information that enterprise customer exposes to SCSB are the organization structure and approval processes/rules. For most small to medium enterprises, the convenience of workflow-enabled e-Bank services can usually override the minor privacy issues.

Organization adoption hurdles

The major problem for organization adoption is the user training at the enterprise-side. On-line user's manual may help. However, current 4000 enterprises are at various computer skill levels. Some of them need classroom or face-to-face instruction.

Solution:

Before the system deployment, every enterprise customer has been assigned a specialist by SCSB as business contact. SCSB trains the specialist internally, and then provide on-site demonstration and instruction for the new system during their scheduled visit to the enterprise customers.

BENEFITS

The deployment of the project benefits both SCSB and SCSB's customers. There are lots of benefits can be observed in the deployed systems. The following table evaluates the major and obvious benefits from different aspects:

Category	Outcomes
Cost Savings	All enterprise customers need not to construct similar approval workflow application systems for financial transactions. The duplicated construction cost can be saved for

	each enterprise. The estimated cost saving for each enterprise is around USD$30,000.
	The increase of e-Bank users leads to less face-to-face transaction. The man-month saving can be conservatively estimated by the following equation: 4000 (enterprise) * 3 (transaction/month) * 12 (month/year) * 0.15 (hour/transaction) = 21,600 (hour). If rate for every man hour is USD$15, the total cost saving is USD$324,000 per year. Note: Assume every enterprise reduces at most 3 face-to-face transactions every month. There are over 4000 enterprises in the e-Bank system.
	Other savings can be observed such as shortened back-office loan approval processing time, reduced progress tracking time between the bank and enterprise.
Time Reductions	For enterprise-side money transfer approval processes, if the approval needs to go through several country offices, the cycle-time can be reduced from 7 days to 3 days.
	The reserved-payment loan process can shorten at least 3 to 5 days in waiting for the loan approval
Increased Revenues	SCSB's EPS (earns per share) increases. The EPS for FY2004, 2005, 2006 are NTD$3.64, $4.43, and $4.98 respectively.
	SCSB's net profit ratio increases. The ratio for FY2004, 2005, 2006 are 45.43%, 49.31%, $54.82% respectively.
	The enterprise customers obtain higher capital utilization through rapid loan applications.
Productivity Improvements	The average effort paid in the loan-approval process is reduced. It reduces 20% effort for each loan approval case.
	The cases that enterprise customer requests for clarifying unclear/suspected transaction content are reduced. SCSB estimated the reduction from 60 cases to 10 cases per month.

BEST PRACTICES, LEARNING POINTS AND PITFALLS

7.1 Best Practices and Learning Points

✓ *The bank provides higher-level security mechanism in terms of workflow-enabled approval processes to strengthen the trust of enterprise owner when doing financial transactions. The higher-level security mechanism works together with network-level security mechanism to ensure safe and legal transaction by avoiding vulnerability in both technical and human aspects. The combined mechanism can encourage more hesitated enterprise to do transaction on the e-Bank platform.*

✓ *The bank-side hosted financial domain oriented workflow applications for enterprise customers are regarded as valuable and reliable services that keep current customers on the platform and attract more new customers.*

✓ *The idea to implement the system by the bank and to operate it at bank-side is a win-win decision. The customers save the cost to implement similar workflow application systems, while the bank reduces the cost of manual transaction and tracking questionable transaction records.*

✓ *On the platform the bank holds more transaction detail in the processes execution. It can then make use of the information and processes capability to compose more value-added services.*

✓ *In the project, the financial transaction process is controlled and tracked by the workflow system. It presents a transparent and auditable financial transaction process, which is required by good enterprise governance policy.*

7.2 Pitfalls

✗ *In the project, it integrated several professional domains, such as financial services model, mainframe system communication, workflow system architecture. The required profession and effort to integrate the three parts together is under-estimated in the beginning of project plan. When the project started to delay in designing generalized template process, some workflow domain experts then joined the project to handle this part.*

COMPETITIVE ADVANTAGES

SCSB still continues invest in enhancing the financial services by BPM and workflow technology. The innovation to host workflow applications for customers to perform financial transaction is the first achievement. In the case study, we also observe that SCSB has show the potential to compose more value-added financial services by linking more processes together based on previous project implementation. In the future, SCSB has to expand the capacity of the system as the growth of enterprise financial business – for more customers and service content.

According to the annual report of SCSB published in July 2007, it identified s short-term and long-term business development plan can move on base on current project result.

Short-term plan:

- Enhance the OBU/DBU mutual-funds and loan business.
- Improve the operation efficiency to fully support the financial product selling.
- Enhance the internal audit and regulation compliance through transparent transaction processes.
- Long-term plan:
- Enhance product portfolio, packaging, and marketing, as well as expanding niche business through strategy alliance.
- Continue to enhance e-Bank financial services, provide first-class financial flow service in the e-Commerce environment
- Continue to integrate information system to increase the efficiency of automated process
- Enhance internal audit and regulation compliance to reduce all aspect of operational risk.

TECHNOLOGY

Most of workflows in SCSB are approval-based processes that guide the e-Bank financial transaction through the enterprise-customer defined approval sequence and business rules. In the project implementation, SCSB choose to adopt Flowring's BPMS product – Agentflow to work as the underlying workflow function support.

The deployment and integrated systems for the project is illustrated in Figure 2. The following are the build blocks and their underlying platform information for the project:

Functions	Vendor / Product Version	Platform
Database Server	Oracle DB 9.2	Solaris 8
BPMS Servers	Flowring Agentflow 2.0.3	IBM AIX 5.3 JDK 1.4.2
Application Servers	IBM WebSphere 6	IBM AIX 5.3
Financial Service Gateway	TIBCO BW BlueStar Silverstream	N.A.
Security PKI solution	HiTrust PKI + RA solution	N.A.

When comparing with traditional workflow application system construction, SCSB's project contains many interesting and non-trivial workflow functions that challenge the implementation team. For example, it has to allow several enterprises to execute workflows but sharing the same workflow server instance and without disturbing each other. Technically speaking, the workflow server should allow partition of its resource into several virtual workflow domains to serve many independent enterprises. Each enterprise can has its own organization and role-binding policy. In this project, the project team manages to fulfill the functions by smart process design at the application-level, and rich function support at the BPMS product-level. Besides the BPMS core functions support, the implementation team believes that the following BPMS features can significantly reduce the implementation effort in similar projects:

- Engine-to-engine communication capability to bridge multiple workflow engines work together
- Good organization structure design and maintenance mechanism, the organization maintainer can be specified and limited at the sub-tree level
- The process activity allows flexible run-time member binding mechanism (e.g. allow dispatch/binding as an event that can be customized by script)
- Rich process portal components that can be composed or contained by other Web pages
- Easy to integrate with mainframe system or SOA component through Web services call or XML message manipulation.

THE TECHNOLOGY AND SERVICE PROVIDERS

Flowring (http://www.flowring.com) devotes itself to provide Business Process Management (BPM) software solution that helps enterprises build process-oriented information system since its establishment in February 1999. Its main product is *Agentflow* -- a full BPMS product suite. From the development of BPMS platform to technical consultancy, the services stretch across different fields to offer an ideal experience of BPM implementation. Through intuitive process thinking, intelligent workspace, streamline knowledge management and humanistic process enterprise, the mission is to help the clients to create the human-centric organizations to pioneer in the e-business trend.

Section 5

South and Central America

Government of Bermuda, Forms and Transaction Engine Project, Bermuda

Silver Award, South and Central Americas
Nominated by PPC, USA

EXECUTIVE SUMMARY / ABSTRACT

In 2003, the Government of Bermuda launched its initial on-line presence to communicate with the island's 60,000 citizens and over 6,000 companies. The initial version of the Bermuda Government Portal focused primarily on disseminating information and providing access to commonly used government forms. In 2006, Bermuda Government sought to expand the portal's capabilities by providing a platform for citizens and business to carry out transactions on the portal. In many cases, these transactions required collaboration and monitoring across numerous government roles, departments, and ministries.

After evaluating various approaches, Bermuda Government settled on Business Process Management (BPM), as both a discipline and a technology, to help facilitate on-line government transactions. An initial slate of government transactions were identified for implementation and deployment to citizens and businesses. Additionally, Bermuda Government established the "Better Process Group" as a BPM Center of Excellence. The "Better Process Group," or BPG, provided governance, education, and a forum for capturing lessons learned. This award submission highlights the initial process project implemented by the Government of Bermuda and the benefits realized by the project.

OVERVIEW

Through several prior attempts the Government of Bermuda sought to allow businesses and citizens to conduct business with Government on-line. However, many of these attempts involved one-off solutions, leveraging different technology platforms and custom coding. Government quickly realized that maintaining and managing these different applications could prove costly and difficult to support. Ultimately, Bermuda Government decided that a consumer-off-the-shelf (COTS) solution would provide the infrastructure, stability, and support required by some of these solutions.

After coming to this conclusion, Bermuda Government created the "Forms and Transaction Engine" project as the mechanism for identifying, implementing, and improving on-line government-to-citizen (G2C) and government-to-business (G2B) transactions. At its core, the project focused on achieving three primary objectives:

- Provide a consistent platform and methodology for developing process-driven solutions that facilitate business and citizen interaction with Bermuda Government
- Promote increased collaboration and information sharing across various ministries and departments in Bermuda Government

- Prove that on-line transactions can be automated and provide measurable return-on-investment and value for both Bermuda Government and its constituents

The Forms and Transaction Engine project was lead by the Department of E-Government and involved cross-ministry collaboration amongst numerous ministries. Early on in the project, the government realized that it needed to acquire a flexible Business Process Management Suites (BPMS) platform that would allow business analysts and developers to effectively collaborate on developing business process solutions. Ultimately, the Department of E-Government settled on the BEA AquaLogic BPM platform for its ease of use and ability to integrate with legacy systems.

Additionally, Bermuda Government realized early on that it would be critical to establish a BPM Center of Excellence to provide a governance and education framework for delivering process solutions. In order to keep its BPM Center of Excellence accessible to everyone in government, the name "Better Process Group" or BPG was chosen to represent the team that would serve as both steering committee and educators.

Initial process solutions were identified based on several criteria, including level of sponsorship, solution complexity, and overall impact to the organization. Out of the initial list of solutions identified, the first solution selected focused on the Department of Statistic's Annual Employment Survey. The Employment Survey was selected as the first project because of the high degree of sponsorship and commitment demonstrated by leadership within the Department of Statistics.

The initial project implemented for the Department of Statistics focused on automating a manual, paper-based G2B process for capturing and reporting employment statistics across the island. The automated process, named the e-Employment Survey, allowed businesses to efficiently complete the government's Annual Employment Survey on-line and to better collaborate with Department of Statistics staff throughout the submission process. The final process solution provided the Department of Statistics with greater visibility into how employers were progressing with their individual survey responses, increased quality control over data submitted and reviewed, and eliminated the need for duplicate entry of data provided by employers. For the initial release of the e-Employment Survey process, over 60 employers participated across the island. However, the process is designed to support the 400+large employers that are anticipated to use the system in 2008.

BUSINESS CONTEXT

A Vision for Collaborative Government

- Bermuda's Department of E-Government was founded to facilitate a more strategic approach to delivering electronic and on-line services to citizens, businesses, and the government's employees. The primary objective of the department is to develop a "joined up" Government environment that promotes collaboration and cross-departmental sharing throughout government.
- The Department of E-Government's Pole Star model defines its guiding principles for creating a process-oriented and collaborative environment for driving efficiencies and improved services to Government's clients. As outlined on the E-Government web page (www.gov.bm), the department's Pole Star model emphasizes six key principles for promoting collaboration and improving internal efficiencies:

- **Dialog** - Dialogue is the means by which E-Government services & efficiencies are discovered, defined developed and deployed.
- **Skills/Knowledge** - Developing the right skills and knowledge base within the Civil Service is key to the effective management & use of e-technology.
- **Innovation** - The deployment of e-services is dependant on the Government's ability to utilize its internal innovative resources. The E-Government Department will work with Government agencies to leverage and position the "innovators" within the Civil Service to facilitate the effective development of e-technology.
- **Partnership** - Government has effectively used IT vendors in acquiring & developing its applications. Creating and sustaining effective partnerships with the vendor community and the private sector is a critical success factor for E-Government delivery.
- **Integration** - The end game for effective E-Government is "joined-up" Government. Wherever the integration of business processes and technology benefits the internal and external client it will be pursued coordinated and deployed.
- **Pragmatism** - The technology deployed should meet the actual need. Technology decisions must be dictated by practical needs and considerations. This principle applies to decisions on need, choice of technology and scope of deployment.

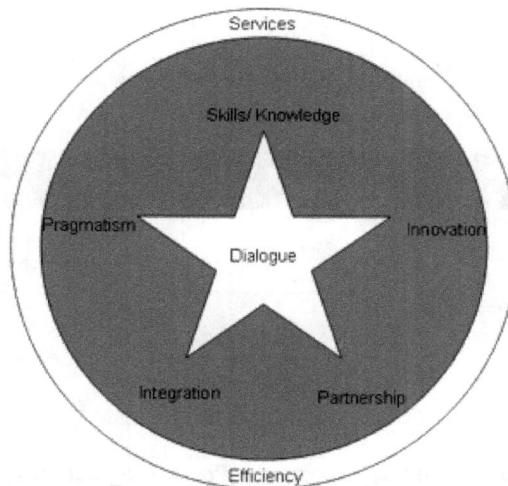

Figure 1: E-Government's Pole Start Model

Extending the Reach of the Government Portal

As one of the Department of E-Government's first initiatives, the Bermuda Government Portal focused on providing the island with information on various government initiatives and access to key government forms and documents. Providing comprehensive access, the Government Portal has become a one-stop shop for accessing information and activities for each department and ministry within Government.

Unfortunately, "information dissemination" was as far as the Government Portal went. Increasingly, users sought to use the portal to interact directly with Government. Many of the electronic forms provided on the Government Portal required visitors to download, print, and manually fill out the paper-based forms.

After completing forms, users either had to fax or mail the forms to the appropriate department. In many cases, citizens and business were required to visit the department's physical office location to drop off the forms. Once a completed form was submitted, it fed into a closed process that had little visibility by managers or the original submitting party. Additionally, the processes associated with these forms crossed many departmental boundaries. For example, submitted job applications are first processed by human resources and then routed to the appropriate department for review. Job applications resulting in an offer employment must be routed back to human resources, and then on to the finance department to set up the new employee in the payroll system.

As with most public sector organizations, departments and ministries within Bermuda Government often operate as independent silos. Only in rare cases, where mandated, do departments and ministries collaborate and share processes that cross departmental boundaries. Often, data captured by a system in one department is re-keyed into a different system used by a different department. The Department of E-Government is seeking to eliminate these "islands of information" by providing a solution that could automate processes that required data to be replicated across multiple systems.

The initial catalyst for the Forms & Transaction Engine project was the need to better utilize the Government's portal platform to extend the overall reach and responsiveness of government to business and citizens. .

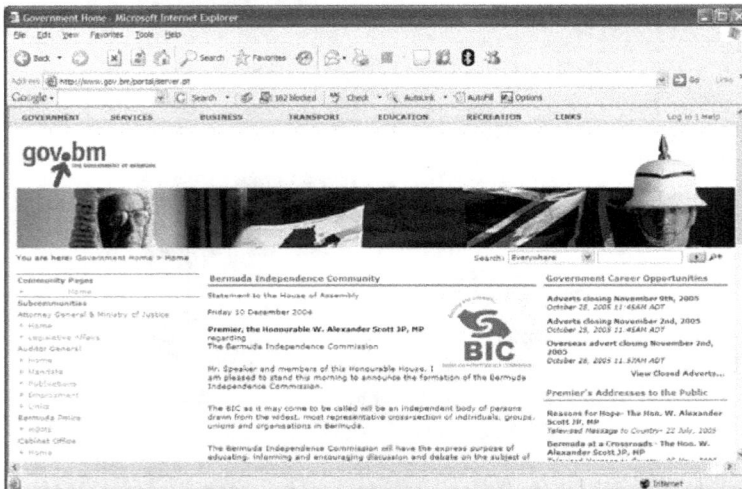

Figure 2: The Government of Bermuda Portal served as the catalyst for the Forms & Transaction Engine Project.

Finding the Innovators

Prior to launching the Forms & Transaction Engine project, the Department of E-Government realized that it would need to identify initial process projects that would enjoy strong support and sponsorship from government leaders. E-Government sought out leaders that were willing to introduce innovation to their respective departments and become champions for process transformation and collaboration throughout Government.

With this in mind, E-Government sponsored the first Forms & Transaction Engine solution with the Department of Statistics. The Department of Statistics had long been viewed as innovators within the Government of Bermuda. The department was often first to adopt new technology and always sought out new ways to leverage technology to improve efficiency. Additionally, leadership within the Department of Statistics saw technology as a key enabler for improving the quality of service to their key constituents.

Prior to kicking off the Forms & Transaction Engine project, the Department of E-Government collaborated with the Department of Statistics to scope out requirements for web-enabling the Government's Annual Employment Survey. This annual survey captures and analyzes volumes of data from the island's employers. All employers are required to participate in the survey, providing demographic information on employees, hiring trends, and vacancies.

The information captured during the annual survey is used throughout government and business communities for policy, economic, and recruitment planning. The original process was highly manual, requiring businesses to fill out paper-based surveys and mail them back in to the Department of Statistics. Once the paper surveys were received by the department, clerks were responsible for keying in the results. This usually required keying in data for hundreds of employees, numerous vacancies, and employment trends.

Many of the island's larger employers, mostly from the re-insurance industry, were pushing the Department of Statistics to place the annual survey on-line in order to streamline the submission process. To meet the demand from the private sector, the Department of Statistics and the Department of E-Government decided to develop an innovative process-driven solution that would introduce efficiency improvements for both government and employers on the island.

THE KEY INNOVATIONS

While many commercial industries have embraced business process management as a key driver for improving productivity, most government and public sector organizations have yet to reap the benefits of implementing BPM technologies and methodologies. As an early adopter, the Government of Bermuda realized tangible benefits and immediate return-on-investment from implementing BPM technology and applying process-oriented methodologies to improve service to constituents.

4.1 Business Impact

As the primary sponsor of the Form & Transaction Engine project, the Department of E-Government sought to leverage BPM to improve collaboration and communication across departments and ministries. The impact of the Forms & Transaction Engine project can be organized into four key categories:
- Faster Time to Market for e-Enabled Solutions
- Standardized Approach to Solution Development
- Improved Services to Constituents
- Identification of Shared Process Services

Faster Time to Market

In many ways, BPM has evolved into a platform and methodology for rapid solution development. Within the Government of Bermuda, the Forms & Transaction Engine project demonstrated how BPM could be used to quickly document process requirements, promote collaboration between business and technical teams, and quickly deploy solutions in three to four months. Using the AquaLogic BPM platform, business analysts were able to document requirements for the end-to-end employment survey process for the Department of Statistics in less than 30 days. These requirements were turned into feature lists that were prioritized and validated by the business stakeholders.

Process analysis sessions were driven by business stakeholders; in some cases literally controlling the mouse and driving the process design using BEA Aqua-Logic BPM's intuitive process modelling interface. This approach helped streamline the requirements gathering process and helped to bring everyone on the same page for capturing process activities, roles, and business rules.

These sessions were also attended by technical team members, which helped to accelerate the transition of knowledge for developing the technical components of the process solution. BEA AquaLogic BPM's innovative design tool allowed analysts and developers to collaborate in the same environment. After the initial process model was designed, the same model could be handed off to the technical team for to continue with developing forms, integration components, and business logic.

Combining agile development principles with the collaborative framework provided by BEA AquaLogic BPM allowed E-Government and the Department of Statistics to complete development of the automated Annual Employment Survey in less than four months. The automated solution, known as the e-Employment Survey, automated the initiation, submission, and logic associated with the annual survey.

Using traditional approaches, the solution might have taken six to nine months to develop. However, leveraging BPM, the solution was developed in less time with fewer resources.

Standardized Approach to Solution Development

Prior to implementing the Forms & Transaction Engine project, each department and ministry utilized various approaches and tools for implementing process-driven solutions. Some departments developed custom solutions using Microsoft or Java-based applications, while others acquired third-party solutions that were closed to customization and often required expensive off-island resources for maintenance and support.

Through the Forms & Transaction Engine project, the Department of E-Government established BEA AquaLogic BPM as a standard enterprise architecture component for implementing process-driven solutions. This approach has allowed Government to begin containing the growth of custom applications developed by numerous vendors. This approach has also allowed Government to introduce a "co-opetition" model that emphasizes collaboration and competition among vendors. Vendors are encouraged to attend training on the standardized BPM platform in order to begin developing process-driven solutions for departments and ministries. In some cases, several vendors participate as a team to support analysis and development of a particular government process.

Improved Services to Constituents

The initial BPM solution developed for the Department of Statistics delivered improved services to the island's business constituents. The e-Employment Survey demonstrated that BPM technology could be leveraged to improve efficiencies both inside and outside of Government. The automated e-Employment Survey solution replaced the paper-based survey process, allowing employers to fill out and submit their completed surveys on-line.

The on-line version of the employment survey provided employers with data validation and verification capabilities, on-line monitoring of progress towards completion of the survey, and the ability to collaborate and interact with Department of Statistics staff throughout the process. Additionally, 100% of the employers that participated in the survey completed the survey by the due date. In previous years, only approximately 88 – 90% of employers completed the survey by the due date.

Identification of Shared Services

Throughout the Forms & Transaction Engine project, the Department of E-Government focused on identifying opportunities for creating shared services and processes that could be reused throughout Bermuda Government. Through each round of process analysis, a common theme of shared services emerged around authentication, role-based access, and process monitoring. Instead of developing authentication and role-based access components for each individual solution, the Department of E-Government realized that it should consider developing a single cost-effective service for businesses and to register to do business with Government.

4.3 e-Employment Survey Process

The as-is process model for the Employment Survey solution was documented through a series of collaborative process design sessions. During these sessions, key business stakeholders from the Department of Statistics modelled the high-level end-to-end process, documenting roles, activities, and process decision points.

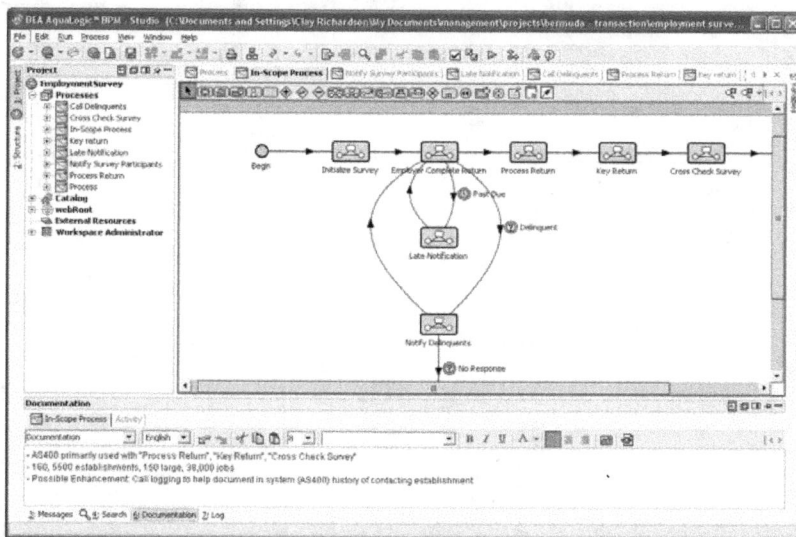

Figure 3: The AS-IS Employment Survey Process documented in the process design tool.

During the collaborative design sessions, analysts utilized BEA AquaLogic BPM to model the process and document questions, suggestions, and critical observations. This helped keep the sessions on track while capturing key areas that required further discussion.

The team utilized the "IGOE" process architecture model (Burlton, 2001) to document strategic goals and objectives, process stakeholders, and key performance indicators. The following four key performance indicators were identified for the as-is Employment Survey process:

- Improve Performance Against Plan - Complete Employment Survey project milestones by the time they are due or before they are due.

- Improve Employment Survey Accuracy - Improve accuracy of data provided by employers and accuracy of data entry by survey clerks.
- Increase Survey Response Rate - Increase percentage of Employment Surveys that are completed and returned by employers.
- Increase Rate-of-Return for Previous Year's Delinquents – Increase the percentage of Employment Surveys that are completed and returned by employers that were delinquent in the previous year.

Using this initial list of key performance indicators, the team created a list of over 75 potential improvements that could positively impact performance. This list of improvements was then weighted based on overall impact and complexity to implement. The top three improvements from each key performance indicator were selected as the basis for designing the to-be process model.

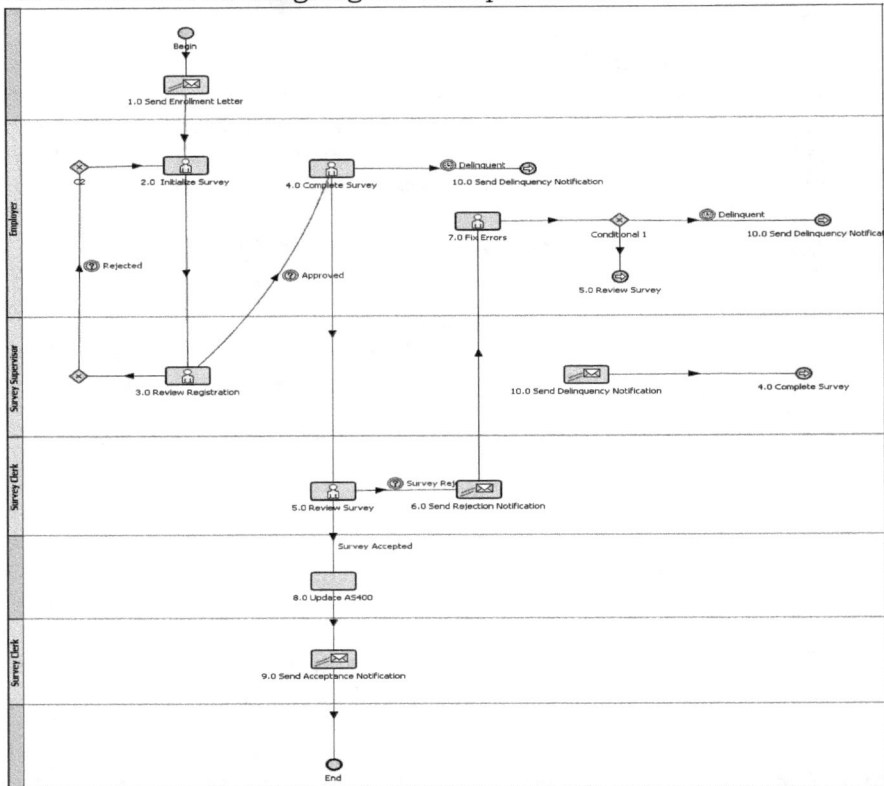

Figure 4: The TO-BE Process Model for the automated e-Employment Survey Solution

The resulting to-be model focused primarily on simplifying data entry and form submission for employers. The Department of Statistics deduced that by simplifying the submission process, more employers would complete surveys in a timely manner, thereby increasing the survey response rate. Additionally, the to-be process focused on improving data entry accuracy by providing process logic and validation checks to ensure that all data was entered properly by employers.

Automatic alerts were incorporated into the to-be model to send e-mail notifications to employers and department staff if surveys are not completed by the due date. Business rules and process logic were also incorporated into the process to automatically route completed surveys to the appropriate clerk for review and acceptance. Rejected surveys were automatically routed back to the appropriate employer for modifications and corrections. In addition, employers were provided with a support process for submitting support requests and questions related to the e-Employment Survey.

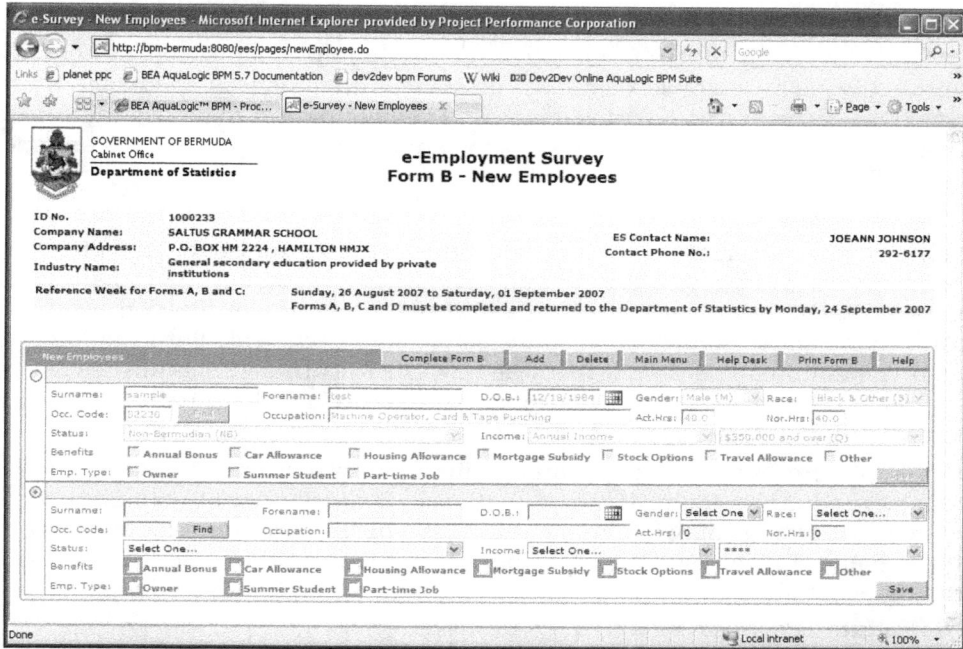

Figure 5: Electronic Forms were tightly integrated with the e-Employment Survey Process

4.4 Establishing the "Better Process Group"

Early on in the Forms & Transaction Engine project, the Department of E-Government realized that it needed to form a cross-government steering committee to help provide governance and support for the various process solutions that would need to be implemented. The "Better Process Group" was chartered as a committee of analysts, developers, and vendors from across government charged with creating standards and best practices for implementing process-driven solutions.

The "Better Process Group," or "BPG" for short, recruited initial members from key government departments to help promote adoption of BPM and to educate analysts, developers, and vendors on the standardized BPM platform. Additionally, the BPG serves as a forum for identifying and prioritizing potential process projects and initiatives within Government. The BPG team meets once each quarter to review the status of various process projects, analyze potential new projects, and to share best practices for process modelling and design.

HURDLES OVERCOME

As with most BPM implementations, the initial hurdles for the Forms & Transaction Engine project centered around introducing a new paradigm and technology platform to the enterprise. While the learning curve and configuration for BPM are not quite as steep as other technologies, it still requires an investment and serious commitment on the part of both lines of business and information technology departments. During the initial stages of the Forms & Transaction Engine project, the Department of E-Government worked closely with the Government's Information Technology Office (ITO) to establish a technical environment that could be shared across government departments.

BENEFITS

Within public sector and government organizations, the benefits of implementing BPM are often measured in terms of productivity improvements, cost savings, and improved services to constituents. An initial ROI analysis was conducted for the first phase of the Forms & Transaction Engine pilot project to assess the benefits achieved by the project. The analysis uncovered tangible improvements and measurable ROI.

6.1 Cost Savings

Each year the Government of Bermuda hires seasonal and part-time employees to support various paper-intensive and manual processes. For the Department of Statistics, these seasonal employees support data entry, verification, and communication for the roughly 6,000 surveys received each year. With the introduction of the automated e-Employment Survey, the Department of Statistics realized immediate cost savings, by eliminating the need to hire seasonal employees for data entry and verification.

Now employers enter the data directly into the on-line survey, which is then routed to managers for review and approval. The department estimates that it realized cost savings of two full-time seasonal employees for the first year of the e-Employment Survey. Additionally, the on-line survey eliminated the need for printing paper surveys and mailing these surveys to employers on the island.

6.4 Productivity Improvements

Migrating from paper-based, manual processes has introduced several productivity improvements to the Government of Bermuda and the island's business community. Many of the government's paper-based processes often require significant quality assurance procedures to ensure that data is accurately and properly entered. These quality assurance measures are often carried out by managers, pulling them from the value-added activities and critical tasks they were hired to do.

The introduction of BPM has minimized the need for quality assurance, since data is automatically transferred from one system to the other in the correct format and with minimal potential for error. Additionally, businesses on the island have realized productivity improvements as a result of the introduction of electronic forms used to capture and route key information. On-line processes have also reduced the latency encountered when forms are returned to businesses for corrections and modifications.

BEST PRACTICES, LEARNING POINTS AND PITFALLS

7.1 Best Practices and Learning Points

- ✓ *Throughout the Forms & Transaction Engine project, the following best practices and lessons learned were documented:*

- ✓ *Start with internal-facing BPM projects to minimize risk and speed adoption*

- ✓ *Conduct weekly or bi-weekly process review sessions to ensure that business stakeholders remain engaged throughout the project*

- ✓ *External-facing BPM projects can sometimes require highly customized user interfaces that can increase development time and overall scope*

✓ *Allow external stakeholders to test-drive the solution before it goes live; this approach increases adoption and reduces the number of questions*

✓ *Engage the technology infrastructure team early on in the project to gain buy-in and support from the IT department*

COMPETITIVE ADVANTAGES

The Government of Bermuda competes within a global market for re-insurance and international finance business. In order to maintain its leadership position within these markets, the Government must constantly seek new approaches to improving the quality of service to citizens, expatriates, and businesses on the island. The Forms & Transaction Engine project is playing a key role in demonstrating to the island's businesses and citizens that Government is on-line and moving into the 21st Century. The Annual Employment Survey process was chosen as the first solution for the Forms & Transaction Engine project as a result of its potential impact on both Bermuda Government and the island's private sector. Many of the large businesses participating in the on-line e-Employment Survey provided positive feedback on the automated solution and responded that they were impressed that the Government is moving its processes on-line.

TECHNOLOGY

The Forms & Transaction Engine project was implemented using BEA AquaLogic BPM and BEA AquaLogic User Interaction Portal. The Government of Bermuda had already implemented its portal using the AquaLogic User Interaction Portal platform. The Department of E-Government sought a BPM solution that would work seamlessly with the existing portal environment, yet could also stand alone if necessary.

The BEA platform provided the flexibility to implement simple processes utilizing out-of-the-box capabilities, while also supporting the need to deploy robust processes utilizing J2EE frameworks such as Struts and Spring. Additionally, the BEA platform provided out-of-the-box connectors to integrate existing applications, web services, and legacy components (including applications developed on the government's AS400 system).

The system configuration for the Forms & Transaction Engine project encompassed three environments: development, staging, and production. The production environment was configured to support high-availability and clustering to minimize downtime. Using BEA AquaLogic BPM's deployment capabilities, the development team was able to easily package all process components and quickly deploy processes for testing and production release.

The final solution was deployed to a Wintel architecture, utilizing SQL Server databases and J2EE web application servers.

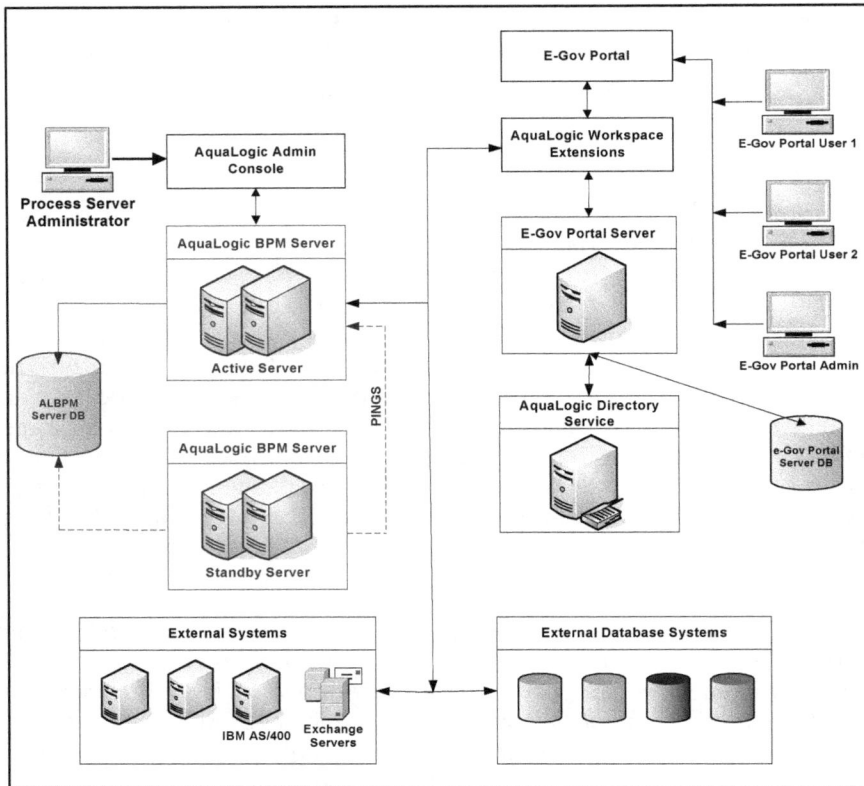

Figure 6: System Configuration for Forms & Transaction Engine

THE TECHNOLOGY AND SERVICE PROVIDERS

Project Performance Corporation (http://www.ppc.com)

Founded in 1991, Project Performance Corporation is a management and tech-nology consulting firm in the business of simplifying complex problems for top government and Fortune 500 decision makers, with specialization in environ-ment, energy, security and information technology solutions. Project Performance Corporation is privately held, supporting a culture of personal and shared suc-cess for every employee. Headquartered in McLean, Virginia, the company has offices in Alexandria, Virginia, and Germantown, Maryland. The company has more than 350 employees. For more information about PPC, visit the website at www.ppc.com.

BEA Systems (http://www.bea.com)

BEA Systems, Inc. (NASDAQ: BEAS) is a world leader in enterprise infrastructure software. Information about how BEA helps customers build a Liquid Enter-prise™ that transforms their business can be found at bea.com.

Grupo Pão de Açúcar, Brazil

Finalist, South America
Nominated by iProcess, Brazil

1. EXECUTIVE SUMMARY / ABSTRACT

This paper describes the evolution of Grupo Pão de Açúcar (GPA), one of the largest retail groups in Brazil, in the implementation of Workflow technology. The company started to use Workflow in 2005, with the Investment Approval Workflow (IAW), which reduced the process completion time in around 80%. Soon after this well-succeeded project, GPA started to expand Workflow technology usage to other business processes.

This paper focuses on the largest Workflow project GPA has implemented, the Travel and Expenses Workflow. Motivated by the need to cut and better control costs, this project has redesigned the travel and expenses processes, achieving relevant financial savings, simplifying the job of thousands of employees and drastically increasing the company's level of control of these processes. The success of this project is now leading GPA to definitively incorporate workflow culture into its operations.

2. OVERVIEW

Grupo Pão de Açúcar, founded in 1948, is one of the retail leaders in Brazil. With a 13.3% market share and total sales of R$ 16.4 billion (R$ 1 = US$ 0,554 in 12/20/2007) in 2006, it has 549 stores distributed through 14 states in the South, Southeast, Midwest and Northeast regions and in the Federal District. With stocks listed in the São Paulo Stock Exchange (Bovespa) since 1995, and in the New York Stock Exchange (ADR level III) since 1997, the company participates at Level 1 of IGC Corporate Governance, an index that brings together companies with leading initiatives of Corporate Governance; of the IBX-50, an index that brings together 50 companies the present the highest Bovespa liquidity indices; and, in 2006, it became a part of Ibovespa, the most important average performance indicator of quotations in the Brazilian stock market.

In recent years, Grupo Pão de Açúcar has become focused on a strong cost reduction strategy, with the objective of reversing their declining profit margins. The Shared Service Center (SSC), introduced in August 2006, plays a leading role in this strategy, as it unifies all of the company's back office activities, making cost reduction and scale gains feasible. This new management model has demanded a greater level of standardization of GPA's various processes, among which the travel and expenses processes, which had previously been done by hand in different ways, with a low level of control and high vulnerability.

The Travel and Expense Workflow fit perfectly into the Grupo Pão de Açúcar's new organizational context. The system came online in May 2007 and automated three different processes: **Definitive Expense** (expense reimbursement process already done by employees), **Temporary Voucher** (expense advance process and employee account rendering) and **Domestic/International Travel** (travel request and involved services process, such as airline tickets, hotel, vehicle rental, per diem, etc.) The system helped the company reach various business and process objectives, in that it institutionalized existing norms, sped up the payment approval flow, almost completely eliminated paper procedures, reduced the involvement of people in the process, markedly reduced the risk of errors and fraud and optimized travel and expenses cost by using a much more effective reimbursement and advance management.

In addition to the Travel and Expenses Workflow, three other workflows have been previously developed: Investment Approval Workflow (winner of the Silver Medal of this Award for South America in 2006), IT Resources Control and Outsourcing Management. Three other projects are in development and will soon be added to this list: Incidents (control of non-conformities in stores), Events (control of marketing events done by the GPA) and Product Registry (control of the registry of new products to be sold in stores).

3.   BUSINESS CONTEXT

GPA has, in recent years, significantly increased investments in process automation. This activity began in 2005 with the introduction of the Investment Approval Workflow (IAW), mainly motivated by the need to comply with the Sarbanes-Oxley Act and to accelerate the execution of processes considered critical. Since then, eight processes have already been automated, including the Travel and Expenses Workflow, subject of this paper.

This number shows, in and of itself, the importance that workflow technology has been gaining for the company. In this context, some factors were determinants for GPA to make such investments, specifically, the Travel and Expenses Workflow:

Need to increase profit margins and maintain competitiveness

Profit margins registered by GPA have been diminishing in the last years. In 2006, net profit was R$ 219.7 million, equal to 1.6% of net income, compared to 1.9% in 2005 and 4.4% in 2000. The company felt the pressure of two international giants in the sector, the French network Carrefour, the new market leader in Brazil, and the American Wal-Mart, third in the ranking. In this heated dispute, the two rivals have been announcing heavy investments in Brazil (the French network intends to invest R$ 1 billion per year for the next three years, and the American one reported investments of R$ 1.2 billion in 2008), making it necessary for GPA to quickly act to prevent an imminent market loss. Close margins and changes in the Brazilian competitive scenario have led the company to adopt a strong cost reduction strategy and productivity and efficiency gains, which makes it possible to operate with lower expenses and greater competitiveness.

Introduction of the Shared Services Center (SSC)

Nearly two years ago, Grupo Pão de Açúcar began a profound administrative restructuring focused on facing and reversing the profit margin reduction trend. GPA's principal and most daring initiative in this sense was the introduction of the Shared Services Center (SSC) in August 2006. SSC's role is to centralize all back office activities that were common to various company units, such as account payables and receivables, purchasing, accounting and human resources. Therefore, activities that before had been repeated in various parts of the organization, in an non-standardized way, were grouped in one single location, allowing for economy of scale, cost reduction and productivity gains, preparing GPA to be able to sustain accelerated growth in coming years. GPA´s SSC has nowadays around 650 employees.

Shared Services Center represents an organizational transformation for GPA, which has begun to transition from a departmental work view to a process work view. SSC behaves like a contracted company, whose client is the company itself (the internal client) and their suppliers (the outside client.) With this, the very service model of these corporate clients was changed, and today is done by a Contact Center, and no longer by GPA departments. SSC also has much more ambitious goals: to provide services to other companies, no longer being a cost center but becoming a profit center.

With SSC, GPA identified the need to implement more effective processes and technology, which gave them the necessary support and control to reach their objectives. In this context, workflow technology has gained even more importance, as it has become imperative to create mechanisms that make it possible to centralize and standardize organizational processes. Reimbursement, advances and travel requests were activities directly related to the scope of SSC – purchasing products/services and expense costing – but were being done in a practically manual way, with no control or uniformity.

Lack of discipline in executing processes

Despite having a high level of internal standardization, travel and expense request processes hardly followed GPA rules. At the first obstacle, like the absence of the hierarchical superior at the time of request, for example, the requests were processed and approved in different ways. Therefore, it was necessary to enforce those rules, in spite of an organizational environment where, for years, thousands of people were accustomed to do these activities without a standard.

Accordance with the Sarbanes-Oxley Act

With stocks listed on the New York Stock Exchange (ADR level III) since 1997, GPA needed to adapt to Sarbanes-Oxley Act (SOX), which has become an important motivating factor for adopting workflow technology in various processes, especially those with financial impact. The Travel and Expenses Workflow represents, with respect to SOX, much greater and more effective control of company expenses.

4.   KEY INNOVATIONS

Business

Expense reimbursement and advance and travel made by GPA employees represent a large investment for the company: from February to November of 2007, approximately R$ 7.9 million of this kind of expense were recorded in the Travel and Expenses Workflow. Considering that the system adoption curve was slower in the beginning, it is estimated that total annual expenses of this nature will be close to R$ 12.5 million. Only in travels between June and December 2007, GPA neared R$ 3.9 million, among airfare, accommodations, vehicle rental and per diems, which should lead to annual spending of approximately R$ 8.6 million.

With this, the Travel and Expenses Workflow had an important impact in terms of GPA business. Following, we highlight the main innovations reached by introducing the system:

Greater control of travel costs

The Travel and Expenses Workflow provided GPA with much more effective control of expenses related to employee travel, making negotiations for reservations, airfare, hotel, vehicles and other related services more transparent. With it, the approvers will have guidelines to compare travel costs, as the request provides all of the quotes sent by the tourism agency. Before, the approvers could only approve or deny options previously selected by the requester, but did not have access to other values found by the agency. It was not rare for the option selected by the requester to be the most expensive, usually because of benefits like schedule convenience, boarding service and mileage. In the new process, the approvers are able to see all of the options, and can question the employee's motive for not selecting the least expensive option. This, in a company who has a cost reduction strategy, represents an important process change, as decisions become transparent, requiring employees to be more rational in their choices.

Centralized Decentralization

While increasing the system user base, from nearly 800 to more than 10,000 people, the Travel and Expenses Workflow became the only method of requesting expense and travel in GPA. Also, previously, the greater part of travel and expense requests were done by secretaries, who were also responsible for store employee requests. This meant that the same person did various requests that, in reality, were not his or hers, creating a distortion in the number of requests and the values released/reimbursed, in addition to a total lack of control. Today, the requester is the final system user and is responsible for their own requests and account rendering.

Safer approval process

An important innovation brought by the Travel and Expenses Workflow was the guarantee that each request would be directed to and approved by the appropriate people. Before, approval was given through signatures, a fragile mechanism subject to error, which gave the Treasury the difficult tasks of validating signatures and detecting possible falsifications. Today, the system has guidelines: approval flow is managed according to the functional hierarchy of the person requesting the expense and user permission is valid using a unique login, eliminating the risk of fraud.

Standardizing the process throughout the company

The Travel and Expenses Workflow helped GPA to institutionalize best practices defined during the process analysis phase, guaranteeing that it was carried out in exactly the manner for which it was created. Also, the system incorporated rules that had already existed in the company, but that were not always known or complied with. Thus, the introduction of workflow technology had an important role so that the company could rise beyond the inertia of the status quo and ensure the adoption of the new process, making it official and making it impossible for it to be used in other ways.

Agility in the analysis and approval flow

A process that previously could have been paralyzed by the first obstacle, today has a logical and completely automated flow. The Travel and Expenses Workflow ensured quicker request analysis and approval for GPA, who could return it to the requester if the predefined rules were not complied with. The approvers receive request data by email and can access the system via internet, wherever they may be, in order to give approval, no longer needing to be physically present to sign a paper, which was the case before. This allowed the directors and executive to evaluate expenses and travel even when they were outside of the company.

Workflow usage leads to process improvement initiatives

The use of the Travel and Expenses Workflow revealed that GPA did not understand deeply their own process. The first version of the system was developed using existing norms, which were often not known before, much less complied with, and which began to be questioned by the users. This created a series of subsequent improvements in the process, as it was realized that some norms were not appropriate to the reality and needs of the company. The result is that system use led GPA to reevaluate their internal practices.

Process

In summary, the Travel and Expenses Workflow automated three different processes:

- **Definitive Expense** – expense reimbursement process already done by employees.
- **Temporary Voucher** – employee expense advance and account rendering process.
- **Domestic/International Travel** – process to request all of the services involved in travel (airfare, hotel, vehicle rental, per diems, etc.)

The Definitive Expense process, while the simplest of the three, is the most used by GPA employees, with an average of 1,630 cases started per month, during the period of June to November of 2007.

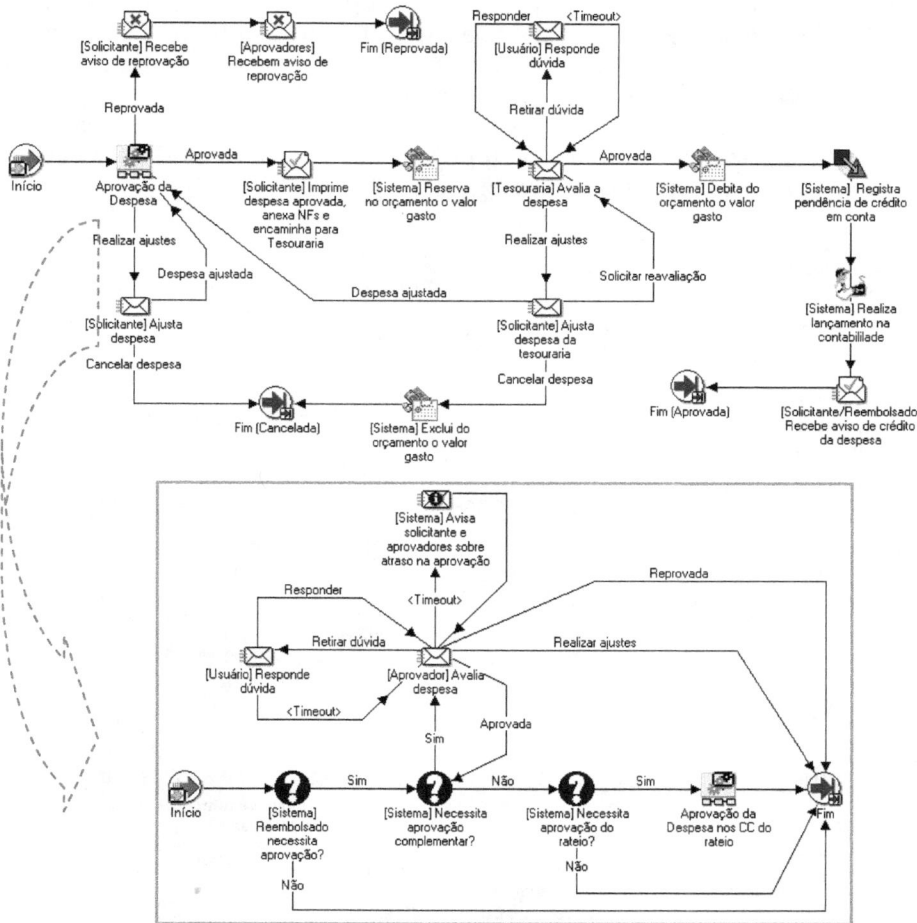

Figure 1. Graphic representation of the Definitive Expense process

The Travel and Expenses Workflow had important impacts when analyzed from the process perspective. The greatest innovations were:

Reversal in the expense payment process

The greatest perceived change from using the Travel and Expenses Workflow was the reversal in the way that GPA reimburses/advances employee expenses. Previously, when an employee made and expense, he/she completed a form with its description, collected the signature of his/her hierarchical superiors and sent the request directly to a bank agency located within GPA network, where he/she withdrew the money. Only after the money had been received did the information arrive at the Treasury, sent by the bank to validate expenses. If there was any discrepancy with the company norms, it was necessary to wait for the employee's good will to make any corrections, or those responsible in the Treasury needed to charge the employee, requiring time and effort.

With the new process, all this was reversed. Today, directors previously approve the request, then it passes through the Treasury conference and, only at the end, if everything is agreed upon, the employee receives the reimbursement, which is directly deposited into his/her bank account, also avoiding moving money by the company.

The image below demonstrates the application through which the approvers have access to the details of the requested travel, with the reservations ("Reserva de Passagem" and "Reserva de Hotel") and the options entered by the tourism agency ("Complementação da Agência"), and those chosen by the traveler are marked (items marked with the ⊘ symbol.) It is also possible to see the processes comment history ("Histórico") and the list of approvers with the date and time of previous approvals ("Aprovadores da Viagem").

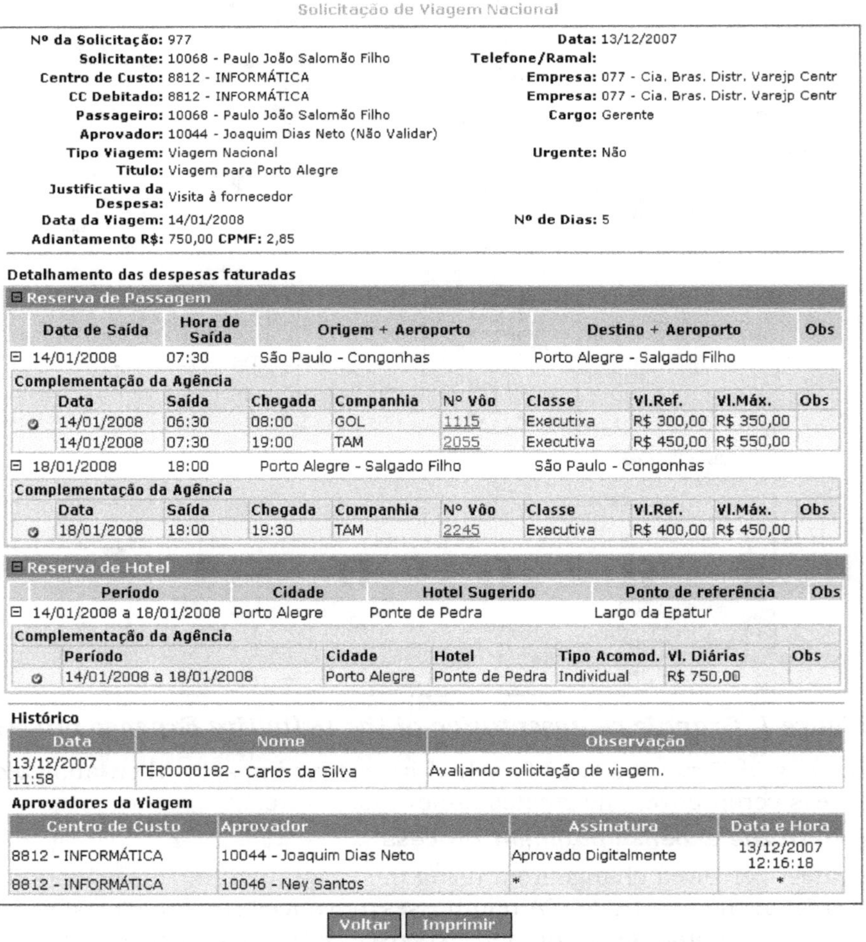

Solicitação de Viagem Nacional

Nº da Solicitação: 977 — Data: 13/12/2007
Solicitante: 10068 - Paulo João Salomão Filho — Telefone/Ramal:
Centro de Custo: 8812 - INFORMÁTICA — Empresa: 077 - Cia. Bras. Distr. Varejp Centr
CC Debitado: 8812 - INFORMÁTICA — Empresa: 077 - Cia. Bras. Distr. Varejp Centr
Passageiro: 10068 - Paulo João Salomão Filho — Cargo: Gerente
Aprovador: 10044 - Joaquim Dias Neto (Não Validar)
Tipo Viagem: Viagem Nacional — Urgente: Não
Título: Viagem para Porto Alegre
Justificativa da Despesa: Visita à fornecedor
Data da Viagem: 14/01/2008 — Nº de Dias: 5
Adiantamento R$: 750,00 CPMF: 2,85

Detalhamento das despesas faturadas

Reserva de Passagem

Data de Saída	Hora de Saída	Origem + Aeroporto	Destino + Aeroporto	Obs
14/01/2008	07:30	São Paulo - Congonhas	Porto Alegre - Salgado Filho	

Complementação da Agência

	Data	Saída	Chegada	Companhia	Nº Vôo	Classe	Vl.Ref.	Vl.Máx.	Obs
⊘	14/01/2008	06:30	08:00	GOL	1115	Executiva	R$ 300,00	R$ 350,00	
	14/01/2008	07:30	19:00	TAM	2055	Executiva	R$ 450,00	R$ 550,00	

Data de Saída	Hora de Saída	Origem + Aeroporto	Destino + Aeroporto	Obs
18/01/2008	18:00	Porto Alegre - Salgado Filho	São Paulo - Congonhas	

Complementação da Agência

	Data	Saída	Chegada	Companhia	Nº Vôo	Classe	Vl.Ref.	Vl.Máx.	Obs
⊘	18/01/2008	18:00	19:30	TAM	2245	Executiva	R$ 400,00	R$ 450,00	

Reserva de Hotel

Período	Cidade	Hotel Sugerido	Ponto de referência	Obs
14/01/2008 a 18/01/2008	Porto Alegre	Ponte de Pedra	Largo da Epatur	

Complementação da Agência

	Período	Cidade	Hotel	Tipo Acomod.	Vl. Diárias	Obs
⊘	14/01/2008 a 18/01/2008	Porto Alegre	Ponte de Pedra	Individual	R$ 750,00	

Histórico

Data	Nome	Observação
13/12/2007 11:58	TER0000182 - Carlos da Silva	Avaliando solicitação de viagem.

Aprovadores da Viagem

Centro de Custo	Aprovador	Assinatura	Data e Hora
8812 - INFORMÁTICA	10044 - Joaquim Dias Neto	Aprovado Digitalmente	13/12/2007 12:16:18
8812 - INFORMÁTICA	10046 - Ney Santos	*	*

Voltar   Imprimir

Figure 2. Domestic travel request approval screen

Better collaboration with business partners

Today the tourism agency that provides services to GPA is integrated into the Travel and Expenses Workflow system, and receives quote requests directly from the employee, without intermediaries. The request arrives at the agency as a task to be completed which is automatically assigned to a tourism agent who makes the quotes and continues the process. The system allows the attendant to include airfare, hotel and vehicle rental options, controlling the period to carry out the quote and sending warnings when the stipulated time has passed. Previously, it was common for a request to stall because of the employee's (usually a secretary) relationship with a specific agent, which, if he/she were unavailable or involved in another activity, would delay the entire process.

In addition to these, the table below shows other important changes in the process offered by the introduction of the Travel and Expenses Workflow:

Topic	Before	After
Documentation	For travels, five copies of a paper form were used; for expenses, one paper form	Custom Web Application
Definition of the approval group	Based on the travel norm, the requester needed to include the name of the approvers in the expense document.	Automatically defined according to the type of expense or reimbursement, his/her cost center and position in GPA's functional hierarchy.
Media	Paper. A form with the expense data was printed and sent to the approvers.	Digital. Information is automatically sent to the people that need to validate and approve the expense.
Process control	Manually done by the requester, which required calling the approvers and checking the process status.	Electronic, with the ability to monitor the process status at any time.
Approval task	The document was sent to the approver, who could immediately approve it or return it to the requester for further evaluation.	Approval tasks are submitted directly to approver's e-mail inbox. The system is responsible for sending a new alert message if the approver takes too long to complete the task.
Comments about the document	There was no space for commenting. Some managers used to justify rejection in the document body.	Every comment is recorded and the comment history is shown to subsequent approvers, allowing improvement in effective collaboration.

Apportionments	Cost centers with shared expense values only found out that they should pay something when they received the accounting report.	Possibility of the cost center to indicate if it is desired to approve the value that will be paid due to an apportionment before the same of the expense to be approved and paid to the employee.
Rendering of accounts	Depended on the initiative of the requester, with no control of deadlines defined in the company's internal norm.	Controlled by the system through time counters, with sending of warning to the requester based on the timeframe defined in the company's internal norm and allowing a block for creating new expenses for those employees that do not meet the established deadlines.
Consulting other employees	When in doubt, the user needed to communicate using email or the telephone and the information was not recorded on the expense database.	The main activities of the system (quote, validation and approval) allow any user to be consulted. The question and answer are recorded on the expense database and can be consulted by anyone participating in the process.
Conversion rates for purchase/sale of foreign currency	Stored in Excel worksheets manually controlled by the Treasury	All of the rates used for buying and selling foreign currency or reimbursement of expenses in a foreign currency are recorded in the system with the travel database, making it possible to check the values effectively spent during travel.

ORGANIZATION

Change for the user (requester)

The most affected group by the Travel and Expenses Workflow were GPA employees. The system had a profound effect on the way in which GPA supports employee's expenses, as it automated processes that were previously done manually with a low level of control. With the availability of the system, the entire company began to use it and was unable to make requests any other way or outside of the system. This means that every employee, independent of hierarchical level, needed to conform himself with the new reality and follow strictly the rules. This was especially difficult for some middle and senior managers, who were used to have an almost absolute power in their departments, including a sort of 'right' to decide which administrative rules would be followed or not.

Change in the service request structure

Since the creation of the Shared Services Center (SSC), expenses are validated in a centralized manner, as the Treasury is one of the areas that were integrated into SSC. The use of the Travel and Expenses Workflow supports this centralized service, as the system is the only point to receive requests to be validated.

5. HURDLES OVERCOME

Management

The Travel and Expenses Workflow was developed to work in an integrated manner with GPA Accounts Payable and Accounting systems. In this aspect, it was necessary to avoid some difficulties during development and approval of the part of the system that would be integrated to legacy systems.

Web services technology was the approach chosen to integrate the Travel and Expenses Workflow and the Accounts Payable system. This approach was adopted because the systems were in very different environments (the workflow directly in the database and the Accounts Payable system in the mainframe.) For this, greater involvement of GPA's IT team was required to develop the web service. Later, during the pre-production phase, the presence of the system analyst responsible for this system was also required, in order to validate that the information was being adequately received.

Likewise, integration with the Accounting system also required the involvement of GPA team. Since this system runs in an external ASP and already has a standard integration interface using file exchange, it was chosen to develop a routine to generate a file in the required format. This routine, however, needed a series of adjustments during the pre-production phase, since the file layout was not clearly documented and some data formatting details were only discovered during testing.

Business

In terms of business, GPA's size, with 549 stores in 14 states, is a challenge to surpass. In the company's headquarters, there was already a rising workflow culture, but that was not the case in the regional offices. The introduction of the Travel and Expenses Workflow needed to consider this scenario and succeeded, with little investment in training (as will be seen later), to overcome this great challenge.

ORGANIZATION ADOPTION

Introduction

In order to avoid that the old process continued to be used in some areas or regions, which would certainly happen if the introduction was done in steps, GPA determined, after tests and the approval of the Travel and Expenses Workflow, that within 15 days all expenses and travels should be requested through the system. This abrupt introduction required the employees to quickly adapt to the new system, and also met difficulties because of the different versions of operating systems in the company and by the fact that the users were spread in various places in the country.

Training

To succeed in training the more than 10,000 potential Travel and Expenses Workflow users, GPA chose to train only the secretaries, who were traditionally the only users of the old expenses and travel process. They, in turn, were responsible for training the employees in their departments. As the system use is extremely intuitive, this training format proved to be effective and users quickly incorporated the new tool.

Inclusion of tax reimbursement (CPMF)

The first version of the Travel and Expenses Workflow did not include in the reimbursement the calculation of CPMF (Temporary Contribution on Financial Movement), a Brazilian tax, with a rate of 0.38%, which is payable on every financial transaction. Not reimbursing CPMF was an obstacle in adopting the system in its first days, as the only way to pay the reimbursements is through deposit in a checking account and the CPMF value relative to the reimbursement was not deposited. Therefore, the employees did not want to take responsibility for the cost not included in the reimbursements and stopped using the system, making requests in the old manner. GPA revised its decision and CPMF reimbursement was included soon after introducing the Workflow.

6.   BENEFITS

Cost Savings

Reduction in travel costs due to better quote comparison

From June to December of 2007, GPA spent nearly R$ 3.9 million in travels, among airfare, hotels, vehicle rental and per diems, leading to a projected annual expenditure of R$ 8.6 million in these items. As previously stated, one of the greatest innovations of the system is that is allows various quotes to be compared for each travel item. This helps approvers to make better decisions, making it possible to choose the items with the lowest price. Thus, GPA has certainly gained an important reduction in travel expenditures.

There are no precise statistics, since, previously, travel requests were recorded only on paper. However, it is clear that the person making the travel request often pre-selected a more expensive trip. For this estimate, we assumed that between 25% and 50% of the travelers requested higher prices airfares. A recent study from the Air Transportation Competition and Regulation Study Center (NECTAR, a research organization part of the Air Force Technology Institute) points out that, on average, the difference between highest and lowest airfares in Brazil for business travels is around 40%. Since it is known that GPA, in the new process, will always choose the lowest airfare, there is an expressive cost benefit.

With the parameters above, we can estimate a conservative airfare cost reduction between 10% and 20%. As, on average, 65% of travel costs are in airfare (R$ 5.6 million), we can estimate financial savings between R$ 560,000 and R$ 1.12 million per year.

In fact, the actual cost reduction is probably much higher, since it has been widely published in the Brazilian press (please see www2.topclip.com.br/gpa/noticia.php?idresumo=133856) that GPA spent more than R$ 10 million in airfares in 2005. Since the company has only grown since then (and therefore the number of travels has certainly not been reduced), the actual cost reduction in airfares may approach 44%, resulting in savings of R$ 4.4 million (US$ 2.4 million).

The same rationale can be applied to hotel reservations, which are estimated to cost R$ 1.2 million per year. In this case, the average variation is 18%. According to the parameters above, this would create savings of between 4.5% and 9% of the total expense, resulting in a financial gain between R$ 54,000 to R$ 108,000.

Also, the new system established that high values (above R$ 2,000) are only withdrawn with special authorizations, avoiding unnecessary advances and requiring the employees to be reasonable in their requests.

Improvement in cash flow management

The Travel and Expenses Workflow is helping GPA to better manage their cash flow. The company gained more time to make decisions such as financial investments or the need for cash coverage. This is because now accounts are reconciled in the morning and no longer in the afternoon, as used to happen, thanks to the automatic integration between the system and the bank, which reports completed payments to the Treasury earlier.

In addition to these precious hours, the Workflow also affects cash flow, as, before, with a low level of process control, the employee could withdraw advances various days before travel. Now there are rules that prevent this from happening – the money is only released the day before traveling --, and any exceptions need to be justified in the system. Taking into consideration the estimate that, annually, advances reach R$ 3.8 million, it is easy to see the positive impact of these measures on the company's accounts.

Also, the reversal of the payment process - first have the proof/justification of the expense to later reimburse the employee - also had an effect, since GPA stopped paying advanced unconfirmed expenses or those that were not in accordance with the procedures. The Travel and Expenses Workflow also controls the deadlines for rendering accounts, reducing the time that the advanced and unspent amounts are in the power of the requester and making it possible for users with late accounts to be blocked and prevented from requesting new expenses.

Reduction in the number of lost reservations

The lack of agility of the old process caused another problem: hotel and airfare reservations made by the tourism agency were often lost because they were not confirmed in good time. When this happened, the entire process needed to be repeated, and generally the quoted price was lost, leading to increase in costs. The Travel and Expenses Workflow allows a tourism agency to have access to the travel approval in real time, making it possible to confirm reservations and avoiding the extra work of the requester and the agency in having to redo the reservation.

Time Reductions

Reduction of approval and validation time

The new approval flow improved the average process time. There was a significant reduction in the approval time and in the validation by the Treasury. The Treasury also had the responsibility of collecting from employees that did not render their accounts or that had corrections to make - time that was eliminated by the reversal in the reimbursement payment process. The following table shows these reductions:

	Before	After
Average process time		
Reimbursements	Uncertain, undefined and not controlled. Each area carried out the process differently, without being	3.6 days
Advances		5.3 days
Travel		17.5 days
Average manager approval time		

Reimbursements	possible to get a history.	12 business hours
Advances		8 business hours
Advances -- Account rendering		12 business hours
Travel – Advances and reservations		12 business hours
Travel – Account rendering		24 business hours
Average Treasury validation time		
Reimbursements		24 business hours
Advances		24 business hours
Travel		72 business hours

Productivity Improvements

Employee focus in their end activity

The Travel and Expenses Workflow allows GPA employees to stop using their time on tasks that were not focused on their jobs. The previous process required the employee to be personally involved in the entire process, from completing the form with expense information to collecting the signatures, to going to the bank to withdraw the money to delivering the bills and receipts to the Treasury. Today, the system does all of the procedures and the money is automatically deposited in the employee's account.

Reduction in the time employees are involved in the process

The adoption of the Travel and Expenses Workflow led to an approximately 60% reduction in the time employees spend on each request. In the previous process, each employee spent on average 25 minutes per request, from completing the form to collecting signatures to going to the bank. With the system, this time dropped to only 10 minutes, on average. During a 6 month period (June to November 2007), there was a total estimated reduction of 4063.50 hours in the time employees spent on the process, thereby estimating a saving of 8127 man-hours per year.

Increase in service capacity

From the moment that GPA began using the Travel and Expenses Workflow, the processes had a wider reach within the company and were done faster. Today GPA is capable of processing a much higher number of requests simultaneously, without overloading a restricted group of employees, as had happened before (in the last 6 months, the average number of processes per month was 2709, close to 1 process every 4 minutes). Each employee makes his/her own request, controls and follows the process with a minimum time involvement, as the system does the activities that had previously been done manually.

Reduction of rework

Various steps in the previous process were potentially subject to rework, from wrongly completing the form to collecting signatures of the wrong people. Rework was significantly reduced after the introduction of the Travel and Expenses Workflow, since the possibility of errors has been minimized.

Treasury was one of the departments that was most affected by this change, as it came to have all of the data consolidated in the system and could validate expenses and interact using the system. In this sense, what had previously been the

Treasury's responsibility – asking for account rendering after the employee had already been reimbursed – became the employee's responsibility, who needs to make all the corrections to be able to receive the money.

7.   BEST PRACTICES, LEARNING OPPORTUNITIES AND PITFALLS

Best Practices and Learning Opportunities

✓ *Creation of mechanisms throughout the process that aided comparison and questioning of estimated travel costs*

✓ *Intuitive user interface, with the participation of the main process users (secretaries), reduced the need for training and aided in the adoption of the system by the entire company.*

✓ *Preparation of a viable application and process prototype, validated by the user while still in the analysis phase, which aids in identifying differences in understanding and helps in closing the functional scope.*

Pitfalls

The development of the Travel and Expenses Workflow showed that integration with complex legacy systems is a subject to be treated carefully. In GPA's case, at the moment of approval, it was identified that the interface with the accounting system defined in the beginning of the project was incorrect, which required adjustments and, consequently, created rework.

8.   COMPETITIVE ADVANTAGES

The creation of the Shared Services Center by GPA represented an organization and cultural change in the company. SSC does not exist for another reason except to reduce costs and obtain gains of scale, achieving competitive advantages in a highly disputed and fragmented market such as the Brazilian retail market.

The introduction of the Travel and Expenses Workflow in this new organizational context was strategic for GPA, contributing to the institutionalization of the new goal brought by SSC: the unification of all corporate purchases in one single location. In the case of this system, the "location" is not necessarily physical and makes it possible for employees spread throughout 14 states in Brazil to have their expense and travel requests processed, decentralizing the requests, but centralizing the process.

It is very clear for GPA that cost reduction is absolutely fundamental to keep its market position. For example, while Carrefour's and Wal-Mart's operational costs are under 18% of their net income, GPA's is above 21%. This leads to higher prices to the consumer, many of which are starting to prefer GPA's competitors. Following this vision, the Travel and Expenses Workflow is completely in line with GPA's strategy, in addition to being a tool that ensures process transparency and control. With overwhelming success of this implementation, the Travel and Expenses Workflow is directly contributing to the GPA's strategic goal – to maintain excellence in customer service while achieving more competitive costs.

9.   TECHNOLOGY

Grupo Pão de Açúcar adopted Oracle Workflow as the platform for development of the Travel and Expenses Workflow. The system infrastructure includes:
- Workflow Server: IBM Server running AIX, Oracle Database Server 9.1.2, Oracle Workflow Server 2.6.2 and Oracle HTTP Server 1.3.22.
- Workstations: Intel (several speeds), 32 to 512Mb, running MS Windows (98, 2000 or XP), Microsoft Internet Explorer up to version 5.5, Mozilla or

Mozilla Firefox browser, Microsoft Outlook, Oracle Workflow Builder (only Process Analyst).

- E-mail server: Microsoft Exchange Server.

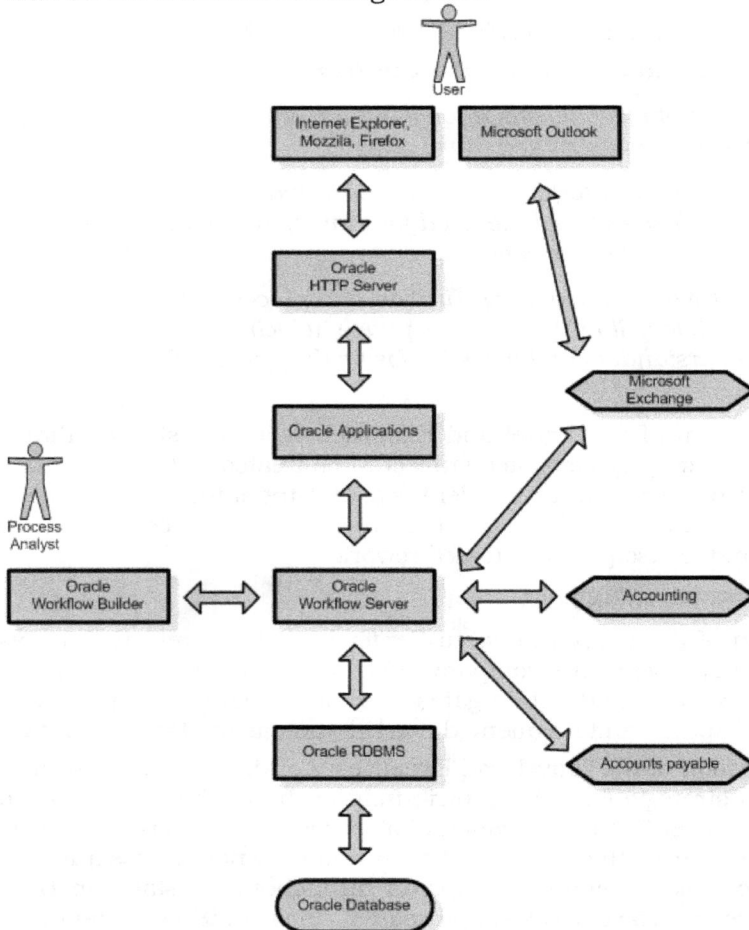

Figure 3. Global System Architecture

10.   TECHNOLOGY AND SERVICE PROVIDERS

Grupo Pão de Açúcar's Travel and Expenses Workflow was developed and implemented by iProcess Soluções em Tecnologia, a Brazilian company specialized in building intelligent solutions in BPM (Business Process Management), Workflow and ECM (Enterprise Content Management) technologies. More information can be found at http://www.iprocess.com.br.

MONEDERO, Argentina

Gold Award, South and Central America, Nominated by PECTRA Technology, Inc., USA.

EXECUTIVE SUMMARY

MONEDERO is a leader in means of payment in the segment of micro payments in the Republic of Argentina. Conceived 100% under the logic of processes management, it presently allows the user to pay, with a single prepaid recharge Contact Less card, his/her everyday spending in the public and private transport network, retail chains and shopping malls throughout the country.

Among its main characteristics are the following:
- 750,000 active users.
- 1,500,000 average transactions per day including expenses and recharges.
- More than 1,000 recharge centers.
- Integration with mobile devices to carry out virtual charges through mobile phones.
- Balance and spending checks online.
- Integration with credit and debit card and with the "Banelco"[1] network.
- Adaptation to simple and fast devices as well as to validation devices (financial POS).
- The PECTRA BPM Suite solution integrates all these operations, functionalities and participants of the value chain.

OVERVIEW

With the purpose of implementing the first subway-ticket payment system under the concept of SmartCard in Latin-America, "Metrovias" SA has faced the development of "Monedero", a *contactless* card conceived 100% under the logic of processes management based on the PECTRA BPM Suite tool.

Moving beyond the boundaries of its origin, Monedero has become the quintessential means of payment in the micro payment segment. Presently it allows the user to pay, with a single *Contact Less* card under a prepaid system, his/her everyday expenses in the public and private transport network, retail chains and shopping malls throughout the country, integrating as well to a network of credit and debit cards, and to the Banelco network.

Monedero has 750,000 active users and processes approximately 1,500,000 average daily transactions including expenses and recharges, including subways, 400 turnstiles and 70 servers process those transactions. It also counts on more than 1000 recharge centers and integration with mobile devices to carry out virtual recharge through cellular phones. Online control of balance and expenses is another advantage to which the network users can access.

The PECTRA BPM Suite solution has permitted the integration of these operations tying together all participants of the value chain and the existing applica-

---

[1] Banelco S.A., is a corporation of 7 member-banks and 18 participant-banks which own a network of ATMs in the Republic of Argentina.

tions based on the company's business rules. The BPM solution - Business *Process Management* – worked as the Integrating Element of Applications (EAI) and facilitated the integration among diverse and complex systems: "the tool's versatility has permitted to modify the business rules in the most critical moments of stabilization of the solution, without major inconveniences, "stated Ariel Perassi, Monedero Product Chief.

ERP (*Enterprise Resource Planning*) and Pectra Events (*Customer Relationship Management)* can be mentioned among the main integrated ones. The latter, a PECTRA BPM Suite vertical application, allowed the organization to administer both internal and external relations in a centralized way and with a safe and easy to access information storage.

On the other hand, PECTRA BPM Suite also permitted the automation of the Automatic Debit Process, which enables the processing of automatic recharges of the card "Monedero" through an X25 Line with debit cards. "The tool permitted working these rules with great flexibility without having to modify developments to enable the configuration of repeated attempts to collect payments and the time in which transactions are effectively carried out. Particularly, this process lowered debit rejection by 40% approximately," continues Perassi.

The implementation of PECTRA BPM Suite made possible the exponential development experienced by the Monedero Network, which has echoed in tangible advantages for the end user, the commercial chain and Monedero as a link between both, which will be described in the present document. Among these, the following can be mentioned: operative efficiency, security, practicality, and control of operations; these are translated in a remarkable increase in productivity, revenue, and business potentiality.

BUSINESS CONTEXT

Since January of 1994 Metrovías S.A. is the concessionary company of all subway lines in the city of Buenos Aires, the "Premetro" and the "Urquiza" Railway, which together transport 300 million passengers annually.

The company – which employs approximately 3000 people and attends 70 km of ways, traveling through 108 stations by means of 692 units – has as its main challenge to offer every day an ever better service to its clients. In this sense, and in order to create value for its users, Metrovías is executing an intense investment plan which covers several levels: communications, infrastructure, cultural actions, and services.

The implementation of a technological solution, based on the concept of intelligent card that will replace money in cash, "not only for each user to pay the fare in the means of transport, but also to carry out commercial transactions in member shops," explains Perassi, was set as a goal under this last category. In this context, the main drivers to initiate the development have been:

- To offer new and better services to users covering a niche not yet exploited: the micro-payment segment.
- To make more agile users' daily transactions, assuring security of operations.
- To let the users have a fast and comfortable access to passengers transport service, turning more efficient the duration and cost of operations.
- To implement the *Smart Card* technology to quicken this process.

In order to satisfy the mentioned necessities, the technological solution had to comply with the following requirements:

- Adherence to the standard / Norm ISO/IEC-14443 A/B (Mifare)
- To use technology which permits multiple applications to share one same device and to be administered within an information structure under the protocols MAD1, 2, and 3 (Mifare Application Directory).
- To guarantee information security.
- To guarantee swift availability of funds.
- To guarantee high performance of the solution when processing transactions.
- To centralize information coming from different systems of the company.
- To provide high value-added services that would materialize in competitive advantages to all participants of the value chain.

In view of these needs, the company decided to base the core solution on the PECTRA BPM Suite tool, which would act as the integrator of applications and services supplied to all the value chain, would allow automating the critical processes of the business, and would provide the Business Intelligence tools for management analysis and decision-making.

THE KEY INNOVATIONS

A successful implementation is a consequence of both the technology utilized and the creation of an integral system that satisfy the necessities of users and agents involved. In this sense Monedero meets these features, as it creates a value proposal that satisfies the needs of all participants in the process, and also uses –in an innovative and efficient manner- the cornerstones of Business Process Management. These two distinctive attributes turned Monedero into the first card of its kind, leader in the segment of micro payments in the Republic of Argentina.

The main innovations of the solution in regard to business, processes, and particularly the organization, which explain the fundamental role played by the BPM tool in Monedero, the extent of the implementation and the level of integration with different and complex systems, are presented as follows.

BUSINESS

In order to dimension the impact that, at a business level, the development of Monedero implied, the main indicators that permit to figure out the exponential growth of the network and how it interrelates all members of the value chain, having PECTRA BPM Suite as the integrating element, are exposed in this section.

Main indicators of business impact
- Active users: 750,000 users.
- Average daily transactions: 1,500,000 transactions including both expenses and recharges.
- Recharge: more than 1,000 cash-recharge centers and virtual recharge through cellular phones.
- Monthly new registrations: 10,000 average new users per month.
- Projections: 2,000,000 cards in March 2008 (massive plan to capture new users).

All these operations are supported by a powerful back office which guarantees transaction speed, security and reliability, integrating every operation performed by each of the agents of the value chain:

Integration of the value chain:

Conceiving the solution with process management logic allowed the integration of end users, the commercial chain, and the employees of Monedero providing a single information access point and customized services, as described bellow:

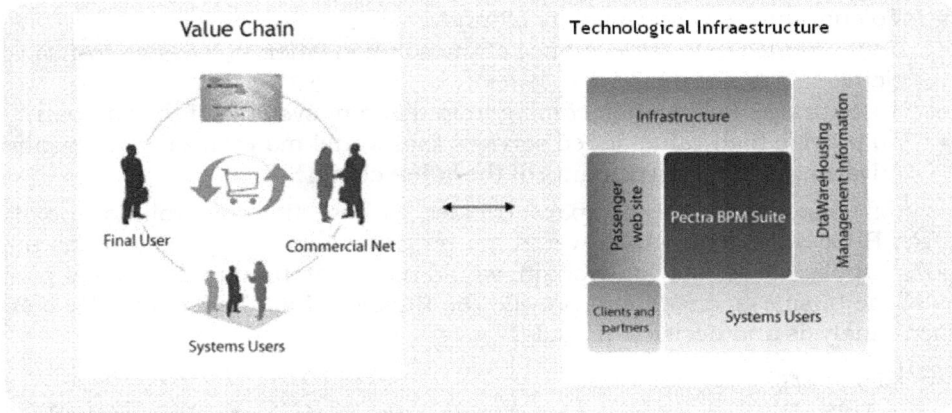

Services to end users:

Basically, Monedero is a prepaid system by means of which users can operate in any shop belonging to the network. Users have to recharge their contact less card in any recharge-center, through their mobile phone, or by means of the integration with their credit or debit card. Among the main services provided by Monedero to end users, the following can be mentioned:

The Monedero Portal: One of the services with the highest value added for the final user has been the production of The Monedero portal. This site allows the user to access all kinds of information regarding his/her card, such as the way to consult the card balance, the expenses or other transactions carried out by this card or associated cards, or other kind of information, such as benefits and promotions of marketing campaigns. "The important thing is that the portal was built by means of the components of PECTRA BPM Suite, with an exclusive log-in for each user; thus, registration it is done directly into the PECTRA data base, where the user is directly assigned an owner-profile which allows him/her an access to all functionalities", describes Pablo Rojas, member of the team that developed, implements, and maintains the solution.

Customer Service center: Monedero manages the customer service center by means of PECTRA Events, a PECTRA BPM Suite vertical that automates processes related to relationship management. The solution integrates the modules of claim handling, client administration and memberships, centralizing the following functionalities:

Customer-capture by means of:
- Cash.
- Credit or debit card.
- With Banelco tickets.
- Access to a client's claims.
- Access to expenses carried out with a card.
- Collection of a client's debt, whether cash or by credit card.
- Renewal of lost, missing, or stolen cards.
- Print and reprint of contracts.
- Collection of statements

Integrated promotion of products and customer loyalty: The integration, native, of PECTRA BPM Suite with PECTRA Events allowed the development of several campaigns and benefits for clients in order to create long term relationships and value-added construction for end users. This integrate ion allows to centralize user membership and transaction data, which in its turn allows to plan and carry out clearly segmented and highly effective campaigns.

Monedero and the commercial chain:
- The operations carried out by external companies which have used the *Contact Less* card as a means of payment, are processed and paid off once they are received.
- The corresponding fees agreed upon for the use of devices and other concepts are charged in this process.
- Their payment is carried out according to the modality agreed upon with the company, which can be a check or a debit in a bank account.
- The companies receive their corresponding sales pay off with details of the operations carried out. Also, they may include other administrative concepts.
- It integrates the network of automatic cashiers and operators of telephone system for virtual recharge, network of devices installed in the companies (toll, parking, busses, subways, railways, shops) where recharge and spending operations are carried out, and the network of credit and debit cards for statement administration.

The PECTRA BPM Suite solution permitted to centralize all these operations and to automate their main related processes. Among them, the automatic debit process is the main one, which resulted in a 40%-reduction of debit rejections, as explained in section Key Innovation / Process.

Functionalities for Monedero members:
The advantages and functionalities that Monedero offers to the employees who access the different integrated systems will be described in depth in the section Key Innovations / Organization. To introduce them, and in order to give visibility to the link between the solution and its third component in the value chain, we anticipate that the functionalities for Monedero members are centered in three main concepts:
- Single sign on (a single log-in to access all applications).
- Business Intelligence (to analyze and link the transactional and qualitative information of end users as well as of the commercial chain).
- Scheduler (Automatic tasks scheduling).

These three parts are supplied by the PECTRA BPM Suite tool, and work as the cornerstone to centralize management information, granting access according to profiles for subsequent analysis and decision-making.

Current reach of the network:

As a result of the services rendered to all agents involved, the Monedero network has experienced exponential growth: born as a means of payment just for sub-ways in the City of Buenos Aires (year 20001), it moved beyond its boundaries to all the micro-payment segment in Argentina.

At present, consumers can pay –with a single Contact Less card- their everyday transactions in the public and private transport network, retail chains and shopping malls throughout the country. There follows the current structure of the network:

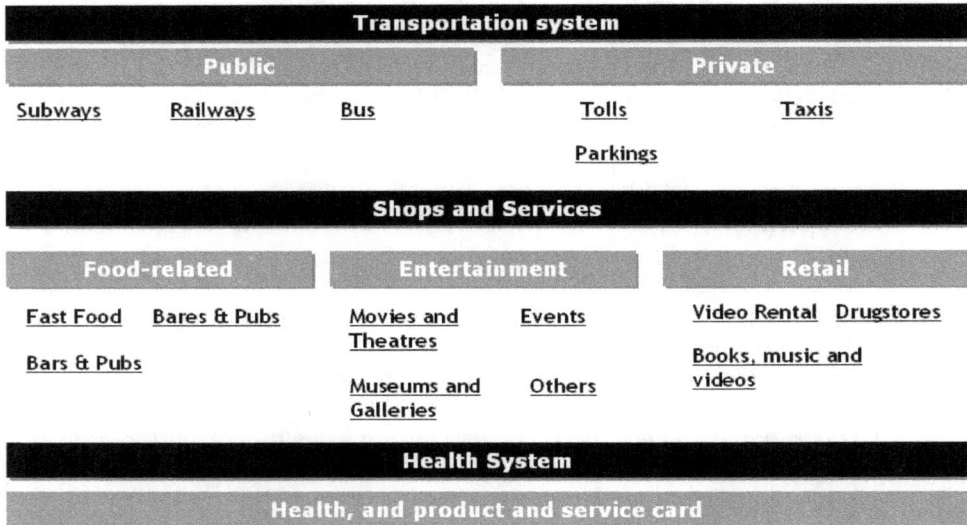

Transportation system				
Public			**Private**	
Subways	Railways	Bus	Tolls	Taxis
			Parkings	

Shops and Services		
Food-related	**Entertainment**	**Retail**
Fast Food Bares & Pubs	Movies and Theatres Events	Video Rental Drugstores
Bars & Pubs	Museums and Galleries Others	Books, music and videos

Health System
Health, and product and service card

Obra Social de la Ciudad de Buenos Aires

PROCESS

The main innovation is that the solution was conceived under the logic of processes management, this being the reason why the BPM solution had a leading role in the development and implementation of the solution, acting as application integrator and allowing:

- To integrate all participants of the value chain with the existing applications, as it has been described in former section.
- To provide a single point of access to all information and critical resources of the business, including structured and non-structured company data.
- A swift integration, filter, and action over the relevant information for the performance of daily tasks, obtained from any internal or external source of the organization.
- To perform high-level integrations with the company's systems, automating critical processes.

Integrations & architecture:

"PECTRA BPM Suite helped us to integrate the applications in a much faster and agile way, making a connection to all applications separately without an integration tool. Consequently, new ideas rose, which PECTRA BPM Suite helped us materialize," explains Ariel Perassi. "Many functionalities have been implemented, matters such as the relationship with the credit cards, the creation of the contact center, and handling payment processes that required a high level of control, as examples of the main ones." The integration scheme employed is the following:

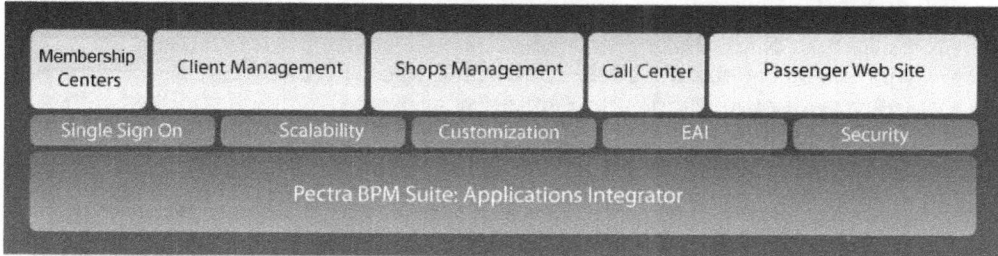

Monedero has a powerful back office, centered in PECTRA BPM Suite, allowing the integration and support of all network operations. The following chart shows its architecture and describes the integration with the main applications of the company.

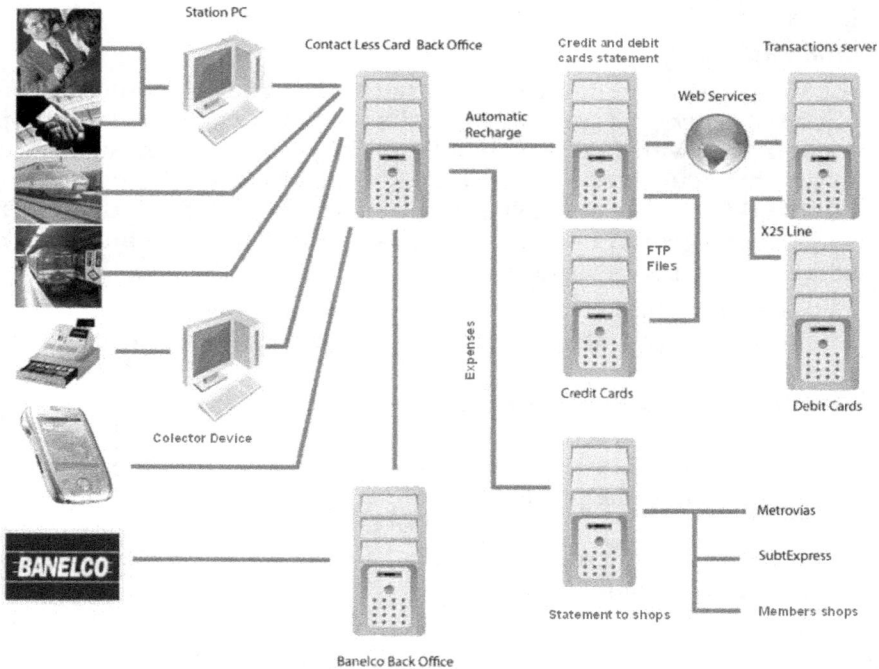

Integration with PECTRA Events:

One of the main integrated systems is that of PECTRA Events (Customer Relationship Management). Its main integrated functionalities are:

Membership centers:

- Charge and discharge module.
  - Cash recharge of the Contact Less card.
  - Sale of products
  - Balance check
  - Inquiry of transactions per user and date for daily closing of operations
- Beginning and ending of user session

- - Beginning of session of a user from the membership centers
  - End of shift of a user from the membership centers
- Statement of sales carried out and money collected.
- Claims reception.
- Claims reception from customers.
- Follow-up of claims.
- Application of business rules according to the received claim.
- Delivery of promotions and communications.
- Client attention center:
- Customer Service Center:
  - Call-center management.
  - 50 automatic action plans.

Stressing the meaning of this point, Perassi states that, "this integration has offered an effective solution: for example, when a user looses his/her card, the card can be cancelled through the contact center without loosing the money balance in it. PECTRA BPM Suite works integrated to the contact center, with an average of 50 action plans shot daily, which are activated autonomously, updating all information in the back office".

Integration with ERP:

Another of Metrovías´ main integrated internal systems has been the ERP (*Enterprise Resource Planning*). In regard, Perassi says that, "once substituted, processes were designed with PECTRA BPM Suite, allowing the integration with the ERP system, which supports the administrative processes of Metrovías, running them on the workflow tools. The ERP solution has been implemented attending to specific interaction needs of each area or department of the company." The main integrated functionalities are as follows:

Process of trade receivables:
- Customer administration (memberships and changes in means of payment)
- Customer invoicing and collection
- Payment of credit cards
- Credit to credit cards
- Customers current account
- Accounting
- Administration of promotions

Process of automatic debits:

A core process that has been automated is that of automatic debits. It has a transaction server specially developed to this end, and the infrastructure of Monedero has been provided with an X25 line connected to different cards, in order to carry out transactions with those. "The centralized system for registering memberships is connected to a transactions server which communicates with the credit card companies and manages their approval. Through a predetermined process, the same system generates the statement for control of the credit card companies," explains Monedero Product Chief.

Among the automated functions in this process there are:
- Statement of operations to be collected
- Collection follow-up according to response.
- A Catalogue of new delivered messages
- Modification of business rules for each response
- Trends of collections and rejections for a cause

- Notification in case of events

"Nowadays we can carry out the automation and configuration of business rules very easily by modifying them as the business evolves, since it is very simple to change them," says Ariel Perassi. "Today, the functioning allows running an automatic circuit (a process) that goes to the credit card, comes back, makes a transaction, and delivers orderly each one of the transactions;

the first to arrive is the first sent; if already collected, it does a certain thing, if not, it does another. This allowed us to give a value added to the business we were carrying out," he concludes.

ORGANIZATION

The development of Monedero under the Process Management logic implied sub-

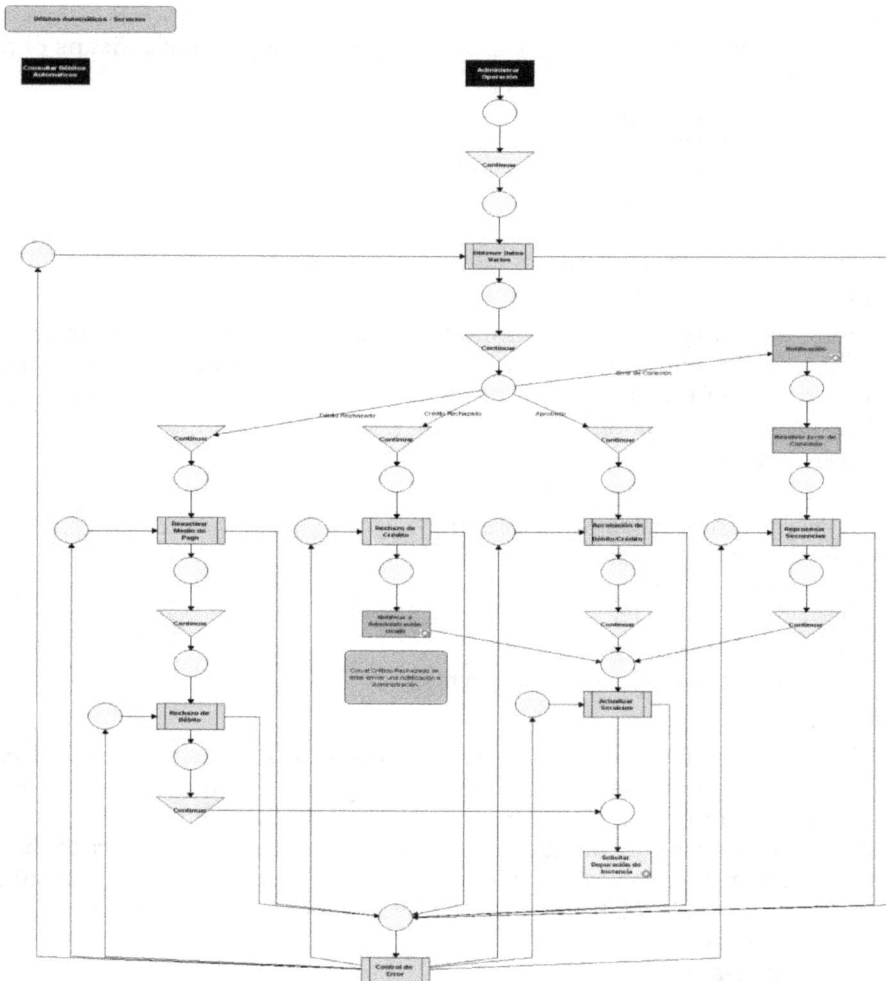

stantial differences in the way work was being implemented in Metrovías, both regarding access to, and treatment of, information, as well as to system access and tasks efficiency.

Three central aspects allowed a remarkable difference in productivity of internal employees of the company:

- Business intelligence

- Scheduler
- Single sign-on

Business intelligence:

Obtaining management centralized information for decision-making, and planning of strategies and commercial and marketing actions is one of the central contributions of the BPM tool. Using data registered in the transactional systems, DataWarehouse has been created, necessary to offer a detailed analysis of Monedero´s management. This allows obtaining quantitative and qualitative information on network transactions, on members of the commercial chain and end-users profiles; at the same time, it also allows its crosschecking and consolidation for the decision-making.

Main Business Intelligence functionalities:

Analysis

- Customer management (ages, dwelling, types of payment, means of payments)
- Registration, resignation.
- Points of Sales
- Transactions
- Way to use Monedero
  - Control panels.
  - Management indicators control modules.

Scheduler:

The Scheduler is a PECTRA BPM Suite tool which allows scheduling tasks which run automatically: notifications in case of events such as mistakes or successful events, follow-up of tasks executed at any given moment and an average calculation of performances, among others.

Main associated functionalities:

- Automatic tasks scheduling
- Diverse forms of tasks scheduling
- Notification of results
- Execution follow-up
- Execution map
- Tasks categorization
- Administration by roles of each task

Single Sign On:

The BPM tool provided one single point of access to all information and critical resources of the business, including structured and non-structures company data. Users can access to all integrated applications with one single user name and password. Access control according to roles also constitutes part of the functionality, in order that each user will access only permitted and functional information. Among the main advantages obtained by Monedero employees are:

- Unified search
- Personalization
- Collaboration
- Security and scalability

Hurdles Overcome

Management & Business

"Fortunately, there were no major inconveniences, only the usual ones in any IT project: Problems that were overcome, some adjustments to be made, some improvements, reductions, which are normal," Ariel Perassi comments. "From the moment that Metrovias made the decision to optimize the organizational structure, to improve and capitalize the organization's knowledge and information, and to make the existing technological structure more modern and efficient, there was full support to the project, collaborating to avoid situations that obstruct it," he adds.

Although this has contributed to the project, one of the obstacles to be solved was the reengineering of some processes in view of the network exceptional growth and the amount of transactions and active cards (at present there are 750,000 cards circulating and an average of 1,500,000 transactions.) In turn, the solution to this problem allowed considering projections for 2008 (2,000,000 active cards) in the reengineering carried out in order to continue granting the solution's performance.

"Another obstacle at the moment of implementing this means of payment occurred when we started to work with another line (the Urquiza train) and we found that, as the route of the train goes through sectors of dwelling were citizens' acquisitive power is middle and low, we started realizing that people who traveled by this route used no banks, they did not have credit or debit cards," Rojas summarizes. In face of this situation rigorous market studies were carried out, which allowed defining in a precise way the target-population and the strategy to turn this means of payment into massive use. Thus, the promotion strategy to turn the system into massive use "was to inform subway users that the ticket is cheaper if acquired through this means," he explains.

Organization Adoption

As a strategy for the implementation of this solution, Change Management actions have been carried out, in order to incorporate the benefits of Monedero network into the organizational culture of the company, which included internal activities of training and communication.

Moreover, a special division to attend Monedero needs has been created, creating an area composed mainly out of the following sectors:

Administration:
- Clearing house and back office maintenance.
- Marketing:
- Publicity, promotions.

Commercial:
- Agreements with shops, communities, commercial possibilities, biddings.
- User service:
- Memberships, claims, call center.
- Service to recharge/shops network:
- Service and support to shops which are part of the recharge network.
- Projects:
- Analysis of new projects such as incorporation of buses, taxis, biddings, integration with Banelco, Link or "Pago Facil" (Easy payment) networks.

Systems:

- Solution technological support. With development, functional analysis, new projects, operations, database, and other areas.

BENEFITS

The implementation of PECTRA BPM Suite in the Monedero network produced tangible benefits for all members of the value chain.

COSTS SAVINGS AND TIME REDUCTIONS

Commercial network

Operative efficiency and financing constitute one of the core results of the implementation in the commercial network, which main benefits are translated into:

- Cost reduction in tickets commercialization
- Reduction in money handling (lower risks)
- Reduction to 1/3 of time in counters
- Reduction of equipment maintenance costs
- Reduction of financial cost
- Quick availability of funds

Sales credit in 72hs

Users

- Reduction in recharge time
- Optimized speed in transactions
- Naught emission and maintenance costs.
- Integrated promotions, cost reduction in access to products
- Surplus recovery

Monedero

Regarding internal benefits of Monedero:

Reduction of debit rejection: "the automation of automatic debits with PECTRA BPM Suite lowered by 40% the number of debit rejections", Ariel Perassi comments. "Now, it is done through an email automatically delivered by PECTRA BPM Suite notifying the rejection, which contributes to the process efficiency," he adds.

The reduction in recharge time: "The procedure of recharge used to take 72hs. With the optimization of processes attained with PECTRA BPM Suite, it now takes about 5 min. The reduction of this gap is very important, and is made possible thanks to the off-line operation, since a turnstile through which 10 people circulate per minute cannot be connected online," Pablo Rojas explains.

- Reduction of turnstile maintenance operating costs. Zero costs.
- Fraud control
- Reduction of recharge time on undergrounds ticket-sale posts.

INCREASED REVENUES

The following indicators on increased revenues of Monedero during this last year (2007) will help appreciate the growth experienced by the Monedero network, as a result of the performance of the tool supporting the network:

Monedero

- Increase in turnover: 25% annual
- Increase in cards registration: between 8% and 10% monthly
- Increase in daily average of transactions: 5% monthly
- Increase in recharge points: 80 % annual (2006-2007)
- Projected increase in turnover for 2008: 20% annual

- Projected increase in quantity of active cards: 300 % annual (massive plan to capture new users).
- Projected increase in total number of transactions: 20% annual
- Fraud reduction of: 2%

PRODUCTIVITY IMPROVEMENTS

The following comparative indicators (which compare the situation prior and after the commencement of the project) describe the productivity improvements that the development of the Monedero network meant for Metrovías:

- Reduction of idle time: 2 %
- Improvement in recharge speed: 100 %
- Optimization of transactions performance: 100 %
- It must be taken into account that these percentages indicate that performance is doubled due to migration from a "dirty" technology, as is transaction per traction, to a "clean" technology as is the contact less transaction.
- This implies a 100% reduction in validation-devices maintenance, 100% improvement in recharge speed (in the case of automatic charge) and a 20% increase in productivity since controls are automated in the Back Office.

BEST PRACTICES, LEARNING POINTS AND PITFALLS

The development and implementation of the project was based on the methodology of Pectra Technology, which boasts 10 years of certified quality under ISO norms 9000:2000. Regarding the implementation of this successful solution we can point out to Best Practices & Learning Points:

- The follow-up of implementation methodology certified by global standards.
- Exhaustive assessment of current and future business context and client needs.
- Exhaustive documentation of processes and surveys.
- Project monitoring and execution carried out jointly with the customer, with milestones and deliverables defined at the beginning of implementation.
- Use of risks and deviation management methodology
- Satisfaction of needs of all participants involved in the value chain of the market targeted by the solution.
- Exhaustive market studies, for a detailed survey of these needs.
- Methodological framework: PMI (*Project Management Institute*)

Based on global quality standards, Pectra Technology works under project management integral methodology: scope, times, risk management, quality, communications, human resources, costs; endorsed by the Project Management Institute:

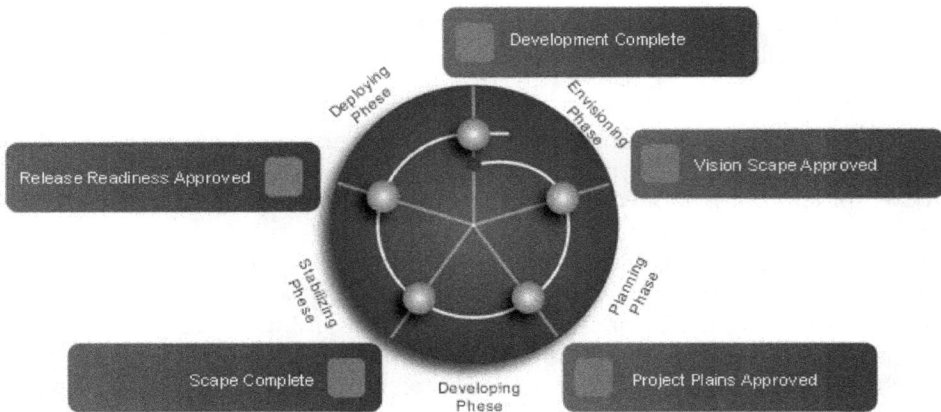

COMPETITIVE ADVANTAGES

Through the development of Monedero, Metrovías has been able to move beyond its business frontiers, obtaining the following competitive advantages:

- Higher control in ticket sales.
- Higher speed in transactions.
- Large volume of information for statistics regarding end users and members of the commercial chain.
- Cost reduction and productivity increase.
- Leadership in an unexploited segment (micro payments).
- Diversification of income sources.
- To attain penetration to diverse niches.
- The strengthening of brand positioning and image offering more and better services.

Facing the new year the following guidelines are proposed in order to carry on with the sustained growth experienced:

- Clients and commercial chain loyalty, to guarantee the current transaction volume.
- Expansion of the currently installed base by means of plans of card massive use and benefits for the commercial network.
- Verticalization of Monedero card in order to penetrate in diverse niches of the market: There already exist two pioneer cases described below (MetroShop and Ob.SBA).

Ob.SBA:

- ObSBA is the social security organization for the city of Buenos Aires.
- It has 260,000 people affiliated and renders health services with a network of 900+ professionals.
- The affiliated members may use his/her card to access professional services rendered (magnetic stripe and an ID) and by means of a contact-less chip, he/she can travel by subway or by Urquiza railways, have access to parking, pay tolls and use the Monedero shop network in a simple and easy manner.

Furthermore, it functions as an electronic purse for purchases in pharmacies and co-payments fees.

Metroshop:

MetroShop is a new credit-card concept with minimum access requisites, low costs and total transparency. By means of a contact-less chip, it offers the possibility of traveling by subway or Urquiza railways easily and simply.

Furthermore, it functions as an electronic purse for minor spending (purchase in kiosks and other shops belonging to the underground network.)

TECHNOLOGY

Infrastructure

For the MONEDERO solution, an infrastructure including 400 intelligent turnstiles and 70 servers which process 1,500,000 daily transactions was created, using a fiber-optics ring installed in the subway stations of Buenos Aires. The Monedero solution uses PECTRA BPM Suite as a platform, a tool that permits the integration with all the applications that make up this solution. All administrative and management processes are diagrammed and implemented on PECTRA BPM Suite reaching approximately 200 processes for this solution.

Cards transactions are registered in a database MS SQL Server 2000 in Cluster, on an MS Windows 2003 Advanced Server platform. Another MS SQL Server 2000 database in Cluster with MS Windows 2003 Advanced Server platform stores information related to customer management, current accounts and administrative processes.

MONEDERO web page and its enabled inquiry system are installed in a server with an 800 MHz processor and 512 MB RAM memory. Web Service for card conciliation and Card Server applications are installed in a 500 MHz processor and 256 MB RAM memory, with an X25 communication plate for the linking with credit and debit cards.

INFRASTRUCTURE	
Development Tools	•Microsoft Visual Studio .NET 2005 •Microsoft Visual Basic 6.0 •ASP
Data Bases	•SQL Server 2000
Web Server	•Internet information services
Platform	•Microsoft Windows 2003
Implemented Architectures	•DNA (Distribute Network Architecture) •SOA (Aplicaciones orientdas a servicios - web services)

TECHNOLOGY

The Contact Less technology utilized by Monedero reduces the likelihood of transaction failures to a minimum, while at the same time offering a system without mechanic contact, which increases the resistance to the card deterioration.

This technology allows, moreover, carrying out a detailed follow-up of the processed information, coming both from recharges and from purchase points. It also stores and carries out the processing of data originated in each turnstile for access to the transport units, data that can be checked with a private password.

It provides as well a centralized interconnection, intercommunicated with credit card companies; a control of black list registers and frauds; and a follow-up of events captured by the Call Center. The encryption model and the adherence to global standards /Norm ISO/IEC-14443 A/B (Mifare) guarantee the security of information.

Devices Fixed terminals: Vx510 Connection: Dial and Lan Mobile terminals: Vx610 Connection: Dial and WiFi Connection: Dial and Gprs	

Section 6

Appendix

Appendix

Awards Winners, Nominees and Nominators

Introduction

LAYNA FISCHER

About the Excellence Awards

Company	Future Strategies Inc	2436 North Federal Highway, #374, Lighthouse Point
Title	Editor and Publisher	FL 33064 USA
E-Mail	layna@FutStrat.com	
URL	www.FutStrat.com	
Phone	1[954] 782-3376	

Ms. Fischer is editor and publisher of Future Strategies Inc., which publishes the business book series **Excellence in Practice** and the annual **BPM and Workflow Handbook** published in collaboration with WfMC.

As chair of WARIA (now BPMFocus), she is also the Awards Director for the annual BPM and Workflow Excellence Awards. The winning case studies are published annually in Excellence in Practice.

Her experience in the IT industry includes being the president and CEO of a multi-million dollar high-technology export company for seven years, during which time she also founded an offshore franchise distribution company. Ms. Fischer was a senior editor of a leading computer publication for five years and has been involved in international computer journalism and publishing for over 20 years. She was a founding director of the United States Computer Press Association in 1985.

Future Strategies Inc., specializes in publishing books on Business Process Management and workflow, Information Technology and electronic commerce. As such, the company contracts and works closely with individuals and corporations worldwide, collaborating on joint projects using state of the art information technology.

Foreword

NATHANIEL PALMER

Title	President, Transformation+Innovation and Executive Director, Workflow Management Coalition	99 Derby Street, Suite 200, Hingham, MA 02043, USA.
E-Mail	nathaniel@wfmc.org	
URL	www.wfmc.org	

Nathaniel Palmer is President of Transformation+Innovation, as well as the Executive Director of the Workflow Management Coalition. Previously he was Director, Business Consulting for Perot Systems Corp, and also spent over a decade with Delphi Group as Vice President and Chief Analyst. He is the author of over 200 research studies and published articles, as well as "The X-Economy" (Texere, 2001). Nathaniel has been featured in numerous media ranging from Fortune to The New York Times. He is on the advisory boards of many relevant industry publications, as well as the Board of Directors of Association of Information Management (AIIM) NE, and was nominated to represent the Governor of Massachusetts on the Commonwealth's IT Advisory Board.

Guest Chapters

PROCESS MEASUREMENT AND ORGANIZATIONAL PERFORMANCE REDUX

Author
Dr. Michael zur Muehlen

Company	Howe School of Technology Management Stevens Institute of Technology	Castle Point on the Hudson Hoboken, NJ 07030
Title	Director, Center of Excellence in Business Process Innovation	United States
E-Mail	mzurmuehlen@stevens.edu	

Dr. Michael zur Muehlen is Assistant Professor of Information Systems at Stevens Institute of Technology in Hoboken, NJ. He directs Stevens' BPM research center (Center of Excellence in Business Process Innovation) and is responsible for the University's graduate program in Business Process Management and Service Innovation. Prior to his appointment at Stevens, Michael was a senior lecturer at the Department of Information Systems, University of Muenster, Germany, and a visiting lecturer at the University of Tartu, Estonia. He has over 14 years of experience in the field of process automation and workflow management, and has led numerous process improvement and design projects in Germany and the US and serves as Enterprise Chief Process Architect of the U.S. Department of Defense Business Transformation Agency. An active contributor to standards in the BPM area, Michael was named a fellow of the Workflow Management Coalition in 2004 and chairs the WfMC working group "Management and Audit." He studies the practical use of process modeling standards, techniques to manage operational risks in business processes, and the integration of business processes and business rules. SAP Research, the US Army, the Australian Research Council, and private sponsors have funded his research. Michael has presented his research in more than 20 countries. He is the author of a book on workflow-based process controlling, numerous journal articles, conference papers, book chapters and working papers on process management and workflow automation. He has also published widely on BPM standards and standard making in general. He is a founding director of the AIS special interest group on process automation and management (SIGPAM). Michael holds a PhD (Dr. rer. pol.) and an MS in Information Systems from the University of Muenster, Germany.

AIR FORCE SOA ENTERPRISE SERVICE BUS C4I SYSTEMS INTEGRATION STUDY

Authors
Dr. Timothy D. Kehoe, Irene N. Chang, David S. Czulada, Howard Kong, Dr. Dino Konstantopoulos, MITRE; with Linus Chow, Charles Medley, Oracle.

Company	The MITRE Corporation	202 Burlington Road Bedford, MA 01730-1420 781-271-2000
URL	www.mitre.org	
Contact	Irene Chang	781-266-9694
Email	inchang@mitre.org	
Company	**Oracle Public Sector**	1910 Oracle Way, Reston, VA 20190
URL	www.oracle.com	
Contact	Linus Chow	703-203-2178
Email	linus.chow@oracle.com	

The MITRE Corporation is a private, independent not-for-profit organization chartered to work in the public interest. As a national resource, MITRE has expertise in systems engineering, information technology, operational concepts, and enterprise modernization to address sponsors' critical needs. MITRE currently manages three Federally Funded Research, and Development Centers (FFRDCs) sponsored by the Department of Defense (DOD), the Federal Aviation Administration (FAA), and the Internal Revenue Service (IRS). MITRE also has its own independent research and development programs that explore new technologies and new uses of technologies. The MITRE Corporation has two principal locations: one is located in Bedford, Massachusetts, and the other is in McLean, Virginia. MITRE also has additional sites located across the country and around the world.

Case Studies

Section 1: Europe

INFOCAJA, SPAIN

Silver Winner

Contact	Diego Marín	Avda. Burgos, 114
		Madrid, 28050
Title	Director de desarrollo de producto	Spain
E-Mail	Diego.marin@infocaja.es	
URL	www.infocaja.es	
Phone	+34 (91) 5103550	

Nominator *BizAgi*

Contact	Federico Ramirez Botero	Carrera 7a #71-52 Torre B of
		1302, Bogotá
Title	Account Manager	Colombia
E-Mail	Federico.Ramirez@bizagi.com	
URL	www.bizagi.com	
Phone	+ 571 3170049 Ext 132	

Integrator *Price Waterhouse Coopers*

Contact	Arturo Derteano	Paseo de la Castellana, 43
		Madrid 28046
Title	Director	España
E-Mail	arturo.derteano@es.pwc.com	
URL	www.pwc.es	
Phone	+34 915 684 116	

As the result of over 18 years of experience in process automation technologies, our company developed the BizAgi® Business Process Management System. BizAgi® is now a leading BPM Solution specialized in the financial sector with a strong presence in Latin America and Europe where it is being used by some of the most important financial institutions. BizAgi® allows process owners to automate or modify complex and dynamic processes faster and more flexibly than any other solution in the market. This is due to a concept called The Relational Process Model. This model fuses the relational data model with modern process theory allowing BizAgi® to automate processes without programming using a Model Driven Architecture and a Data Driven Process Engine.

LPH VRANOV, SLOVAKIA

Finalist

Contact	Jan Mandulak	Pod dolami 838
		Vranov 093 02

Title	Production Director	Slovakia
E-Mail	dmandulak@lph.sk	
URL	www.lph.sk	
Phone	00421 57 48604	

Nominator ***Technical Univer-sity of Košice, Slovakia***

Contact	Vladimir Modrak	Bayerova 1
		Prešov 080 01
Title	Lecturer	Slovakia
E-Mail	modrak.vladimir@fvt.sk	
URL	web.tuke.sk/fvtpo/indexuk.htm	
Phone	00421 51 7722828	

NATUZZI FURNISHING & ACCESSORIES BUSINESS UNIT, ITALY

Gold Winner

Contact	Amedeo PICCINNO	Via Iazzitiello, 47
		Santeramo in Colle, Bari
		70029
Title	Operations Manager - BU Furnishing & Accessories	Italy
E-Mail	apiccinno@natuzzi.com	
URL	www.natuzzi.com	
Phone	+39 080 8820623	

Nominator ***openwork, Italy***

Contact	Francesco BATTISTA	Via Conservatorio, 22
		Milan 20122
Title	Marketing Director	Italy
E-Mail	francesco.battista@openworkBPM.com	
URL	www.openworkBPM.com	
Phone	+39 3355794429	

openwork® is a pure Independent Software Vendor concentrating all efforts exclusively on its openwork Business Process Management suite. openwork features an original methodology that makes use of daily business, non-technical language and approach, introducing high-abstraction tools to map, share and maintain organizations shape and working rules. Those agile tools also allow to reflect organizations evolutions, keeping them always aligned with changing business needs. openwork is then able to act as an interpreter of graphic representation of organizations shape and working rules, enabling paper manual processes to become alive into finalized real-world web applications, integrated with other existing IT systems. openwork is the final solution of a crucial problem: modeling business organizations and processes, getting at the same time suitable fitting-like-a-glove BPM web applications, cutting down low added-value activities, technical complexity and costs. openwork suite including also Workflow Management, Document Management and Business Activity Monitoring capabilities has already been used to build hundreds of complete solutions for customer companies of any sector and size.

University Hospital Virgen del Rocío

Finalist

Contact	Carlos Parra Calderon	Manuel Siurot S/N
		Sevilla, 41013
Title	Chief of research and Technological	Spain
E-Mail	carlos.parra.sspa@juntadeandalucia.es	
Phone	697-954-864	

Nominator *University Hospital Virgen del Rocío*

Contact	Carlos Parra Calderon	Manuel Siurot S/N
		Sevilla, 41013
Title	Chief of research and Technological	Spain
E-Mail	carlos.parra.sspa@juntadeandalucia.es	
Phone	697-954-864	

Section 2: Middle East Africa

Eskom, South Africa

Gold Winner

Contact	Kevin von Berg	3 Menston Road
		Westville, 3630
Title	Corporate Specialist (Customer Service)	South Africa
E-Mail	Kevin.VonBerg@eskom.co.za	
URL	www.eskom.co.za	
Phone	+27 (0)31 204 5627	

Nominator *ciboodle*

Contact	Jennifer Donn	India of Inchinnan
		Renfrewshire PA4 9LH
Title	Marketing Executive	United Kingdom
E-Mail	jennifer.donn@ciboodle.com	
URL	www.ciboodle.com	
Phone	+44 (0)141 533 4345	

ciboodle, formerly Graham Technology, is a wholly owned subsidiary of Sword Group. Specialists in process centric customer interaction software for contact centres, our unique approach to customer interaction gives agents a comprehensive view of customer data across multiple channels, and is the only enterprise scale BPM based CRM product to focus exclusively on contact centres. ciboodle helps large organisations across North America, EMEA and Asia Pacific drive operational efficiency and improve customer experience. Headquartered in the UK, ciboodle has offices in Australia, Indonesia, South Africa and North America. Customer References: Vodafone, Standard Bank, Eskom, BT, ScottishPower, Friends Provident, Pacificorp, Ergon Energy, Pacificorp.

Section 3: North America

CONAGUA, MEXICO

Finalist

Contact	Juan Carlos Garcés del Angel	Insurgentes Sur 2416 Col. Copilco El Bajo
		Ciudad de Mexico 4340
Title	Gerencia de Distritos de Temporal Tecnificado	Mexico
E-Mail	juan.garces@cna.gob.mx	
URL	www.cna.gob.mx	
Phone	51-74-40-00 ext. 1242	

Nominator **PECTRA Technology**

Contact	Fabio Rocca	2425 West Loop South, Suite 200, Houston, TX. 77027
Title	Manager Pectra	United States
E-Mail	frocca@pectra.com	
URL	www.pectra.com	
Phone	1[713]335 5562	

PECTRA Technology's award-winning Business Process Management system, PECTRA BPM Suite□, is a powerful set of tools enabling discovery, design, implementation, maintenance, optimization and analysis of business processes for different kinds of organizations. PECTRA BPM Suite□ is an application that automates the processes and the most critical tasks in the organization, generating optimum levels of operational effectiveness. It fulfills all requirements demanded by today's organization, quickly and efficiently. Furthermore, it increases the return on previous investments made in technology by integrating all existing applications. Based on BPM technology it incorporates the concepts of: BAM (Business Activity Monitoring) providing management with user-friendly graphic monitoring tools, to follow up any deviation in the organization's critical success factors, with capabilities to control and coordinate the organization's performance by means of graphic management indicators; WORKFLOW offering powerful tools to automate and speed the organization's business processes, improving communication and work-flow between people working in different areas; carrying out the work more efficiently and producing customer satisfaction, lower levels of bureaucracy and cost-reductions in day-to-day operations; EAI (Enterprise Application Integration) enabling integration with all existing technologies in the organization, regardless of their origin or platform, coordinating them to help the organization achieve its goals more efficiently; and B2Bi (Business to Business Integration) enabling the control and coordination of each and every link in the organization's value chain, providing robust tools for business process management, and enterprise application integration, making it possible to totally integrate suppliers, clients and partners in an easy and flexible way.

GEISINGER HEALTH SYSTEM, USA

Gold Winner

Contact	David Partsch	100 N. Academy Ave Danville, PA 17822
Title	Program Director	United States
E-Mail	dpartsch@geisinger.edu	
URL	www.geisinger.org/	

Phone	1[570]271-5013	
Nominator	**TIBCO, USA**	
Contact	Emily Burns	3303 Hillview Avenue
		Palo Alto, CA. 94304
Title	Product Marketing Manager	United States
E-Mail	eburns@tibco.com	
URL	www.tibco.com	
Phone	1[857]991-1878	

TIBCO Software Inc. (NASDAQ:TIBX) provides enterprise software that helps companies achieve service-oriented architecture (SOA) and business process management (BPM) success. With over 3,000 customers, TIBCO has given leading organizations around the world better awareness and agility—what TIBCO calls The Power of Now®. TIBCO provides one of the most complete offerings for enterprise-scale BPM, with powerful software that is capable of solving not just the challenges of automating routine tasks and exception handling scenarios, but also the challenges of orchestrating sophisticated and long-lived activities and transactions that involve people and systems across organizational and geographical boundaries.

LOUISIANA SUPREME COURT, USA

Silver Winner

Contact	Peter Haas	400 Royal St
		New Orleans, LA. 70130
Title	Director of Technology	United States
E-Mail	phaas@LASC.ORG	
URL	www.lasc.org/	
Phone	1[504]310-2461	
Nominator	**Oracle Corporation, USA**	
Contact	Linus K Chow	3015 Nicosh Circle
		Falls Church, VA. 22042
Title	Principal Consultant	United States
E-Mail	linus.chow@oracle.com	
URL	www.oracle.com	
Phone	1[703]203-2178	

Oracle (NASDAQ: ORCL) is the world's largest enterprise software company. Oracle delivers the unified SOA platform for business transformation and optimization in order to improve cost structures and grow new revenue streams. Oracle BPM Suite and SOA Suite are market leading software suites that allows enterprises to integrate modeling, execution and measurement of end-to-end business processes involving complex interactions between people and IT systems. Oracle customers across the world have achieved greater efficiency, control and agility by optimizing the business process lifecycle and improving the alignment between business and IT.

WELLS FARGO FINANCIAL INFORMATION SERVICES

Gold Winner

Contact	Rachel R. Aukes	800 Walnut Street,
		F4030-030, Des Moines, IA.
		50309
Title	WFFIS Continuous Improvement Team	United States

E-Mail	rachelaukes@wellsfargo.com	
URL	www.wellsfargo.com	
Phone	1(515) 557-8556	

Nominator   **Lombardi Software**

Contact	Wayne Snell	4615 Seton Center Parkway Suite 250 Austin, TX. 78759
Title	Sr. Director of Marketing	United States
E-Mail	wsnell@lombardi.com	
URL	www.lombardi.com	
Phone	1(512) 382-8200 x377	

Lombardi is a leader in business process management (BPM) software for companies, systems integrators and government agencies. We offer award-winning BPM technology, know-how and services to help our customers become Process-Driven. Lombardi products are built on open standards and provide ongoing prioritization, planning, visibility and control of business processes, increasing the speed and flexibility with which organizations can manage their business process activity and decision-making. Lombardi is behind some of the largest, most successful BPM implementations in the world.
Our Teamworks BPM software suite helps companies to design, execute, and improve their business processes. Teamworks for Office™ makes it easy for anyone to participate in business process management using the familiar Microsoft® Office System products. Lombardi Blueprint™ is the only on-demand collaborative process planning tool that enables companies to map processes, identify problems and prioritize improvement opportunities. Our customers include leading financial services institutions, insurers, manufacturers, healthcare, telecommunication, retailing and public/government agencies. For more information, visit **www.lombardi.com**.

Section 4: Pacific Rim

DAEWOO SHIPBUILDING & MARINE ENGINEERING (DSME), KOREA

Finalist

Contact	Kwang-Phil Park	1, Aju-dong Geoje-si Gyeongsangnam-do 656-714
Title	Senior Engineer/Information Technology R&D Team	South Korea
E-Mail	kppark@DSME.co.kr	
URL	www.dsme.co.kr	

Nominator   **DNV Software, Norway**

Contact	Espen Woyen	Veritasveien 1 Hovik N-1322
Title	Head of Department	Norway
E-Mail	Espen.Woien@dnv.com	
URL	www.dnv.com/software/	
Phone	+47 67 57 82 19	

MALLESONS STEPHEN JAQUES, AUSTRALIA

Silver Winner

Contact	Derek Hamill	Level 61 Governor Phillip Tower 1 Farrer Place Sydney NSW 2000
Title	Manager Development and Integration	Australia
E-Mail	derek.hamill@mallesons.com	
URL	www.mallesons.com	
Phone	+61 2 9296 3345	

Nominator *Metastorm, USA*

Contact	Gina Karr	500 East Pratt St. Baltimore, MD. 21202
Title	Corporate Communications Manager	United States
E-Mail	gkarr@metastorm.com	
URL	www.metastorm.com	
Phone	1[443]874-1260	

With a focus on enterprise visibility, optimization, and agility, Metastorm offers market-leading solutions for Enterprise Architecture (EA), Business Process Analysis & Modeling (BPA) and Business Process Management (BPM). As an integrated product portfolio, Metastorm Enterprise™ allows organizations to maximize business results by unifying strategy, analysis and execution. Metastorm is the only solution provider to bring together these critical disciplines on a single software platform to enable an understanding of enterprise architecture and strategy, accurate impact and opportunity assessment, effective process execution, and accelerated value realization for organizations worldwide. For more information on powering strategic advantage with Metastorm Enterprise, visit www.metastorm.com.

MINISTRY OF LABOR, REPUBLIC OF KOREA

Finalist

Contact	Hey Keyng Im	Jungangdong 1, Gwacheon city Gyonggi province 427-718
Title	Grade-5 official	Korea
E-Mail	galdol@molab.go.kr	
URL	www.molab.go.kr	
Phone	82-2-2110-7053	

Nominator *HandySoft Global Corporation*

Contact	Garth Knudson	3141 Fairview Park Drive Suite 850 Falls Church, VA. 22042 United States
Title	Director of Marketing	
E-Mail	gknudson@handysoft.com	
URL	www.handysoft.com	
Phone	1[703] 645 4515	

Integrator *HandySoft Global Corporation*

Contact	Chang Gyum Kim	776-15, Yeoksam-dong, Gangnam-gu

		Seoul 135-928
Title	PR Manager	Korea
E-Mail	cgkim@handysoft.co.kr	
URL	www.handysoft.com	
Phone	+82 02 3479 5406	

Founded in 1991, HandySoft is the leading global provider of Business Process Management (BPM) and dynamic tasking software and solutions. In 1994, HandySoft spearheaded development with workflow automation and by 1997 became the global leader in workflow management and the first to include process modeling with business rules capabilities, forms development, and user interfaces into the same solution platform. In 1999, HandySoft launched BizFlow®, a BPM Suite combining full human-driven workflow development with process monitoring and application integration. Now, almost 10 years later, BizFlow® version 11 is the leading BPMS platform for designing and executing process-driven applications. BizFlow® is built on standard platform technologies such as JAVA, BPMN, BPEL, Web Services, SOAP, XML, and WSDL. And it provides an entire suite of BPM functionality including process modeling, simulation, business activity monitoring, dynamic tasking, and critical path analysis. HandySoft attributes its success to its dynamic relationship with its more than 500 customers and partners worldwide.

HandySoft's dedication and achievements in innovation can be seen through the Company's consistent receipt of industry praise. For five consecutive years HandySoft has maintained its standing as a Gold Award recipient in the Global Awards for Excellence in BPM and Workflow, sponsored jointly by BPMFocus.org, WfMC and OMG, in recognition of the Company's global excellence in Workflow implementations. In addition, for several consecutive years, HandySoft has also retained its standing as one of the Top 100 Companies That Matter in Knowledge Management (KM). Today, HandySoft provides collaborative process management and groupware software, services and solutions for business-to-business collaboration, business process management, process asset management, enterprise knowledge portals, tasking, compliance and business activity monitoring. To help our customers dynamically adapt to an ever-changing global business environment, we will continuously develop and improve "handy" solutions that are easy to install, configure, deploy, and use to achieve immediate and long-term return on investment.

SATYAM COMPUTER SERVICES LIMITED, INDIA

Finalist

Contact	Surya Gadiraju	C5, TSR Towers, Raj Bhavan Road Somajiguda Hyderabad Andhra Pradesh 500082
Title	Head, eSupport	India
E-Mail	surya@satyam.com	
URL	www.satyam.com	
Phone	91 9849558863	

Nominator   Satyam Computer Services Limited, India

Contact	Surya Gadiraju	C5, TSR Towers, Raj Bhavan Road Somajiguda Hyderabad Andhra Pradesh 500082
Title	Head, eSupport	India
E-Mail	surya@satyam.com	
URL	www.satyam.com	

Phone	91 9849558863

SHANGHAI COMMERCIAL AND SAVINGS BANK, TAIWAN

Gold Winner

Contact	An-Chang Lo	238, Sec. 2, Tun Hua S.Rd., Taipei
Title	Deputy Executive Vice President	Taiwan
E-Mail	loac@scsb.com.tw	
URL	www.scsb.com.tw	
Phone	886-2-2378-0111 ext.110	

Nominator *Flowring Co. Ltd., Taiwan*

Contact	Lin Wan Ju	5F., No. 52., Sec. 1, Nanjing E.Rd., Taipei 104
Title	Sales Assistant	Taiwan
E-Mail	monicalin@flowring.com	
URL	www.flowring.com/	
Phone	886-2-25636568 ext.319	

Section 5: South and Central America

GOVERNMENT OF BERMUDA, FORMS AND TRANSACTION ENGINE PROJECT, BERMUDA

Silver Winner

Contact	David Atwood	40 Church Street Hamilton, HM NX
Title	Director of e-Government	Bermuda
E-Mail	datwood@gov.bm	
URL	www.gov.bm	
Phone	441 292 4595	

Nominator *Project Performance Corporation, USA*

Contact	Clay Richardson	1760 Old Meadow Road McLean, VA. 22102
Title	Practice Leader	United States
E-Mail	crichardson@ppc.com	
URL	www.ppc.com	
Phone	1(703)748-7544	

Project Performance Corporation is a management and technology consulting firm in the business of simplifying complex problems for top government and Fortune 500 decision makers. PPC specializes in enterprise and infrastructure solutions, software development, web services, and program and project planning. Working closely together, our practices include over 350 skilled and experienced consultants from a broad spectrum of disciplines who provide high-value-added solutions for our clients and an optimal environment for employee experience and growth. Committed to quality at every level of the workforce, PPC has been externally certified at CMMI Maturity Level 3 and is ISO 9001:2000 Registered. Our disciplined practices emphasize risk minimization; agile, on-time, in-budget performance; and proven, replicable processes.

GRUPO PÃO DE AÇÚCAR, BRAZIL

Finalist

Contact	Paulo Salomão	Rua Manuel da Nobrega, 930
		São Paulo 04001-003
Title	IT Coordinator	Brazil
E-Mail	paulo.salomao@grupopaodeacucar.com.br	
URL	www.grupopaodeacucar.com.br	
Phone	+55 (11) 3886-9283	

Nominator   *iProcess, Brazil*

Contact	Vinicius Amaral	Rua Washington Luiz
		820/301 Porto Alegre
		RS 90010-460
Title	Director	Brazil
E-Mail	vinicius.amaral@iprocess.com.br	
URL	www.iprocess.com.br	
Phone	+55[51]3211ext.4036	

MONEDERO, ARGENTINA

Gold Winner

Contact	Pablo Rojas	Bartolomé Mitre 3342
		Buenos Aires C1201AAL
Title	Director	Argentina
E-Mail	projas@traditum.com	
URL	www.monedero.com.ar	
Phone	54 011 5368 6800	

Nominator   *PECTRA Technology, Inc., USA.*

Contact	Fabio Rocca	2425 West Loop South, Suite
		200, Houston, TX. 77027
Title	Manager Pectra	United States
E-Mail	frocca@pectra.com	
URL	www.pectra.com	
Phone	1[713] 335-5562	

PECTRA Technology's award-winning Business Process Management system, PECTRA BPM Suite, is a powerful set of tools enabling discovery, design, implementation, maintenance, optimization and analysis of business processes in the organizations. PECTRA BPM Suite automates processes and critical tasks generating optimum levels of operational effectiveness. It fulfills all requirements demanded by today's organization, quickly and efficiently. Furthermore, it increases the return on previous investments made in technology by integrating all existing applications. PECTRA incorporates the following concepts: BAM (Business Activity Monitoring); Workflow; EAI (Enterprise Application Integration) and B2Bi (Business to Business Integration). Also, its functionality PECTRA BPM Mobile, allows every user to execute tasks from any mobile device in a very simple way through an interface designed on Services Oriented Architecture (SOA). PECTRA BPM Mobile increases organizations' productivity through fast access to information, providing dynamism and synchronization to the operations. PECTRA BPM Suite increases productivity, saving time and reducing costs in any organization.

Additional BPM and Workflow Resources

- AIIM (Association for Information and Image Management)
  www.aiim.org
- AIS Special Interest Group on Process Automation and
  Management (SIGPAM)
  www.sigpam.org
- BPMN (Business Process Management Notation)
  BPMN.org
- BPM Focus (previously WARIA)
  bpmfocus.org/
- IEEE (Electrical and Electronics Engineers, Inc.)
  www.ieee.org
- ISO (International Organization for Standardization)
  www.iso.ch
- Object Management Group
  www.omg.org
- Open Document Management Association
  infocentrale.net/dmware
- Organization for the Advancement of Structured Information
  Standards
  www.oasis-open.org
- Society for Human Resource Management
  www.shrm.org
- Society for Information Management
  www.simnet.org
- Wesley J. Howe School of Technology Management
  attila.stevens.edu/workflow
- Workflow Management Coalition (WfMC)
  www.wfmc.org
- Workflow Portal
  www.e-workflow.org

Valued Reader Discount 2008

- *Workflow Handbook* series, 2001-2008 Retail $95.00
- *Excellence in Practice Series* Retail $49.95
- *BPMN Modeling and Reference Guide* $39.95

Buy any book using *this* order form for instant 50% discount*.
Fax: +1 954 782 6365   Order Online at FutStrat.com

Year	Title

View complete title descriptions online at www.FutStrat.com.
* If ordering online, insert **"Book Order"** in the discount code box to get this 50% *Valued Reader Discount* discount on all our books (Print or Digital), as many copies as you wish but limited to only once in ONE order.

SHIPPING INFORMATION
Name:
Title/Occupation:
Company:
Address:

Phone: Fax:
Email: *Please write clearly!*

PAYMENT INFORMATION:

No.	COPIES	@ $ each	= $
		FL state tax 6%	= $
		Subtotal	= $
No.	Shipping	(see rates below)	= $
		TOTAL	= $

☐ Check (in US$ drawn on a US Bank to Future Strategies Inc.)
☐ VISA   ☐ MASTERCARD   ☐ AMEX

Credit Card No.   Exp. Date
Name on Card   Today's Date:
Signature

Mail or fax this order to:

Future Strategies Inc., Book Division
2436 North Federal Highway, #374, Lighthouse Point, FL 33064 USA
Tel: +1 954 782 3376 / Fax: +1 954 782 6365
email: books@FutStrat.com or order www.FutStrat.com

Shipping: PRIORITY MAIL SHIPPING CHARGES: USA Priority Mail $8.00; Canada/Mexico $11.00; UK/Europe $16.00; Pacific Rim $19.00; Africa/South America $19.0
Distributors/Bookstores/Libraries/Educational Institutions, please call for special discounts and shipping schedule.)

www.ingramcontent.com/pod-product-compliance
Lightning Source LLC
Chambersburg PA
CBHW061352210326
41598CB00035B/5957